LEADING IN PLACE

In *Leading in Place*, the authors open up new avenues in the debate on leadership by drawing the reader's attention to the ways in which women can be—and are—leading in organizations and communities in sometimes unconventional, often unrecognized, ways.

Through surveys and interviews, this practitioner–academic team has conducted a thorough and fascinating study of women in various leadership roles, from paid high-level executives to community volunteers. The book bridges the chasm between what the experts write about leadership and what is experienced in organizations and communities. It pushes the reader to think about how unconscious biases have influenced perceptions of leadership in research and organizations. They suggest leadership research should be updated to integrate 21st century realities by moving past both bias towards male prototypes, as well as the 'great women' genre, revealing a wealth of experience and knowledge, including insights about leading in place.

With strategies for addressing issues around leadership at both the individual and organizational levels, this book will provide students of leadership as well as professionals with insights that challenge the ways we think about women leaders and leadership more generally.

Rita M. Hilton, Ph.D., is an organizational and leadership development expert and an ICF executive coach. She currently serves as Director of Talent and Organizational Development for a US government agency.

Rosemary O'Leary, Ph.D., is the Director of the School of Public Affairs and the Edwin O. Stene Distinguished Professor of Public Administration at the University of Kansas, USA.

"Now more than ever, leadership is a concept that requires a set of new eyes, a fresh perspective, and a unique vantage point of exploration and reflection. *Leading in Place* does all of these things and more. An examination of leadership from a female perspective truly fills an important void in the body of knowledge surrounding this important influence related process."

Christopher P. Neck, Arizona State University, USA

"In their survey of close to 300 women, Hilton and O'Leary provide a rich, in-depth picture of leadership in practice, illustrating how women leaders make a difference and serve as important resources for their organizations. Their work here is outstanding and most impressive. This book represents a significant contribution to the literature on leadership and is a must read for researchers as well as practitioners."

Norma M. Riccucci, Rutgers University, USA

"Readers of *Leading in Place* will exclaim, 'That's my experience. Why hasn't someone written about this before as leadership?' With this book, Hilton and O'Leary engage in breakthrough thinking by recognizing and naming the central role individuals play in exercising leadership without the top position to fill a void, move a goal forward, or take advantage of an opportunity on behalf of the organization. This book represents women from millennials to baby boomers, and they do not agree on long-held assumptions concerning bias and behavioral expectations. In the end, *Leading in Place*, with its case studies and rich dialogue, is a needed addition to the many books on leadership and, more importantly, sets a standard for studying women in leadership."

Catherine Gerard, The Maxwell School of Syracuse University, USA

LEADING IN PLACE

Leadership Through Different Eyes

Rita M. Hilton and Rosemary O'Leary

Routledge
Taylor & Francis Group

NEW YORK AND LONDON

First published 2018
by Routledge
711 Third Avenue, New York, NY 10017

and by Routledge
2 Park Square, Milton Park, Abingdon, Oxon, OX14 4RN

Routledge is an imprint of the Taylor & Francis Group, an informa business

© 2018 Taylor & Francis

Library of Congress Cataloging in Publication Data
A catalog record for this book has been requested

ISBN: 978-0-8153-5185-6 (hbk)
ISBN: 978-0-8153-5188-7 (pbk)
ISBN: 978-1-351-14000-3 (ebk)

Typeset in Bembo
by Sunrise Setting Ltd, Brixham, UK

CONTENTS

ILLUSTRATIONS

Figures

Tables

Boxes

PREFACE

Our Elevator Speech

Imagine that you are our boss and you stop us in the elevator at work. You know that we—a practitioner and an academic researcher and writing team—have been working on a book on the topic of leadership using surveys and interviews of women. You want a rundown. You just read *The New York Times* article on why women don't make it to the boardroom with the subheading: "It's not a pipeline problem. It's about loneliness, competition and deeply rooted barriers" (Chira, 2017). You are taken aback because 1) you just don't see it this way, and 2) you're concerned about recruiting and retaining the best talent ... and quite frankly don't believe gender plays a role in outcomes. Don't we all want to believe everyone has equal access, a fair shot at, achieving leadership positions?

You ask us about the latest thinking and research on the topic of leadership. You want to know what are the top ideas, findings, and recommendations that will come from this book ... and you only have two minutes on the elevator to listen! Here is our (fast talking) response to you:

1. Outdated conceptions of leadership pose a fundamental challenge for individuals and organizations. We coin the term 'Leading in place' to describe a gender-neutral phenomenon of leadership that unfolds beneath the CEO and top executive team level, without positional authority (or over and beyond positional authority), that keeps teams and organizations moving towards mission achievement in the workplace. Outside the workplace, it unfolds across community and volunteer organizations, typically without formal designated position. Leading in place is a spectrum of behaviors proactively enacted in response to observed need, whether in response to

gaps left by those with designated positions of leadership or in response to perceived opportunities beyond existing boundaries and practice. Leading in place is a proactively self-selected activity.

2. We make the point that 'women leading' has long been a widespread occurrence but it is not widely recognized or rewarded by most societies or organizations. This is in part because women tend to emphasize leadership as behaviors rather than position. This runs counter to organizational systems and cultures based on stereotypical male prototypes of leadership, implemented (by men and women) in ways that are biased toward a traditional male perspective. We argue that women, and men, 'leading in place', with or without position, is beneficial not only to all places of work, but to society as a whole. 'Leading in place' needs to be rewarded as a desired form of leadership around the world.

3. To be clear, we are *NOT* suggesting that women are or ought to be restricted to leading in place. We are ardent supporters of women in formal positions of leadership. We have found evidence that appears to support the notion, however, that some have tended to lead in place. This may be partially attributable to a range of factors: personal life-balancing choices; pervasiveness of unintentional and unrecognized bias in leadership assessment, development, and selection; and the failure of organizations to create missions, cultures, and results that motivate appreciable numbers of women to prioritize commitment to those organizations.

4. If you examine evolution of leadership research, as well as organizational practice, it's possible to see a revolution unfolding for the 21st century. The experience of women possibly illustrates a vanguard, a 'new way' that will expand how we think about and enact leadership across domains. We suggest that the observed phenomenon of women not making it to top positions of leadership is at least partially a function of how leadership is conceived, recognized and rewarded. Women clearly do experience themselves as leaders. But women's stories vary: there is no one way to be a leader. The challenge of increasing representation of women in visible positions of leadership is as much a challenge of addressing and adjusting the way roles are structured and operative leadership prototypes, as it is preparing and supporting women to compete in existing structures.

5. A disturbingly significant minority of our respondents perceive that organizations are biased against recognizing emergent leadership and providing opportunities. What we heard from a broad cross section of women, and had validated by six highly experienced executives, reveals a clear disconnect. Many women have stories of organizations failing to recognize or develop them as leaders if they display collaborative behaviors such as promoting team over individual (i.e., promoting results, not personal profile), encouraging information-sharing, structuring processes that welcome broad input, and emphasizing constructive communication. Ironically, if well-executed, and

consistent with organizational objectives, all of these behaviors contribute to engaged workforces and effective organizations.

6. We argue that in order to describe and operationalize a robust conception of leadership, thinking and practice need to be updated. Women's voices have to be integrated into mainstream views, not treated as if they are a niche perspective. Simultaneously the implicit model of organizations as hierarchies, that underlies much of research and practice, needs to be updated to capture reality in the 21st century. Organization leaders, and researchers, need to critically examine whether their model of leadership assumes either a male prototype and/or an outdated hierarchical organizational model, and consciously make room for multifaceted, modern leadership. If organizations are not providing transparent access to leadership roles for people of varying styles of leadership, or if women are not seeing themselves as leaders, or if we as a society are not seeing the problem, then the 'women' part of the equation is not the place to start. An out-of-whack view of leadership has to be looked at first.

7. Leadership research is highly fragmented across disciplines and off base with regard to practice, particularly with reference to women. We need to start from the understanding that leadership is an interpersonal, perceptual phenomenon. One way forward is to examine the stories of women's experiences with leaders and their views of themselves as leaders because stories are the way that humans make sense of perception and experience. We need to build new leadership theories by understanding a cross section of women's stories, rather than focusing on the 'great woman' stories of the elite.

We predict that organizations will increasingly evolve towards holacracies, requiring significant numbers of adaptive workers who are willing to lead in place. This will require redefining roles and structures to recognize and reward different styles of leadership. Moving forward in the 21st century, the most innovative organizations will embrace the phenomenon of leading in place—and those who embody it. We as a society need to validate and reward those who lead in place, as well as those who lead well in formal positions of leadership.

Reference

Chira, S. (2017, July 23). Why women aren't C.E.O.s. *The New York Times*, p. SR1.

ACKNOWLEDGMENTS

This work started as a labor of love, arising out of a stream of individual conversations we each had with peers, students, clients, around the topic of women and leadership. We, the authors, shared a strong view that the focus of publicly unfolding conversation about the under-representation of women in senior leadership positions across industries was misplaced. This was confirmed and repeatedly echoed by others—male and female. We wanted to know how the conversation might be framed, and informed, if a broad cross section of women's voices were integrated into the conversation.

We received immediate and generous responses from a number of quarters when we reached out. We received support from men with long experience in the workplace and proven commitment to finding and promoting the best talent. We received an overwhelming response from nearly 300 women when we asked them to share their views on and experience of leadership. The extent of input gleaned from the exercise was a gift. It kept us going on the project as competing demands crept up for each of us. We remain particularly grateful and indebted to each of our interviewees for their time and the thoughtfulness of their authentic contributions. While we take responsibility for this work, it simply would not have happened without others' willingness to contribute to our endeavor. We also wish to thank the anonymous reviewers who reviewed early excerpts. Their feedback helped improve the book.

Rita: In addition to the women who so generously shared their time and stories, I have tremendous appreciation and thanks for colleagues and friends who shared their thoughts, perspectives, and support for this project. Fellow leadership development practitioners to whom I owe particular thanks include Bob Anderson, Michael Casey, Susan Collins, and Teresa Woodland. While they bear no responsibility for the content or thoughts expressed in this book, each provided collegial support and assistance at critical junctures.

This would not have been possible without my family. I would not have taken the path I chose; and I would not have been able to bring this project to completion. Phil was partnership in action, covering so many demands while I was distracted with this troublesome 'fourth child'. Christopher and Samuel were willing to engage in enlightening, if sometimes challenging, conversations from 'the other side' and provided technical support beyond compare—with good humor. Mariah, none of it would have happened without you: from inception through editing. My love and thanks to each of you.

Rosemary: I can hardly believe that Rita and I worked on this book for five years. We were buddies in our Ph.D. program 30 years ago, took separate paths after we graduated, and then reunited to write this book. The idea for the book came from Rita, who approached me with the idea of bringing a variety of women's perspectives and voices to conversation about women and leadership. This led to the idea of people—often women—leading in place. I have lost count of the hundreds of conversations we have had about this phenomenon, and I mean hundreds. I thank Rita for hanging in there with me when, as one of my Ph.D. students put it, "life interfered with my life": My parents died, I became an empty nester, my husband had cancer surgery, I took a new job across the country, and I entered university leadership. It has been an honor and a privilege to have you as a friend and co-author, Rita.

No one co-authors a book like this without a boatload of help. I thank my research assistants Zach Bauer, Kevin Campbell, Renee Dinsmore, Misty Grayer, Cody Johnson, and Chelsea Morton for help with coding interviews, analyzing surveys, reviewing the literature, and proofreading version after version. I thank the women we interviewed and surveyed for sharing their experiences with, and perspectives on, leadership openly and with such thoughtfulness. I thank my friend Sean O'Keefe, former head of NASA, Secretary of the Navy, and CEO of Airbus, as well as Ambassador Susan Schwab and four other expert CEO-level reviewers who asked not to be identified, for providing helpful 'reality checks' once the first draft was written. I also thank my husband, Larry, my daughter, Meghan, and my step-children Leanne and Nate for serving as sounding boards for my ideas, frustrations, and joys as this project unfolded: You keep me balanced and make me laugh, and for that I will be eternally grateful.

PART I

The Challenge

1

INTRODUCTION

Why This Book?

Experts with a bully pulpit espouse a virtually limitless stream of assertions about leadership. We're told what constitutes leadership and how to get up the ladder into visible positions. There is limited thoughtful treatment of whether leadership paradigms bootstrapped from male-dominated systems of the 19th and 20th centuries fit *anyone*, female or male; or whether the paradigms effectively serve organizations and society. There is a known high rate of failure among those who move into leadership positions, organizations are plagued by relatively weak levels of engagement among staff and ethical scandals are becoming all too common across sectors.

Rather than asking "why don't more women migrate into formal leadership positions?," we are interested in the more fundamental question: What insight would listening to women's perceptions and experience of leadership contribute to refreshing thought and practice? Certainly the perspective belongs in conversations around developing models and practice of leadership appropriate to the 21st century.

Leaders set direction and influence others to get things done.[1] There is no one way for this to play out. There are a range of options in any given situation with a given set of actors: the dynamic is, and always will be, imperfectly understood. In abstract, leadership can be thought of as a three-dimensional puzzle; a complex, dynamic set of simultaneous equations. Along one dimension, equations address the individual(s) leading: who are they as humans, what are their skills and abilities, what behaviors do they deploy, what is going on in their life. Another set of equations address the same issues for those being led, the followers. Together, these form the crux of the imperfectly understood alchemy of leadership. The third dimension, and this is the fuzziest, is bounded by an extensive set of equations referring to a broad span of contextual (internal to organizations) and environmental (socio-political-economic) factors within which the first two unfold.

Equations for each dimension have to be well-specified, and solved simultaneously, in order for effective, productive mission achievement to unfold (whether shareholder value as in the private sector or program performance in the public sphere). There isn't *an* answer.

This book touches on threads from across the three dimensions to serve two purposes. One is to provoke thinking around leadership generally in order to accelerate research and practice that better fit 21st century realities than those of the 20th century. This sets the stage for our more specific but directly related purpose of contributing to a more robust understanding of women and leadership by bringing a cross section of women's voices to bear on thinking about leadership. We're not starting this conversation. We're suggesting 1) that a specific adaptation or elaboration in thinking about leadership be made to recognize a modern phenomenon, and 2) that moving in this direction will increase understanding of the under-representation of women in top *positions* of leadership. Together, these would ideally increase traction around improving opportunities for, and recognition of, women who lead.

Outwardly, thinking on the topic of leadership arising across disciplines has evolved considerably from mid-20th century roots. The evolution (or revolution) appears to have accelerated in recent years. However, the topic of biases (conscious or unconscious) implicit in the framing of early work, and how they may continue to constrain thinking, requires more attention. We believe that remnants of 20th century thinking manifest in two unfortunate ways. An initial understanding of leadership as positional and organizations as hierarchical has obscured the rising reality of leading in place. Insufficient attention to the influence of male leader prototypes on thinking and practice results in failure to recognize that women have been and are leading. Together, these help partially explain why women as a category are so under-represented in top leadership positions.

Leading in Place Is a Rising Phenomenon

We introduce the concept of leading in place. The extent of increased complexity in organizations, and the dynamism of environments in which they operate that have unfolded in the last decades are hard to overstate. While change has been more dramatic in the private than public sector, in terms of organization and leadership practices, where the private sector leads the public sector tends to follow. The extent of complexity in organizations and dynamism in environments remain inadequately represented in foundational framing of work on leadership. We point to a very specific type of leadership that has evolved—leading in place—that does not receive sufficient attention in either thinking or practice.

Leading in place describes a gender-neutral phenomenon of leadership that unfolds beneath the CEO and top executive team level, without positional authority (or over and beyond positional authority), that keeps teams and organizations moving toward mission achievement. Leading in place is a spectrum of behaviors proactively enacted in response to observed need, whether in response to gaps left by those with designated positions of leadership or in response to perceived opportunities beyond existing boundaries and practice. Behaviors deployed while leading in place address gaps targeted. Examples of potential targets include team trust, strategic clarity, cross-boundary innovation and change, or myriad other factors that keep sub-units of organizations resilient and moving towards mission achievement. Examples of behaviors include coaching and recognizing others to promote strong shared team leadership, or systematically initiating boundary-spanning behaviors. At one end of the spectrum of leading in place, individuals step in to compensate for gaps associated with existing leadership limitations (e.g., when a supervisor is in over his/her head); at the other end of the spectrum individuals anticipate and act to head off potential vacuums associated with complexity. In the best of circumstances, leading in place is a proactively self-selected activity—for which one should be recognized and rewarded. Individuals and organizations all have a stake in how opportunities are created for leading in place, how the phenomenon is recognized and encouraged. Leading in place is a specific complement to positions of leadership: it is not a substitute for positions. How leading in place and leading from position can best be intentionally structured and play out in organizations remains to be seen. All will benefit as organizations adjust to increasingly facilitate and recognize leading in place.

Conversation about Women and Leadership Is Skewed

In a country founded on the principle that all *men* are created equal, conversations about access and equity are always in order. Emphasizing the question of *women* and leadership, though, masks the reality that we appear to be at a moment during which the construct of *leadership* itself warrants attention. Thoughtful consideration about how we understand it, how we define it, how we recognize it, how we reward it and how we select individuals for positions of leadership are of paramount importance.

The under-representation of women in visible and acknowledged positions of leadership may be just the symptom. The underlying ill is an antiquated, constraining conception of leaders and leadership. In the tale of Cinderella, was the shoe the problem? Or was the real problem that it kept getting jammed on the wrong feet? Maybe some women have been refusing to get shoe-horned into situations that don't work for them; maybe those selecting leaders have been looking in all the wrong places.

The combination of Slaughter's (2012) *Atlantic* piece on 'Why women still can't have it all' and Sandberg's (2013) *Lean in* sparked a rash of intense conversations among women about leadership. Many of the conversations to which we were privy ran the same course: Slaughter and Sandberg are both right; and they each trip a little too lightly past troubling blind spots.

Slaughter, speaking from her experience of stepping away from an academic position to commute and fill a government policy job, rightly pointed out that the system can be stacked against women for a number of reasons. She also appeared to miss the reality that different jobs yield entirely different lifestyles. Every individual gets to set their own priorities and make choices accordingly: high-level government positions place virtually limitless demands. It is for some, it's not for others. Any individual, male or female, would likely have to make tradeoffs (consciously or unconsciously) between fulfilling such a role and being a present parent (even if they weren't commuting).

Sandberg, reflecting on her journey to a top executive team role at a tech start-up, rightly encouraged women to not get in their own way, to define their ambitions then step up and commit to delivering. She also somewhat glibly undersold the reality that access to the type of advantages of connections, hands up, and *leaning on* others from which she appeared to benefit clearly factored into her success and are simply not available to all. Individuals, male or female, can be capable, hard-working, exhibit leadership capacity—and not make it into top positions if serendipitous mixes of sponsors, power bases, and selection systems not captive to informal, unexamined preferences don't line up. No one makes it to top positions without substantial assists, whether active (e.g., impressing powerful people via effort or capability) or passive (e.g., socio-economic status, access via education).

Clearly, biases—intentional or unconscious, individual or collective, held by observers or by women themselves—can get in the way of women migrating through leadership pipelines (Ibarra & Hansen, 2011). We believe there's a less subtle hindrance as well. Most prototypes or conceptions out there about leadership are implicitly backward-looking. They remain anchored in some conception of 'corporate man' leaders and leadership elaborated after World War II. It evolved towards the end of the 20th century into a conception of a leader competent to function in a dynamic, continuously disrupted globalized economy, but it remains essentially anchored in an understanding of organizations as structured, hierarchical and implicitly linear. It may be time to realize the unfolding revolution and intentionally re-conceive leader prototypes—and position distribution within organizations.

Socio-economic realities and organizations of the 21st century do, and will continue to, look very different from those of the mid- to late-20th century. Ensuring effectiveness and productivity into the future requires a willingness to engage in perspective-taking on the foundations of research and practice grounded in old realities that may be skewing views, practice, and results today.

Women Have Been, and Are, Leading in Place

While leading in place is a gender-neutral phenomenon in 21st century organizations, women in particular have been negatively affected by inattention to this phenomenon. Women have been leading in place for some time, but this reality has been missed because the practice of leading in place is not consistent with artifacts of 20th century conceptions: i.e., implicit hierarchical structure of organizations, and male prototypes of leadership.

Although this book focuses on *women* and leadership, we start by looking at leadership generically. In order to make sense of how a concept as broad as 'leadership' plays out from the perspective of one group, it's important to look at the underlying phenomenon itself. Put differently, consider the familiar 'Potato Head' toys. You start with the essential (body, feet), *then* move on to differentiating (e.g., Mr. or Mrs., conventional or loony). The same logic applies to human interaction: one must start with the basics before addressing the complexities.

Leadership study and research have shifted over time to look at leadership in relation to positions along specific steps in hierarchies: lower and middle layers of organizations, then towards top levels of organizations.[2] Until very late in the 20th century, these positions were typically occupied by men. This reality, coupled with the fact that until only very recently the bulk of research and popular discussions of leadership have tended to implicitly neglect leadership that occurs anywhere but at or near the top, there is a significant gap in our understanding of women and leadership. This book is intended to mitigate this gap by developing a deeper understanding of the many spheres in which women lead, by providing examples of the exercise of leading in place by women in organizations, and scrutinizing limitations that past understandings of leadership may be imposing on current individual and organizational outcomes.

We suggest that the observed phenomenon of women not making it into top positions of leadership is at least partially a function of how leadership is conceived, recognized, and rewarded. Women lead: whether in remunerated roles in the workplace or non-remunerated roles in communities. This reality is not widely recognized or rewarded by most organizations. Further if organizations are not providing transparent access to leadership roles, or if women are not seeing themselves as leaders, or if we as a society are not seeing them, then the 'women' part of the equation is not the place to start. An out-of-whack societal view of leadership has to be examined first.

To be clear, we are *NOT* suggesting that women are or ought to be restricted to leading in place. We are ardent supporters of women in formal positions of leadership. We have found evidence that appears to support the notion, however, that some have tended to lead in place, and explore that phenomenon in this book. This may be partially attributable to a range of factors: personal life balancing choices; pervasiveness of unintentional and unrecognized bias in leadership assessment, development, and selection; and failure of organizations to create missions, cultures, and results that motivate appreciable numbers of women to prioritize commitment to those organizations. Or it may be because of other factors. We believe that a cross section of women's voices and views have to be integrated into the conversation and thinking on the phenomenon of leading in place in order to develop a robust understanding of drivers and solutions.

The evidence presented in this book that indicates that women are, and have been, leaning in and leading comes from our survey of 274 women and 20 subsequent in-depth interviews. Many of these women held (or hold) high-level positions of leadership. Many chose (or choose) to lead in place. Some experienced (or experience) being constrained to leading in place by biases baked into organizational leader development and selection practices.

In our interviews, we reached out to a cross section of survey respondents and asked them to share their stories of leadership. Humans make sense of the world through stories, and they can usefully illuminate human dynamics as complicated as leadership. Stories can powerfully crystallize some of the challenges women face as a result of perceptions and practice. Here are two brief stories we heard. More will follow.

> Becky started, but did not finish college. She is a mother of three living in rural West Virginia, who founded and runs a real estate business selling both local homes and recreational properties to non-residents from wealthier surrounding areas. She also volunteers at an annual local festival, a significant contributor to the local economy. She has taken a lead role in promoting collaboration among local businesses to create and promote small-scale community-building events. When asked to share about her experiences as a leader, she responds, "I'm just a country bumpkin, a momma of three who has found her niche in the community she grew up in." Her view of herself encapsulates one of the challenges of women in leadership. A capable, motivated woman taking initiative to improve the economy and health of her community doesn't see herself as a leader.
>
> Sabine is a highly educated, accomplished corporate executive with broad enterprise experience. She is looking to move from her current position to the next level and has received consistent signals from several senior leaders that she should move into an executive role overseeing product development that's about to come open. She shows up at work one day to learn that someone else has been appointed to the role: a male colleague. Senior leaders who saw her and knew the organization understand her appropriateness for the role. Others made a unilateral appointment without examining assumptions and fit across an equal access pool of candidates. This highlights another of the challenges of women and leadership: exclusion of women leaders from opportunities at top positions via non-transparent processes.

In order to validate our findings, we interviewed six experienced executives: three were (or are) organizational leaders (2 men, 1 woman), three were (or are) top human talent managers for large organizations (3 women). Taken together, the data appear to substantiate that leading in place is a significant phenomenon that warrants attention. Further, we provide evidence that reaching beyond those with a bully pulpit to attend to a cross section of women's voices enriches understanding. Women are leading, but their perceptions of and experiences as leaders are insufficiently recognized. Some executives and organizations recognize the need to adapt and innovate in the face of this reality. However, insights on effective practices have not yet entered the mainstream.

Organization of the Book

This book comprises three sections, and three interludes of interview excerpts. *The Challenge*, the first section, contains three chapters (including this Introduction). Chapter Two addresses current understandings of the phenomenon of leadership. Chapter Three proposes key opportunities for building a new understanding of leadership to better meet 21st century realities. This section closes with the First Interlude, focusing on pivotal points in interviewees' leadership development.

The Story from Many Voices includes four chapters and two interludes. Chapter Four discusses the importance of stories in making sense of leadership, highlighting the value-add of bringing a cross section of women's voices to the conversation. Chapter Five covers in-depth views and stories of leading in place. This is followed by the Second Interlude, which highlights thinking on what constitutes leadership success. Chapter Six presents results of the survey we conducted, focusing on what women shared about their experience of and with leaders. Chapter Seven continues with survey results, shifting to look at respondents' experience *as* leaders. The Third Interlude addresses experiences beneficial for developing women as leaders— including those leading in place. *What to Make of it* draws the previous sections together and turns toward the future. Chapter Eight highlights key findings from our research, complemented by the results of validation interviews with six experienced practitioners. We close with a more personal Epilogue: A letter to our (and others') daughters as they start their leadership journeys. We also include an appendix that contains all the responses we got to the question 'what three words of wisdom would you give a young woman starting on her leadership journey?' The responses reflect a range and depth of views that merits attention.

Notes

1   This succinct description is attributable to Stephen Zaccaro, George Mason University.
2   Considering nested or layered systems of leadership is a relatively recent approach in research. For a clear look at the challenge based on military experience, see *Team of teams: New rules of engagement for a complex world* (McChrystal et al., 2015).

References

Ibarra, H., & Hansen, M. T. (2011). Are you a collaborative leader? *Harvard Business Review*, 89(7/8), 68–74.

McChrystal, S., Collins, T., Silverman, D., & Fussell, C. (2015). *Team of teams: New rules of engagement for a complex world*. New York, NY: Penguin Random House.

Sandberg, S. (2013). *Lean in: Women, work, and the will to lead*. New York, NY: Random House.

Slaughter, A. M. (2012). Why women still can't have it all. *Atlantic Monthly*. Retrieved from www.theatlantic.com/magazine/archive/2012/07/why-women-still-cant-have-it-all/309020/. Last accessed: January 9, 2018.

2

HOW LEADERSHIP GETS CONSTRUED

"Hillary Clinton will win the presidency on Nov. 8; it probably won't be a landslide, but it won't be particularly close."[1]

While virtually all of us recognize good leadership when we encounter it, we don't all have uniform explanations for *why* someone is a good leader. Equally, leaders do not always transition successfully between contexts. For example, David Petraeus was characterized as an innovative and effective leader while commander of a military operation in Iraq. He stumbled, however, when transplanted to a quasi-civilian environment at the CIA. He was not a different person, but a style and set of expectations developed in the military context may not have worked well in a very different context of an intelligence agency staffed with long-serving civilians used to particular culture and conventions. Does this mean Petraeus was not an effective leader? Or does it mean that he exerted effective leadership in one context, but failed in another? Petraeus' story was international news because of his lauded success in the Army and expectations associated with his move to the CIA. However, similar scenarios can be found across levels of organizations in virtually every sector. When it happens at the top, it makes news.

Teresa Sullivan, another example, was installed as president at the University of Virginia in 2010 after succeeding as an administrator at two large state universities (Texas and Michigan). In 2012 she was blind-sided by a very public and ugly effort to remove her. That she was seemingly caught completely unaware appeared to evidence lack of savvy about politics and power among stakeholders. She did not have a record of similar missteps in her previous roles. Did she lack political savvy, did she simply misread her new environment, or did dysfunctions exist within the university so that no candidate would have avoided such a public crisis?

If leadership is not some fixed skill or quality, what is it? Individuals' perception, experience, and expression of leadership vary over time and context.

Leadership failures and misfits generate a variety of costs for organizations. At best, they create drag on mission achievement. At worst, they derail organizations. Whether public or private, formal or informal, effective leadership keeps organizations going. Focus on the topic intensified towards the late 20th century, as previously stable hierarchical corporate and political structures were impelled to new forms by socio-economic developments. Books, scholarly journals, internet commentary, schools, consulting businesses, and entire careers are devoted to topics of leadership and leader development.

Outlines of Leadership Research

It is not possible to do justice to the full range of work on leadership in this short volume. A vast body of available research has mapped an extensive intellectual terrain.[2] We provide a broad-brush view of how the topic is studied addressing mainstream spheres[3] and then touch on concepts central to most modern work in the field.

Broadly speaking, both scholarly and popular work tackling questions either of what comprises leadership or how leadership plays out tend to focus on one of the three dimensions laid out in Chapter One: Identity (who leaders are/how they behave as people); function (what leaders do); and contingency (how context shapes the answer). As we noted at the beginning of the book, leadership in the world is best conceived of as a series of simultaneous equations between these three axes. While the three tend to blend and overlap in the dynamic of reality, isolating the dimensions for purposes of this study facilitates our ability to better specify the respective equations.

Productive conversation requires further clarification beyond the extremely broad (and sometimes fuzzy) dimensions of identity, function, and context. It is necessary to hone in on exactly what is being studied, at what level, and via what unit. Facets of interest can be thought of as: sphere, level, and status,[4] defined as follows:

Sphere: Leadership (whether effective or not) manifests in every sphere of human experience. For example, community, religious groups, schools, government agencies, and commercial entities.

Level: Levels of leadership can be cut several ways. For example, from the outside, 'organizational leadership' can be taken to mean a) the collective of employed managers, b) the top executive, and/or c) the board of directors. Alternately, from within the same organization, leadership might refer to any point in the ranks, or might span line managers through middle and senior management all the way to the CEO. Whom one is actually referring to when talking about leadership is likely to be determined by where one fits in the organization.

Status: Real complexity begins to intrude when discussing status. First, there is an entire literature on the difference between being a manager or administrator and a leader. Ideally, the former are also the latter—but if this were always the case we would tend to see better results across all spheres of existence. Second, differences exist between formally recognized (i.e., designated) positions and enacted influence (i.e., emergent leadership—those who lead without assigned position—see Box 2.1). Again, ideally, meaningful overlap exists between these two. However, anyone reading this can likely access examples they've encountered of misalignment between the individual who was assigned a leader position—and the individual who was the de facto leader. This can happen across spheres and levels (e.g., on high school sports teams, voluntary organizations, corporate offices, or academic departments). Significantly, and this has been folded into thinking on leadership in recent years, it is often said that there is no leader in the absence of followers.

Not all work in the leadership field specifies assumptions and targets with relation to these underlying aspects. When these parameters are not clearly specified, accurately assessing the applicability of research to practice can be problematic. While the sphere is typically easy to specify there is much greater equivocation on the other two aspects. Thus, the study of leadership requires navigating tension between delineating what is being studied to make research possible and ensuring sufficient fidelity with reality to inform and guide practice. The bulk of academic research on leadership is undertaken from within schools of either psychology or business/management.

BOX 2.1 EMERGENT LEADERSHIP

Emergent leaders typically act without assigned position—taking on tasks, promoting collaboration and shared understanding, influencing others to get results. Emergent leadership is recognized by followers, even if the emergent leader does not in fact have authority of position or conscious intention of exerting leadership. It has typically been thought of as a complement to those with positions of leadership, behaviors by which informal groups or teams perform, or a likely predictor for those who will rise to positions of leadership. Emergent leadership *is* leadership. We use the term leading in place to identify **intentional, proactive** emergent leadership that unfolds below the top designated positions of the leadership (e.g., CEO and top management team) layer in any organization. Leading in place specifically incorporates the intention of the individual leading, not only others' perceptions.

The Approach from Psychology

Both industrial/organizational and social psychologists have focused on the topic of leadership. Psychologists tend to focus on either what are called 'within person' individual differences (see Figure 2.1) or 'between person' dynamics (see Figure 2.2) of leaders and followers. Within-person research focuses on traits, characteristics, and capacities of the individual leader, as well as how these are expressed. Between-person research tends to focus on the leader-follower dynamic, the leader-group dynamic, or a combined approach bringing together the leader-follower dynamic with leader and follower individual characteristics and behaviors.[5]

Whether applying the within-person or between-person frame, looking at only one side of the leader equation generates a skewed understanding. Living in

Within-person research focuses on just that: traits,characteristics, capacities, and cognitive processes of the individual as well as how they manifest. Others are considered background factors.

FIGURE 2.1 The Within-Person Frame

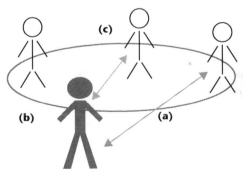

Between-person research can focus on: **(a)** simple bilateral leader-follower dynamics, with particular reference to leader characteristics and/or behavior; or **(b)** dynamics between leader and team or group, with limited reference to specific variation among group members; or **(c)** bilateral leader-follower dynamics with reference to both leader and follower individual characteristics and/or behaviors.

FIGURE 2.2 The Between-Person Frame

the world is a team sport. So it's nonsensical to consider a leader without simultaneously considering how that leader is perceived and affects the experiences and behaviors of others. Leadership does not comprise only particular characteristics or behaviors possessed by an individual.

Leadership requires people to follow leaders, and these followers add complexity to the equation on two levels.[6] In order to comprehend the unfolding of leadership, dynamics have to be considered from the within-person and between-person vantage points of both leader and follower. At the within-person level, leaders and followers each hold distinct experiences and perspectives. These influence how they engage at the between-person level, and what they take away from interactions.[7] In practice, it gets even more complicated, as *in situ* in organizations, aspects of level and status exert potentially confounding influence on interactions.

Research on within-person factors has focused heavily on traits, much of it organized around the 'big five'[8] personality traits (i.e., openness, conscientiousness, extraversion, agreeableness, neuroticism). Research on personality and leadership continues.[9] Building on early work in social psychology, the field has also expanded to focus on the reality of leadership as a between-person social dynamic. Research has diffused across a spectrum to delve into how observable and/or theoretically measurable within-person differences influence interactions between individuals.[10]

Methods used have varied over time and matter profoundly when considering the application of research results to practice. Much of the earliest work arose from military studies around and after the two World Wars. Research on leadership in and for the private sector and public bureaucracies took off in the second half of the 20th century. It is important to pause and note that a variety of data gathering practices have been used. Much of the academic research has used students, either in laboratory experiments or via study of project teams. This approach has two strengths. First, it has often been the only way researchers could access study participants. Second, it provides the level of control required in order to focus on individual differences and interpersonal dynamics. It is legitimate. It also does have limitations, of which the field itself is quite aware. An indication of this is the rise in field studies. A search of the American Psychological Association database[11] using the terms 'leadership' and specifying the method of 'field study' indicates that between 1980–2017, 398 studies using field study methodology were published in peer reviewed journals included in the database. Narrowing the period of interest to 2010–2017 reveals that 353 studies using field study methodology were published in peer reviewed journals included in the database. By far the majority (i.e., 87%) of studies of leadership accomplished via field studies have been published in the last seven years. The extent to which experimental conditions (if an experiment with students), or prevailing context and sample characteristics (if a field study) line up with most settings in the world matters.

Drawing from the vast literature that has been generated, we present five elements briefly here, as they figure significantly in current understanding of human behavior generally and discussions of leadership specifically: affect, self-efficacy,

---

BOX 2.2 EFFECTS OF AFFECT . . .

Affect has been tackled from levels of personality, as well as more malleable emotions, feelings, and moods. These are all highly intertwined with cognitive processes in ways we do not fully understand. Our affect can influence not only what we *feel* but also what we do—or do not—*see*, and possibly what we believe.

There is extensive literature on the effects of affect in relation to leadership and the workplace. For example, core affect has been studied extensively in relation to leader personality and behavior. The effects of all manifestations of affect have been considered in relation to workplace behaviors, judgments we make about leaders, and job satisfaction. As cognitive neuroscience continues to progress, understanding and insight will continue to be refined and expanded.

From a practical perspective, anti-bullying campaigns and efforts to increase emotional intelligence of workers (leaders and followers) all relate directly to human affect—and individual self-management.

---

self-awareness, emotional intelligence, and prototypes. There is accruing evidence that they all impact expectations and perceptions (of ourselves, of others, of experience). (See Box 2.2.) Perceptions and expectations define the world of the possible in the dynamics of leadership.

- *Self-efficacy*[12] *is fundamental to how individuals perceive themselves, hence can affect how they present and perform.* It can colloquially be thought of as 'confidence', but is more narrow and specific. Self-efficacy refers to an individual's belief in their ability to perform a specific task or succeed in a particular situation. It drives how we perceive ourselves in relation to tasks or challenges, hence it influences how we approach them. While it appears to be malleable (e.g., through practice of a given task), it can bound what is possible for individuals. For example, if I don't believe I can swim, I might not try. Alternately, I might try but with a self-defeating narrative scrolling in my head that causes me to tense up and not be able to find a breath or stroke rhythm, so that I flail and fail. If women don't see themselves as leaders, they can be dissuaded from taking on positions or distracted while executing in them.[13]
- *Self-awareness refers to an individual's ability to assess themselves and also to consciously assess how they are perceived by others.*[14] Healthy self-awareness covers the full landscape as we ourselves see it (e.g., motivations, 'what is going on' internally, strengths, weaknesses, performance, etc.), but equally entails attending to how others might be experiencing and assessing us. Self-awareness is fundamental to maturity and critical to the leadership dynamic. The fact that

limits on self-awareness can derail leaders does not appear to be culturally bound (Cullen, Gentry, & Yamarino, 2015).

- *Our affect (i.e., the way we're 'feeling') influences what we perceive, and how we process those perceptions.* The ways in which affect influences social processes has been extensively studied (e.g., see Forgas, 2001), including how it can specifically play out in the workplace (e.g., Rock, 2009). At the deepest level, we each have relatively stable tendencies towards either positive or negative affect. On a more passing level, we have moods and emotions. These all influence what we see, and how we react. We all experience conflict or tension with family and friends. Sometimes the other party has genuinely done something to cause us harm or irritation. Sometimes we're just in a bad mood, or distracted, and get rubbed the wrong way. The same can unfold in leaders' thinking and behavior, as well as followers' reactions to and perceptions of leaders.

- *Emotional intelligence, or EI, refers to the ability to identify and manage one's own emotions, as well as identify and influence others' emotions.* Goleman (1995) popularized the concept, stressing it as a complementary counterbalance to the prevailing wisdom that intellectual intelligence (i.e., IQ) was a universal predictor of abilities including leadership. EI ties together affect and self-awareness, going beyond to cover the reflexive role of emotions in human interaction. EI requires attention to both within-person and between-person dimensions of affect and self-awareness. The ability to identify and manage one's own feelings constitutes the starting point. A higher level of skill is the ability to notice and attend to others' feelings and signals. Adept practice of emotional intelligence requires stepping back, and, as necessary, reading others' emotions and perceptions to moderate one's own presentation (i.e., display feelings effectively, behave appropriately). Stretching even further, the ability to enrich one's understanding by adopting others' perspectives and being able to empathize with them, even if you don't see a situation the same way, describes highly developed emotional intelligence. A growing body of research appears to indicate it is integral to leader performance (e.g., Wong & Law, 2002). Some degree of EI is integral to effectiveness across spheres of life. Requirements may vary across workplace roles, levels, and contexts, but emotional intelligence constitutes a precondition of influencing and engaging with others rather than simply directing or micromanaging them. The range and complexity of relations increases, as does the need for stepping back both to see a bigger strategic picture and to protect oneself from the stresses of the role.

- *Prototypes frame our expectations of others; influencing our evaluations of, and reactions to, them.* Prototypes are (typically unconscious) pictures or expectations we hold. They frame how we assess others; and often what we see. What this means is that our prototypes—expectations or model of what a leader *should* be—will influence our assessment of all leaders we encounter in any sphere.

There is an entire thread of study on 'implicit leadership' built upon operation of prototypes. (For a review, see Shondrick & Lord, 2010). Prototypes can be thought of as an unconscious glass slipper we carry around with us to which we try to fit leaders we encounter; a leader will act like, look like, 'this'. Prototype is a neutral concept; but obviously, prototypes are culturally influenced, and not immune from biases individuals (or organizations) may hold. Prototypes are important both in relation to who makes it into designated positions of leadership (i.e., who fits the selection 'template') and how leadership behavior manifested by an individual is perceived by others (i.e., emergent leadership).

The Approach from Other Fields

There is not an absolute, discrete line of leadership research across fields. The study of and conclusions regarding leadership behaviors and efficacy, what is required of individuals, and how the dynamic plays out in organizations, is distributed across disciplines: business, public administration, popular press. While these literatures are not always mutually informed, they tend to draw heavily upon leadership theories and research arising from psychology. For example, it's hard to overstate the impact that research on such concepts as authentic leadership or emotional intelligence has had on applied research and practice in management in recent years. In general, however, a focus on how individuals (either leaders or managers) behave to attain desired organizational outcomes distinguishes business/management approaches. Leadership as seen through this lens is of interest more as an end to specific means than as a process in itself. Achieving organizational objectives, contributing to the bottom line, is an ever-present concern.

As a consequence, this approach tends towards looking more at leaders in action through cases and applied studies than experimental design. Relevant questions concerning discrete aspects of individuals as leaders, and how leaders interact with others matter *in relation to* organizational outcomes. For example, there are entire threads of literature on leadership in nursing and health care, in education, in marketing, and in public administration. There are also industry-generic threads on decision-making, sense-making (Weick, 1993), strategic planning, organizational culture, innovation, entrepreneurship, and communication. Whether at the individual level of a business unit, or more generally in a world where return to shareholders is of paramount importance, what matters is whether leaders lead and manage the organization's talent pool towards that end.

The case-study approach, a method frequently applied in management and practice literatures to study both organizations and individuals, can facilitate attention to the influences of context and environment on leadership. It has been deployed in any number of ways to contribute to understanding leadership as it plays out. It has also led to some particularly skewed results. For example, in the public sphere, NASA tends to be a target for case studies: hardly a typical federal bureaucracy (Beggs, 1984; Lambright, 1992; Morris & Williams, 2012). At the individual level, the 'great man' approach of studying individuals in visible positions, though often the only practical option for learning about leaders in context, has significant drawbacks. First, researchers often are not able to access typical leaders. Second, they may not observe what is really going on when they do focus on individuals. For example, in the late 1990s before the fall of Enron in 2001, then-CEO Ken Lay was featured as an exemplar of leadership. This was before the company imploded under his leadership, destroying shareholder assets and costing many their livelihoods.

More recently, Sheryl Sandberg provided her autobiographical case study of leadership, concluding that women need to *Lean in* (Sandberg, 2013). One way of construing the message, which landed unevenly, is "try a little harder, ladies, and that glass slipper will fit." Intriguingly, there is some evidence that this 'great woman' genre may not motivate women towards leadership positions any more than the 'great man' version (Hoyt & Simon, 2011).

Findings on Leadership Research Have Been All Over the Map

Scanning the leadership literature across disciplines and practice can be a mind-bending experience. Leaders should be charismatic, which typically implies a degree of narcissism.[15] Leaders should be transformational[16], which implies possession of emotional intelligence. Leaders should be authentic[17], but only to a point.[18] The range of findings poses problems for the consumer, whether an individual or an organization. Upon which research findings should workplace selection and leader development be built? What level of confidence can there be that in the complex, dynamic environment of the workplace the desired results will be achieved? Evidence from the private sector varies, but estimates suggest that somewhere between 50–70% of those promoted into entry and mid-level leadership positions fail; they leave or are removed from positions within 18–24 months.

Failure is not necessarily a bad thing, if individuals reflect on and learn from the experience. In fact, wisdom in leader development circles indicates that leaders become stronger and gain resilience by learning and growing through failure. This is consistent with research on building 'productive failure' opportunities into curriculum design (Kapur & Toh, 2013). Even if we assume that some percentage of cases include productive failure, it's pretty clear that significant misalignments are playing out. Comparable data on public sector selections are not available, but based on employee engagement and anecdotal data, as well as very public failures of leaders to exercise due diligence in performance of their roles that result in very real harm to citizens (e.g., Veterans' Health Administration and Flint Water scandals), there is reason to believe that public sector rates may be comparable.

What Is 'Known'?

Some see emerging coherence in the vast enterprise of leadership research (for example, Meuser et al., 2016). But, as claimed by seminal figures in the enterprise of theorizing about and conducting research on leadership, theory needs to be more relevant to, and more closely approximate, real world complexity. We are not making a novel observation—concerns arise from across the field—whether on the methodological front (Brutus & Duniewicz, 2012) or in calls for more robust theory (Avolio, 2007; Hackman, 2010; Lord & Dinh, 2014).

In closing remarks at a conference of academics oriented towards a business/management take on leadership, Hackman (2010) noted that a pessimistic summary might conclude "leadership [is] little more than a semantic inkblot, an ambiguous word onto which people project their personal fantasies, hopes, and anxieties about what it takes to make a difference"(p. 107). Choosing a more constructive tone, Hackman proceeded to focus remarks on directions for further work that might generate "knowledge about leadership that is more robust, cumulative, and useful than what we collectively have produced so far" (p. 107).

While room for developing theory more effectively grounded in reality exists, an upside of the extent of research available is the presence of recurring threads. Consistent with the definition of leading in place with which we started, we highlight three threads which appear to have broad and consistent support from across the literature.

- The primary job of leaders is to *influence others to get things done,* to accomplish shared goals.
- Framing and *promoting shared sense-making* (getting others 'on the same page') constitutes a critical tool leaders employ.
- *Self-awareness* and skills of perspective-taking constitute preconditions for being able to accomplish either of the other two.

The first two threads describe what leaders do; the third focuses on the individual's ability and strengths that subtend the doing. We address each in turn below. Since self-awareness is foundational we address it first, then the other two in turn.

Effective Leadership Requires Self-awareness

Self-awareness influences effectiveness across domains of life. It undergirds emotional intelligence as well as the skill of perspective-taking which is necessary for effectively doing all the things leaders do: influencing, motivating, coaching, assessing, developing others, as well as managing their own stress. As already noted, perspective-taking enables individuals to step outside their own frame or view to comprehend others' feelings and perspectives, and further to bring that back as a filter on their own perspective. It is an iterative process, a process of reflection requiring thought and energy. A certain maturity is required to do this, especially in emotionally charged or otherwise pressured situations. A habit of perspective-taking not only builds understanding of others' standpoint, it also naturally deepens our own. Having our own perspectives or thought processes challenged may not always be comfortable but it builds complexity of thought and stretches capacity to understand situations. Hence, it contributes to enhanced insight and improved decision-making: clearly a good skill if one hopes to influence others, with or without formal position.

Leaders Influence Others to Ensure Accomplishment of Shared Goals

The phrases 'influence others' and 'shared goals' constitute a crux of leadership. Leaders influence not only followers, but peers, superiors, and customers/stakeholders as appropriate by level. Second, in the context of interaction with these constituencies, they engage in sense-making that promotes shared comprehension of the goals, the environment, and what's necessary to navigate the latter to achieve the former. Sense-making enables teams to articulate goals, make sense of their internal or external environment, and operate together to achieve those goals.

Influence others: How this happens varies by setting, organization type, and level. What happens is stable across setting, organization type, and level. Leaders develop relations with others in order to influence those others to work towards certain ends, whether that be shareholder value, better educational outcomes, or processing invoices on time. While sphere and status (as well as resources available) vary substantially between an executive of a global conglomerate and a community organization, for example, leadership behaviors exhibited may have quite a bit in common. The executive might get a group of colleagues together on the proverbial golf course to build relations. A local activist, on the other hand, might choose a coffee shop, public library, or church social hall; for a parent militating for school change it might be someone's living room. The principles underlying the processes to which leaders attend remain constant.

In strictly hierarchical settings (an increasingly rare environment in the 21st century), influence may result from the exercise of authority residing in one's position. Fear and intimidation along the lines used in sweatshops and mines of the late 19th and early 20th century are, hopefully, increasingly rare although it's naïve to believe these models don't still exist. In most contexts, authority alone will get a leader very little. Organizations that allow climates of intimidation or abuse of power to go unchecked end up with low engagement and high turnover—or maybe worse, low engagement and low turnover. Simply having a designated position of leadership is not enough. Followers know when they are not respected and valued, and organizations have just either degraded or given up an important resource. Enlightened and effective leaders in the modern world mostly use relationships,[19] not position, to influence others by developing connections of trust and/or standing. Position matters, and if they're effective, leaders with position will always have power. More and more in our modern world of complex, diffuse work and social relations, however, emergent leaders without designated position will likely play an ever more pivotal role.

Moving forward in the 21st century, the most innovative organizations will embrace the phenomenon of leading in place—and those who embody it. This logic is implicit in companies that have adopted management models eschewing hierarchy. Zappos, an online retail company that was an early adopter of self-management[20] structures, may be the best-known example. Zappos, and unknown numbers of other organizations, are moving to hyper-flat structures, stripping away as many designated leader positions as feasible in order to empower individuals to collaborate, maximizing opportunity for fluidity and productivity. This may be emergent leadership at its logical extreme.

As noted in the discussion of status at the beginning of this chapter, emergent leadership is recognized by followers, even if the emergent leader does not in fact have either the authority of an assigned position or the conscious intention of leading. Organizations confer positions; followers confer leadership based on their perceptions of and experience with individuals. We've all had the experience of being in situations in which one person is nominally in charge, but most in the group actually look to someone else for guidance, be it a public agency, business, a campus organization, or a community group.

Sense-making: 'Shared goals' is a deceptively simple phrase. Even with crystal-clear goals (and they often aren't), ensuring goals are shared by all involved (i.e., that everyone has the same understanding and commitment to operate towards their achievement) requires deep attentiveness from leaders. In order to function effectively, groups—whether informal coalitions, formally constituted teams, or political parties—must engage in shared sense-making. Chaotic or incomplete sense-making results in breakdown and ineffective functioning as Weick (1993) illustrated in a seminal article (case study) in which he applied the concept of sense-making to understanding the 1949 Mann Gulch forest fire in which 13 firefighters lost their lives. Extensive work on how sense-making plays out—or doesn't—in organizations has followed.[21]

The importance of sense-making applies in any environment where conditions fluctuate and more than one person is involved in goal achievement. In order to function effectively as a team over time, any group needs to share both an identity as a team and an understanding of how they function in a complex environment. For example, sales teams need to understand not only how they perform when times are good but also when setbacks occur, such as stress in the broader company.

Quick—what was the objective of the 'Occupy Wall Street' movement that started in September 2011 when protestors took over Zuccotti Park in

New York City? Few of us probably immediately access a clear answer to that question. Further, the number of answers likely equals the numbers of respondents. Groups without leaders typically do not function reliably. This doesn't mean that one formally designated leader must exist, just that without leadership to facilitate sense-making, groups cannot coalesce and perform effectively over time.[22] They inevitably dissolve—sometimes without disbanding. As the extreme example, Occupy Wall Street both dissolved and disbanded.

Leadership, whether residing in a position, in one person (with or without position), or distributed across individuals, differentiates teams from groups. The former, with leadership, are able to develop shared sense-making, regardless of external pressures, that supports goal achievement. The latter do not benefit from consistency and commitment that comes from shared sense-making, so usually do not endure. The ability to drive, to support, to contribute shared sense-making is definitive of effective leadership, whether accomplished by an individual with a designated position or by one who leads in place.

Leadership Unfolds across Spheres of Life

Leadership unfolds across all spheres of life . . . or doesn't, to the detriment of all. That said, in order to place boundaries around our work, we refer primarily to the workplace. Our conception of 'the workplace' is broad and covers a spectrum of socio-temporal spaces. It includes not just what are traditionally thought of as the 'workplace' such as for-profit, non-profit, and governmental organizations. It also embraces community, voluntary, and other organizations in which women expend their effort to accomplish goals other than personal goals. The reality is that non-remunerated activities make substantial contributions to the society and long-term productivity of the national economy, even though they are less amenable to measurement than remunerated work. They unfold successfully and continue over time only because individuals step up to lead.

Notes

1 Quote downloaded from a Barron's online article which is no longer available online: www.barrons.com/articles/greg-valliere-clinton-will-win-easily-1476381940 (posted October 13, 2016 2:05 p.m. ET). However, a version can be accessed at: www.barrons.com/articles/greg-valliere-clinton-will-win-easily-1476381940.

2 For an authoritative review of much of the literature, currently in its 8th edition, see Yukl (2012). For more detailed treatment of individual topics, see the edited *Handbook of leadership theory & practice* (Nohria & Khurama, 2010).

3 Due to unique prevailing conditions in the realms of military and political leadership, distinct branches of inquiry address these topics. The topic of what differentiates leadership in these realms from other varieties—if anything—engenders substantial conversation among leadership nerds. We ignore, but are not ignorant of, that debate.

4   This statement alone might set some gasping—it implies 'contingent' theory: i.e., that there is no 'universal' dimension to leadership, but that it necessarily varies across contexts. It is not our intention to favor one category of theory over another. Our objective is clarity of discourse.

5   Within the genre, theories tend to be constructed in fairly broad terms. But in order to conduct studies to 'test' theories, hard constraints have to be drawn around variables of interest. Relatively narrow aspects of individuals (e.g., selected personality traits such as openness or neuroticism), or limited specified behaviors (e.g., developing others) are studied.

6   It should be noted there is robust literature on followership.

7   Meindl (1995) provided early exploration of the followers' perspective, highlighting the complexity of socially constructed processes.

8   For a review and first meta-analysis of research from this frame, see Judge et al. (2002).

9   For a current review framing exploration of the darker side of personality and leadership, see Harms, Spain, & Hannah (2011).

10 For an effort to draw it together, see Meuser et al. (2016).

11 For more information, see: www.apa.org/pubs/databases/psycinfo/index.aspx

12 For seminal work see Bandura (1977). For more recent applications tying the concept directly to leadership, see Yang, Ding, & Lo (2016) or Caillier (2016).

13 See Shipman & Kay (2014) for a review and specific reference to women's stories.

14 For a clear review of the construct and excellent treatment of one way in which it may play out for female leaders, see Sturm et al. (2014). Notably, the constructs of self-efficacy and self-awareness have recently been directly connected in theory as foundational to leader effectiveness, see Caldwell & Hayes (2016).

15 Sankowsky (1995) provided early discussion of the downsides of charismatic leaders. More recent scholarship focuses on disaggregating how various individual differences play out in social interactions to differentiate productive charisma from more destructive narcissism: see, for example, Galvin, Waldman, & Balthazard (2010).

16 Burns (1978) introduced the construct, which was elaborated and established as integral to the leadership lexicon by Bass (1985)—and a subsequent stream of research.

17 Early work on this topic by Luthans & Avolio (2003) generated an entire industry of research and application.

18 In his book *Leadership BS,* Pfeffer (2015) took issue with many prescriptions for leaders developed without reference to context. He included 'being authentic' in revealing true feelings as behavior that might not always serve leaders or their organizations.

19 Relationships constitute the primary modality of influence. Effective leaders of course also intentionally deploy resources (e.g., budget, network connections) to support followers and facilitate goal achievement. Effectiveness of how these resources are deployed is intimately related with interpersonal relations. Deployment that unfolds in a transparent manner, promoting and preserving trust, contributes to positive team outcomes—even if not all members benefit equally. Outcomes associated with obscure or underhanded decision processes can undermine team outcomes (although it might serve limited numbers of individuals).

20 For more information on Zappos' specific approach and story, see: www.zapposinsights.com/about/holacracy. For an early review of 'leaderless teams' (i.e., teams without designated leaders) or what the authors call 'holacracy' see Bernstein et al. (2016).

21 Weick (2010) also analyzed the failure of sense-making in the run up to the Bhopal disaster. For a more recent and fascinating application of the concept to development of Wikipedia content, see Nagar (2012).

22 For an exploration of what this reality means for social activism in an era of social media, see Tufecki (2017).

References

Avolio, B. (2007). Promoting more integrative strategies for leadership theory-building. *American Psychologist*, 62(1), 25–33.

Bandura, A. (1977). Self-efficacy: Toward a unifying theory of behavioral change. *Psychological Review*, 84(2), 191–215.

Bass, B. M. (1985). *Leadership and performance beyond expectation*. New York, NY: Free Press.

Beggs, J. M. (1984). Leadership: The NASA approach. *Long Range Planning*, 17(2), 12–24.

Bernstein, E., Bunch, J., Canner, N., & Lee, M. (2016). Beyond the holacracy hype. *Harvard Business Review*, 94(7/8), 38–49.

Brutus, S., & Duniewicz, K. (2012). The many heels of Achilles: An analysis of self-reported limitations in leadership research. *The Leadership Quarterly*, 23(1), 202–212.

Burns, J. M. (1978). *Leadership*. New York, NY: Harper and Row.

Caillier, J. G. (2016). Linking transformational leadership to self-efficacy, extra-role behaviors, and turnover intentions in public agencies: The mediating role of goal clarity. *Administration & Society*, 48(7), 883–906.

Caldwell, C., & Hayes, L. A. (2016). Self-efficacy and self-awareness: Moral insights to increased leader effectiveness. *Journal of Management Development*, 35(9), 1163–1173.

Cullen, K. L., Gentry, W. A., & Yammarino, F. J. (2015). Biased self perception tendencies: Self-enhancement/self-diminishment and leader derailment in individualistic and collectivistic cultures. *Applied Psychology: An International Review*, 64(1), 161–207.

Forgas, J. P. (Ed.). (2001). *Handbook of affect & social cognition*. Mahwah, NJ: Psychology Press.

Galvin, B. M., Waldman, D. A., & Balthazard, P. (2010). Visionary communication qualities as mediators of the relationship between narcissism and attributions of leader charisma. *Personnel Psychology*, 63(3), 509–537.

Goleman, D. (1995). *Emotional intelligence: Why it can matter more than IQ*. New York, NY: Bantam Books.

Hackman, J. R. (2010). What is this thing called leadership? In N. Nohria & R. Khurana (Eds.), *Handbook of leadership theory & practice* (pp. 107–116). Boston, MA: Harvard Business Press.

Harms, P. D., Spain, S. M., & Hannah, S. T. (2011). Leader development and the dark side of personality. *The Leadership Quarterly*, 22(3), 495–509.

Hoyt, C. L., & Simon, S. (2011). Female leaders: Injurious or inspiring role models for women? *Psychology of Women Quarterly*, 35(1), 143–157.

Judge, T. A., Bono, J. E., Ilies, R., & Gerhardt, M. W. (2002). Personality and leadership: A qualitative and quantitative review. *Journal of Applied Psychology*, 87(4), 765–780.

Kapur, M., & Toh, P. L. L. (2013). Productive failure: From an experimental effect to a learning design. In T. Plomp & N. Nieveen (Eds.), *Educational design research—Part B: Illustrative cases* (pp. 341–355). Enschede, The Netherlands: SLO.

Lambright, W. H. (1992). The Augustine report, NASA, and the leadership problem. *Public Administration Review*, 52(2), 192.

Lord, R. G., & Dinh, J. E. (2014). What have we learned that is critical in understanding leadership perceptions and leader-performance relations? *Industrial and Organizational Psychology*, 7(2), 158–177.

Luthans, F., & Avolio, B. J. (2003). Authentic leadership development. In K. S. Cameron, J. E. Dutton, & R. E. Quinn (Eds.), *Positive organizational scholarship: Foundations of a new discipline* (pp. 241–261). San Francisco, CA: Barrett-Koehler.

Meindl, J. R. (1995). The romance of leadership as a follower-centric theory: A social constructionist approach. *The Leadership Quarterly*, 6(3), 329–341.

Meuser, J. D., Gardner, W. L., Dinh, J. E., Hu, J., Liden, R. C., & Lord, R. G. (2016). A network analysis of leadership theory: The infancy of integration. *Journal of Management*, 42(5), 1374–1403.

Morris, L. E., & Williams, C. R. (2012). A behavioral framework for highly effective technical executives. *Team Performance Management*, 18(3–4), 210–230.

Nagar, Y. (2012). What do you think? The structuring of an online community as a collective-sensemaking process. In B. Collier & J. Bear (Eds.), *Proceedings of the ACM 2012 conference on Computer Supported Cooperative Work* (pp. 393–402). Seattle, WA: ACM. Retrieved from http://cci.mit.edu/publications/CCIwp2011-06.pdf. Last accessed: January 9, 2018.

Nohria, N., & Khurana, R. (Eds.). (2010). *Handbook of leadership theory & practice*. Boston, MA: Harvard Business Press.

Pfeffer, J. (2015). *Leadership BS: Fixing workplaces and careers one truth at a time*. New York, NY: Harper Collins Publishers.

Rock, D. (2009). *Your brain at work*. New York, NY: Harper Collins Publishers.

Sandberg, S. (2013). *Lean in: Women, work, and the will to lead*. New York, NY: Random House.

Sankowsky, D. (1995). The charismatic leader as narcissist: Understanding the abuse of power. *Organizational Dynamics*, 23(4), 57–71.

Shipman, C., & Kay, K. (2014). *The confidence code: The science and art of self-assurance—what women should know*. New York, NY: Harper Collins Publishers.

Shondrick, S. J., & Lord, R. G. (2010). Implicit leadership and followership theories: Dynamic structures for leadership perceptions, memory, and leader-follower processes. In G. P. Hodgkinson, J. K. Ford, G. P. Hodgkinson, & J. K. Ford (Eds.), *International review of industrial and organizational psychology* (pp. 1–33). Hoboken, NJ: Wiley.

Sturm, R. E., Taylor, S. N., Atwater, L. E., & Braddy, P. W. (2014). Leader self-awareness: An examination and implications of women's under-prediction. *Journal of Organizational Behavior*, 35(5), 657–677.

Tufecki, Z. (2017). *Twitter and tear gas: The power and fragility of networked protest*. New Haven, CT: Yale University Press.

Weick, K. E. (1993). The collapse of sensemaking in organizations: The Mann Gulch disaster. *Administrative Science Quarterly*, 38(4), 628–652.

Weick, K. (2010). Reflections on enacted sensemaking in the Bhopal disaster. *Journal of Management Studies*, 47(3), 537–550.

Wong, C., & Law, K. S. (2002). The effects of leader and follower emotional intelligence on performance and attitude: An exploratory study. *The Leadership Quarterly*, 13(3), 243–274.

Yang, C., Ding, C. G., & Lo, K. W. (2016). Ethical leadership and multidimensional organizational citizenship behaviors: The mediating effects of self-efficacy, respect, and leader–member exchange. *Group & Organization Management*, 41(3), 343–374.

Yukl, G. (2012). *Leadership in organizations* (8th ed.). Upper Saddle River, NJ: Pearson, Prentice Hall.

3

TAKING ANOTHER LOOK

The Employment Landscape Varies over Time—With Implications for Demands on Leadership

The workplace is evolving quickly, in response to economic pressures, technological innovations, the demographic profile of the labor force, and cultural expectations. There are far-reaching implications for individuals' careers and lives. We can't know exactly what this means for the workplace of 20–30 years from now. Effects to date are clear, however, and evolutionary trends reflect a degree of convergence. Except for pockets of the economy such as utilities (and possibly some government jobs), the days when an employee held the same job or worked for the same employer for life appears an artifact of the past (for an accessible and interpretive review see Pedula, 2011; for an in-depth treatment of what it means in an industry habituated to formal tenure commitments, the academic sector, see Gappa, Austin, & Trice, 2007). Substantial effort is being deployed to understand what this means for individuals and organizations alike.[1]

The US economy has transformed towards a globalized, knowledge- and other services-based economy. Services now account for roughly 80% of the US GDP and the same percentage (i.e., 80%) of those employed in the US were categorized as somehow related to service industries (Ward, 2010). Healthcare, social assistance, education, and professional services industries are expected to continue to grow faster than the average of all categories of employment (US Bureau of Labor Statistics, 2015). Hot topics of research on workers' experiences in modern workplaces emphasize engagement and motivation.

Pieces on how millennials are reshaping the workplace are ubiquitous in both research and popular publications. Millennials, the most diverse generation in the US to date, have grown up with technology, and appear not to be eager to step into the largely linear, hierarchical working world of their parents and grandparents (for a good review of the phenomenon see Ng, Schweitzer, & Lyons, 2010). In an advisory piece to executives (Brack & Kelly, 2012) one team concluded that millennials believe "there are multiple opportunities to stop along the way, with great views they can instantly snap with their camera phones, post to Facebook, and add a status update, all before the next stop." On average, millennials prefer a more socially responsible, interactive workplace that contains substantial feedback. The view that norms of employment relationships will continue to develop in order to balance worker and employer interests appears pervasive (see for example, Tomlinson & Modica, 2015; Mercer, 2017). Whether generational differences will exert definitive influence on work environments, or whether progression through the life cycle (e.g., advent of family responsibilities) will significantly alter expectations and perceptions remains to be seen. Likely, influences will run both ways. (See Box 3.1.)

Discussions of what the combination of relatively rapid and continuing socioeconomic and demographic changes mean for workplace leadership generally—and more specifically how the changing structure of work organizations and workforce composition will shape demands on leadership—has garnered less attention. Certainly, some are thinking in this direction (e.g., Laloux, 2014), but it does not get as much press. There is every reason to believe that trends of the early 21st century will continue for the foreseeable future. Demographic shifts, rapid technology development, continuing disruptions in the global economy and drives to find more environmentally friendly footing for the national economy all point towards the likelihood that the labor market of the future (and employer–employee relations) will be characterized by relative fluidity. The demographic side of this is important. Implications extend beyond numbers and

---

BOX 3.1 FLEXIBLE BY CHOICE . . . ?

Boomer and Gen X women have chosen flexible, alternative, and part-time arrangements in significant numbers. Women constituted 66% of those working part-time in 2014. Of the total women working part-time only 19% reported doing so for economic reasons (e.g., they couldn't find a job with full-time hours). The vast majority (81%) chose part-time for non-economic reasons (e.g., family obligations).

Is it that full-time jobs that allow 'work-life balance', are not available to women—or do they just not want them? Is it that, as a category, women are simply more willing to apply their own, as opposed to employers', calculus in approaching the integration of work and life?

www.dol.gov/wb/stats/percentage_lf_work_pt_sex_reason_2014_txt.htm

compositions in the aggregate. Expectations, especially about recognition of con-tribution and work-life balance, are shifting. This will have tectonic implications for organizations' abilities to retain a diverse talent pool and manage themselves if strategic understanding is not integrated into leader selection and development practices now.

Research Has Influenced—and Skewed—Practice

Leadership theory and research findings have migrated into the workplace in a variety of ways. An early wave was evidenced in leader selection and assessment practices; more recently, there has been a rise in research-based leader develop-ment practices. Following World War II, there was a drive to translate social psy-chology and leadership research and practices developed by the military to the civilian realm. Competency modeling, assessment centers, and calibrated rating scales for interviewing all grew out of psychology research. These tools have been systematically developed and applied across sectors to differentiate between those who exhibit leadership and those who don't; between viable and not-viable candidates for leadership roles. The drive initially was to introduce science to selection, and use measurable factors other than intelligence. Substantial gains have accrued to organizations and individuals through the application of research findings into talent management practices. Improvements in selection increase the likelihood of successfully matching individuals and roles. When implemented effectively, increased attention to employee development, satisfaction, engagement, organizational culture, and other factors serve employees and organizations alike.

Three very real drawbacks in the translation of leadership theory and research into practice have become visible over time, however. First, the demands of academic conventions may inflict unintended consequences as research findings get translated into practice. Second, competencies, a primary tool translated from research into practice, may have less robust utility than assumed. Third, biases (conscious and/or unconscious) exacerbate unintended consequences from two angles: implicitly embedded into research, and/or unchallenged in organizations.

Academic Convention and Reality

Put simply, research findings may be communicated with just a little too much confidence. And a corollary, those translating the most current research findings into practice may not step back and ask enough questions. Theorizing, and con-ducting studies to disprove or validate one's theory about humans and human behavior in social dynamics, is an imperfect business. If something is reliably rep-licable across a variety of settings and times, such as measuring temperature, then we're operating in the realm of declarative knowledge. When considering human behavior and interactions—particularly in complex environments across periods of socio-economic and cultural development—there is a natural limit to what can be 'known' declaratively. A project to replicate a cross section of psychological studies in fact made quite a splash when published—via the Open Science Collaboration (2015) of the journal *Science*. Results could be replicated unequivocally for only 39 out of 100 studies.

This is not news to academics studying leadership, whether psychologists engaged in experimental research or management researchers producing case studies. However, in aggregate, the milieu in which academics compete—for publication, tenure, and the status of 'expert'—values the kind of certainty achieved through statistics and an implicitly unbounded definition of generalizability. Psychologists would not be lauded for intellectual integrity if they submitted results for publication with language along the lines of:

> We believe there may be something to this, but the exact degree of certitude that can be attached to these results is unclear. We looked at an isolated slice of humans and neither varied, nor could control for, highly relevant 'real world' factors such as level of stress at home, life cycle stage, or stability of values structure. More troubling, there is growing evidence that college undergraduates (or even graduate students) in the lab have at best little resemblance to adults in the workplace. We have neither the intention nor resources to repeat this experiment with this same sample in ten years. Further, even if we could, dispersion across spheres might compromise sample size. Nevertheless, we believe these findings are useful because ... etc., etc.

They would not get published, not get taken seriously, and end up without tenure. Faculty across disciplines face similar pressures. A claim along the lines "We think this leader is really interesting, but believe that x factors dictate that this case is unique and caution against simple extrapolation to other environments, without considering these serious constraints" would likely not lead to successful establishment in their field. For example, Jeffrey Pfeffer built a reputation on studies of time (among other topics) with generalizable conclusions. He did not start his career debunking others' findings as *'Leadership BS'* (Pfeffer, 2015).

Discussions about how design and method might significantly limit generalizability can unfold as part of the peer review process: rarely are they detailed in publications. Further, disciplinary boundaries themselves create challenges. Interdisciplinary work is difficult, regardless of the topic. Constructs, findings, and methods vary and it can be hard for researchers coming from distinct fields to collaborate effectively. It takes more effort than simply staying within the conventions of a given field. Those actually doing the work implicitly understand the limitations; those applying it often face pressures to downplay them.

Those engaged in consuming and translating research findings into practice (e.g., consultants, practitioners, and those publishing in the popular and business press) may not always pay sufficient attention to differences between experimental and real-world settings. It takes time and effort to think through and test for these. Both resources are often in short supply for practitioners, and executives typically have limited resources and low tolerance for methodical testing. In our age of urgency and limited attention span,[2] clients and readers want a take-away that makes a difference and provides a solution *now*. As a consequence, a tremendous amount gets published about leadership and leader development in a tone of greater certainty than is actually warranted. Further, research can get translated or consumed in ways that exacerbate limitations.

The overhanging costs of false certainty litter the organizational landscape. A key symptom of this problem is the under-representation of women in leadership ranks. If competency models, assessment centers, interview rating scales, and all the other devices structured into selection and development systems were alone sufficient and effective, then results would be more consistently positive and there would be more women in top leadership positions across industries. Not only would there be more representative gender distribution in leadership ranks, but leaders in organizations would be maintaining engagement, creating inclusive, resilient cultures, and pushing but not overwhelming those who work for them. Many on the front lines of work in the current era do not report these experiences. Instead, organizations are scrambling to understand either how to engage and/or recruit talent.

Competencies

A landmark accomplishment, from human resource practitioners' perspective, was AT&T's establishment and use of assessment centers (post WWII) to identify managerial talent. AT&T conducted a longitudinal 'Management Progress Study' (Bray, 1964) of their talent pool, following workers who were selected into management. Results of the study were translated into a predictive model for selecting candidates via assessment centers. Over time, this assessment method and use of competencies for which to select became intertwined.

Conceptual definition of what constitutes a competency remains fuzzy. They can be thought of as amalgams of characteristics and behaviors expected to be related to the likelihood of success in a given role. The expected relationship is established by statistically relating behaviors and characteristics with successful role accomplishment. Done correctly, establishing competencies is a labor-intensive effort. So, companies or their consultants go through elaborate processes to create competency models for a given role. Human resource staff and managers in organizations remain on the lookout for individual contributors and team members that exhibit these competencies. They also assess candidates for leadership positions against components of those models. These practices spawned a lucrative market likely worth hundreds of billions of dollars by the time one accounts for associated IT investments.

Particularly in a service and knowledge economy, human capital (or what has come to be called talent) constitutes a significant asset for any organization. Smart investment strategy requires ensuring one has top quality talent. This, in turn, requires selecting and developing only the most likely to succeed as future organizational leaders. Applying scientifically validated means of making those selections increases the confidence with which such investments can be made.

The accuracy and reliability of these scientific mechanisms, however, may have been oversold. Two potential weaknesses of models have come to concern research and practitioners alike. First, in a clear illustration of the downsides of false certainty in a complex and changing world, simply extrapolating from what worked in the past may be a faulty strategy. Approaches that serve well in a stable environment may be less useful in chaotic and complex environments. Competencies established with old data (e.g., even three or five years old) may not actually serve organizations well. Second, unanticipated biases may have gone undetected till recently. While the intent of selection models and practices has been to ensure a robust, level field for selecting, assessing, and developing leaders, application of implicitly biased models in changing environments may yield just the opposite. For example, Catalyst (a non-profit organization whose mission is to promote inclusion of women in the workplace) published a report (Warren, 2009) detailing potential biases in systems and applications.

Biases and Disquieting Questions

We acquire leader prototypes through our socio-cultural environments and exposure, and though they shape our expectations we do not usually reflect on them. We take these into the world with us, and essentially sort leaders we encounter, *as well as ourselves as leaders*, against these models. These leader prototypes have been studied for decades with fairly stable results. For example, there is substantial evidence that many (men and women) hold prototypes of leaders as male (Eagly & Karau, 2002; Nye & Forsyth, 1991; Forsyth, Heiney, & Wright, 1997). It is impossible to know the extent to which such unexamined biases, whether from researchers, subjects, decision-makers, or others, skew research and organizational practice around leadership. This is unavoidable. We're human. However, it may be more pernicious than disciplines as a whole are willing to take on board.[3]

Are systems used to select, assess, and develop leaders built upon sufficiently robust concepts of leaders to recognize equally leadership capacities and potential across genders and other demographics? Are those implementing systems (i.e., talent managers, current leaders, *and* peers) equipped with sufficient self-awareness to ensure that they see and evaluate all candidates fairly?

Human cognition unfolds in complex and only partially understood ways. Add a social dimension and the degree of complexity expands quickly. Typically, we remain unaware of cognitive short cuts we use that strongly influence how, as individuals and as organizations we define, perceive, and react to leaders. Researchers and practitioners can unintentionally fall prey to both bias in leader prototypes and implicit or unconscious bias in evaluation of observed behavior. There has been increasing attention to the issue of how bias may be introduced whether through leader prototypes of subjects or in action in organizations (see Junker & van Dick, 2014, for a review). Some research focuses specifically on the question of gender (e.g., Hoyt & Murphy, 2016; Walker & Aritz, 2015). Yet there is still significant distance to go in understanding unexamined distortions—particularly as they influence framing of research, and therefore findings. It is revealing, for instance, that a groundbreaking effort to find integrating themes across leadership research (Meuser et al., 2016) over a 14-year period (i.e., 2000–2013) appeared to relegate research on women and leadership to the area of 'diversity theories' (p. 1389).

Individuals who don't conform to characteristics and behaviors associated with operative prototypes can get squeezed out on both ends. If an organization has a selection model built essentially on a male leader prototype, as many do, women can face challenges getting selected into leadership roles. They just don't fit the model. In such circumstances, even if women do make it into leadership roles, they can fare poorly in evaluations. This can happen either because they're not seen as exhibiting desired leadership characteristics and behaviors, or because they are judged negatively for exhibiting 'male' characteristics and/or behaviors. Both those with formal leadership roles and those who lead in place can be judged differentially by gender—across levels.

Typically, those evaluating men and women differently for the same behaviors are not aware that they're doing it. Instead, unconscious biases influence assessments without raters even being aware that they hold such biases (Bargh et al., 2001; Wegner, 2002). Bias doesn't come from one demographic: it's not that simple. Women can hold a male leader prototype, and be as inclined as men to judge women more harshly, an effect that has been observed across cultures (Cuadrado, Garcia-Ael, & Molero, 2015). It takes a high degree of self-awareness to first identify one's own biases, and second, develop compensatory mechanisms to ensure they don't color evaluations of others. No one demographic is prone to making unreflected judgments—it's simply human. (See Box 3.2.)

The implications of such biases play out in multiple ways in the workplace, from selection all the way through task assignment, assessment, development, and decisions about promotion. Human resource (HR) professionals are well aware of potential biases associated with implementing instruments and protocols and have practices to minimize these risks. However, if, as is coming to be recognized, the instruments, protocols and systems that HR practitioners use to select and develop leader candidates are founded on theory that is inherently biased, there are far-reaching and as yet unmitigated risks.

The preponderance of psychological theory of the late 20th century, and the work of leadership researchers and practitioners influenced by it, by no means ignored the effects of biases and stereotypes. However, they have not consistently been either explicitly folded into, or controlled for, in the vast majority of research

BOX 3.2 EVIDENCE OF WEAK COMMITMENT, OR DECISION-MAKING?

A current theme in popular practice emphasizes the importance of the capacity to step back. This is based on neuro-cognitive research linking cognitive 'down time' with improved health as well as creativity; and therefore effectiveness. Exhortations abound to engage in 'mindfulness' practices, or take vacations, any way of stepping back, as means of cultivating both innovation and resilience.

Yet women who choose to proactively step back are often judged to not be serious professionals, to be taking an 'off ramp'. Maybe they simply are taking risks and exhibiting sound decision-making (consistent with their priorities). Just because it doesn't suit the interests of a particular employer at a particular juncture, such action should not translate into a judgment on the individual's commitment or capacity. Would a choice to move on to an alternate employer elicit the same judgment?

on leadership. Women, as a category, are not the only ones affected by this lapse; it has implications for the workplace generally.

If leader selection and development practices designed in the past have built-in biases—either in the prototypes underlying competency construction or in rating processes—steps can be taken to identify and mitigate these. It is not a small undertaking, requiring significant effort, resources, and, as in any organizational adjustment, leadership commitment. Criteria and processes can be structured to minimize known or common biases; and raters can be trained to become aware, and mitigate the impact, of their respective biases. Google, for example, invested in efforts to design systems and promote practices to reduce the potential influence of biases in selection and promotion (Bock, 2015).

The study of, and interventions to counteract, negative effects of unconscious biases in the workplace and public policy have burgeoned in recent years. There are limits to what is known about effective practice in ensuring that bias is understood as a wide range of potential skews or filters that influence thinking of each and every individual—as opposed to a narrow set of specific stereotypes that are known to disadvantage some groups. The very public storm around a memo written by a Google employee (Matsakis, Koebler, & Emerson, 2017) highlights such challenges. Without defending or accepting points made in the 'manifesto' (as opposed to sensationalized characterizations), it is possible to hear an employee militating for discussion around a charged topic. It is also possible to hear a disgruntled individual that might benefit from increased socialization in the workplace. Without being the author, the author's manager, or peers, it is impossible to know which reading, or weights between interpretations, is accurate. However, the intensity of reactions both within Google and online highlights that theorists and practitioners alike face a steep challenge to translate knowledge about the role of heuristics or bias in human cognition into practice that improves experience and results for *all,* guarding against the risk of getting stuck at underscoring or reinforcing difference and divisiveness. Notably, while biases around demographic diversity (e.g., gender, generation, self-identity dimensions) have been, and are being, tackled there appears to be far more limited attention in practice to expectations and biases around leadership style. Ironically, effective leadership positions organizations to promote psychological safety (see Edmondson & Lei, 2014) and hence get the best out of diverse talent pools.

It's Time for an Upgrade in Thinking about Leadership

Thomas Kuhn's landmark *Structure of scientific revolutions* (1962) invited readers to consider that scientific understanding might not result from linear, constant-rate accumulation of knowledge, but instead from a more choppy process. Kuhn reviewed the pattern of centuries of scientific studies and discoveries. The sense he made of the evidence was that scientific understanding evolved through cycles of 'normal' (or steady state) science, periods in which one way of seeing things prevailed, followed by 'revolution'. According to Kuhn, revolutions happen as paradigm-breaking theories or discoveries that cannot be fit with prevailing scientific stories gain traction and acceptance . . . not necessarily when they are first put out there but *when they become widely integrated into thinking.* Scientific revolutions can be clearly recognized and described with the benefit of hindsight; less clearly so during the period in which they unfold. Revolutionary at the time, Kuhn's understanding of how scientific knowledge evolves has come to be the common view. His work shifted the prevailing paradigm.

A conceptual revolution around leadership is most definitely unfolding; it simply remains to be seen what's on the other side. At this moment in the 21st century there is an opportunity to both observe from a distance—and accelerate—a shift in paradigms surrounding leadership generally, as well as women's experiences and power as leaders more specifically. Emerging trends towards complexity and adaptive leadership theory in the literature, and towards promotion of adult development theory and mindfulness by leader development practitioners, are encouraging. Each pushes us towards revisiting how we implicitly picture a leader. Complexity theorists (Uhl-Bien, Marion, & McKelvey, 2007) have suggested recognizing varieties of leaders, and leadership roles, in complex organizations. Simultaneously, an entire literature has developed around the concept of shared, or more recently 'collaborative' leadership, in which no one individual has a position of authority analogous to that of traditional hierarchies. Shared leadership is typically studied in the case of intact teams. Collaborative leadership addresses this, but more specifically also focuses on dynamics across organizational boundaries, such as inter-agency task forces or a merger team. We maintain that in order to describe and operation-alize a robust conception of leadership that reflects these new complex realities and options, women's voices have to be integrated into mainstream views, not treated as if they are a niche perspective.

In sum, three phenomena appear to be converging. First, gender roles and expectations have transformed dramatically since the mid-20th century and con-tinue to evolve. Second, there is widespread recognition among researchers and practitioners alike that concepts of leadership are plagued with no small amount of ambiguity and may not be well-grounded in modern reality. Third, the early years of the 21st century have seen dramatic advances in understanding the brain and how neuropsychology operates in human sense-making and interaction. By weaving these three phenomena together, the outlines of more modern concep-tions of leaders and leadership emerge. Returning to the Cinderella analogy, will rigid, fragile glass shoes requiring Herculean levels of effort to appear graceful while walking be abandoned in favor of shoes that can be unisex, flexible, and easily accommodate a variety of gaits?

The literature on diversity and teams is broad and expanding (Jackson & Joshi, 2011). Evidence indicates that inclusive teams incorporating individuals differing along a range of dimensions, holding shared goals, produce better results than homo-geneous teams (Mohammed & Angell, 2004). This is true whether diversity is 'surface-level' along (typically) observable factors as gender, race, or age or 'deep-level' along non-observable dimensions such as thought processes, socio-economic background, or experience (Harrison, Price, & Bell, 1998). There are limits, however; organizational culture and contextual factors appear to constrain or create bound-aries.[4] Generally, as long as individuals make genuine efforts to work together, don't get derailed by interpersonal conflict, and operate in facilitative contexts, variety in team composition contributes to outcomes. This result corresponds with common sense: when has inbreeding ever led to great outcomes? Research on social cognition in teams addresses the effects of composition (homogeneity/heterogeneity) across differences. Interactions and thought processes within teams require some degree of differences among actors or decision and performance processes can be artificially (and sometimes disastrously) skewed towards 'groupthink' (Janis, 1982) by homoge-neity of thinking, experience, or compliance with shared norms.

External factors such as social values (often expressed in laws and regulations) and customer/stakeholder expectations also increasingly require a degree of diversity. The law restrains employers and organizations from discriminating against groups in employment. In our connected world, diversity has grown to be an expected value throughout most of society, even if only for utilitarian purposes.[5] Institutional shareholders may not care about diversity on a given company's board of directors, but if company reputation and therefore value takes a hit, they will take notice.

Nevertheless, both anecdotal reports and aggregate data reflect that distribu-tions of roles and opportunities across genders in the workplace do not align with known good practice. Is this evidence of a failure of leadership itself? Does the way that leadership is conceived create artificial barriers? Is this evidence of failures within organizations? Do behaviors of leaders (whether conscious or unconscious) fail to create facilitative environments thus placing boundary conditions on women? Is there some other explanation? Might the answer be "all of the above"?

Emergent leaders *are* leaders. Theory and research increasingly recognize this and explore enabling conditions (e.g., for an examination with specific reference to women, see Lemoine, Aggarwal, & Steed, 2016). However, organizational charts and/or reward structures rarely explicitly incorporate emergent leaders.

In our complex modern era, the phenomenon of leading in place deserves more attention—in how it is recognized, supported, rewarded, and integrated into organizational decision-making processes. Those who lead in place keep teams and organizations functioning. Leaders with position are necessary for organizations—whether private-sector, governmental, non-profit, or community. For most organizations in the modern, fast-paced world, however, they are not sufficient. Behaviors of leading in place, whether they come from one or multiple individuals contribute in significant ways towards goal achievement. They are fundamentally distinct from 'individual contributor' behaviors that simply do what is expected. The end result is that they go underappreciated and under-supported. Failure to account for, develop and adequately recognize talent that facilitates goal achievement (without position) costs companies. It particularly fails to account for leadership contributions that women make and leaks women from the potential leadership pipeline.

Notes

1 Consultancies are pushing forward to help corporate leadership understand what it means in terms of organizational structure and employee development. For an example from industry, see Bersin et al. (2017).

2 See *The Shallows* by Carr (2011) for exploration of changing cognition.

3 Although anecdotal only, it's worth a short story here. Early versions of this manuscript benefitted greatly from several reviewers and we remain grateful for the thoughtful, constructive feedback received. It was revealing, however, that one self-described expert in the field observed that since the work covered 'leadership and women' the manuscript must belong in the feminist literature (as opposed to mainstream leadership).

4 For examples of work exploring diversity and context, see: Parola, H. R., Ellis, K. M., & Golden, P. (2015). Performance effects of top management team gender diversity during the merger and acquisition process. *Management Decision*, 53(1), 57–74; Schneid, M., Isidor, R., Li, C., & Kabst, R. (2015). The influence of cultural context on the relationship between gender diversity and team performance: A meta-analysis. *The International Journal of Human Resource Management*, 26(6), 733–756; Balkundi, P., Kilduff, M., Barsness, Z. I., & Michael, J. H. (2007). Demographic antecedents and performance consequences of structural holes in work teams. *Journal of Organizational Behavior*, 28(2), 241–260; or Dwyer, S., Richard, O. C., & Chadwick, K. (2003). Gender diversity in management and firm performance: The influence of growth orientation and organizational culture. *Journal of Business Research*, 56(12), 1009–1019.

5   Consider Koch Industries effort to create a new reputation (Gold & Hamburger, 2014). TV spots did not picture the conservative political finance powerhouse Koch brothers themselves. The spots featured a variety of individuals who likely shared little in common with the Kochs—but did either look like, or appeal to, the target audience.

References

Bargh, J. A., Gollwitzer, P. M., Lee-Chai, A., Barndollar, K., & Trötschel, R. (2001). The automated will: Nonconscious activation and pursuit of behavioral goals. *Journal of Personality and Social Psychology*, 81(6), 1014–1027.

Bersin, J., McDowell, T., Rahnema, A., & Van Durme, Y. (2017, February 28). The organization of the Future: Arriving now. *Deloitte Review*. Retrieved from https://dupress.deloitte.com/dup-us-en/focus/human-capital-trends/2017/organization-of-the-future.html?id=us:2el:3dc:dup3817:awa:cons:hct17. Last accessed: January 9, 2018.

Bock, L. (2015). *Work Rules: Insights from inside Google that will transform how you live and lead.* New York, NY: Twelve, Hachette Book Group.

Brack, J., & Kelly, K. (2012). Maximizing millennials in the workplace. *UNC Executive Development.* Retrieved from www.kenan-flagler.unc.edu/executive-development/custom-programs/~/media/DF1C11C056874DDA8097271A1ED48662.ashx. Last accessed: January 9, 2018.

Bray, D. W. (1964). The management progress study. *American Psychologist*, 19(6), 419–420.

Carr, N. (2011). *The shallows: What the internet is doing to our brains.* New York, NY: W. W. Norton & Company.

Cuadrado, I., García Ael, C., & Molero, F. (2015). Gender-typing of leadership: Evaluations of real and ideal managers. *Scandinavian Journal of Psychology*, 56(2), 236–244.

Eagly, A. H., & Karau, S. J. (2002). Role congruity theory of prejudice toward female leaders. *Psychological Review*, 109(3), 573–598.

Edmondson, A. C., & Lei, Z. (2014). Psychological safety: The history, renaissance, and future of an interpersonal construct. *Annual Review of Organizational Psychology and Organizational Behavior*, 1(1), 23–43.

Forsyth, D. R., Heiney, M. M., & Wright, S. S. (1997). Biases in appraisals of women leaders. *Group Dynamics: Theory, Research, and Practice*, 1(1), 98–103.

Gappa, J. M., Austin, A. E., & Trice, A. G. (2007). *Rethinking faculty work: Higher education's strategic imperative.* San Francisco, CA: John Wiley and Sons.

Gold, M. & Hamburger, T. (2014, September 8). Koch Industries adopts new public posture to neutralize opponents, recast image. Retrieved from www.washingtonpost.com/politics/koch-industries-adopts-new-public-posture-to-neutralize-opponents-recast-image/2014/09/07/a85e8484-3502-11e4-a723-fa3895a25d02_story.html?utm_term=.ac5d8606ee80. Last accessed: February 10, 2018.

Harrison, D. A., Price, K. H., & Bell, M. P. (1998). Beyond relational demography: Time and the effects of surface-and deep-level diversity on work group cohesion. *Academy of Management Journal*, 41(1), 96–107.

Hoyt, C. L., & Murphy, S. E. (2016). Managing to clear the air: Stereotype threat, women, and leadership. *The Leadership Quarterly*, 27(3), 387–399.

Jackson, S. E., & Joshi, A. (2011). Work team diversity. In S. Zedeck (Ed.), *APA handbook of industrial and organizational psychology, Vol 1: Building and developing the organization* (pp. 651–686). Washington, DC: American Psychological Association.

Janis, I. (1982). *Groupthink: Psychological studies of policy decisions and fiascoes.* Boston, MA: Houghton Mifflin.

Junker, N. M., & van Dick, R. (2014). Implicit theories in organizational settings: A systematic review and research agenda of implicit leadership and followership theories. *The Leadership Quarterly*, 25(6), 1154–1173.

Laloux, F. (2014). *Reinventing organizations*. Brussels, Belgium: Nelson Parker.

Lemoine, G. J., Aggarwal, I., & Steed, L. B. (2016). When women emerge as leaders: Effects of extraversion and gender composition in groups. *The Leadership Quarterly*, 27(3), 470–486.

Matsakis, L., Koebler, J., & Emerson, S. (2017, August 7). Here are the citations for the anti-diversity manifesto circulating at Google. *Motherboard*. Retrieved from https://mother board.vice.com/en_us/article/evzjww/here-are-the-citations-for-the-anti-diversity-manifesto-circulating-at-google. Last accessed: January 9, 2018.

Mercer. (2017). Inside employees' minds. Retrieved from www.mercer.com/content/dam/mercer/attachments/global/inside-employees-minds/gl-2017-inside-employees-minds-financial-wellness.pdf. Last accessed: January 9, 2018.

Meuser, J. D., Gardner, W. L., Dinh, J. E., Hu, J., Liden, R. C., & Lord, R. G. (2016). A network analysis of leadership theory: The infancy of integration. *Journal of Management*, 42(5), 1374–1403.

Mohammed, S., & Angell, L. C. (2004). Surface- and deep-level diversity in workgroups: Examining the moderating effects of team orientation and team process on relationship conflict. *Journal of Organizational Behavior*, 25(8), 1015–1039.

Ng, E. S. W., Schweitzer, L., & Lyons, S. T. (2010). New generation, great expectations: A field study of the millennial generation. *Journal of Business Psychology*, 25(2), 281–292.

Nye, J. L., & Forsyth, D. R. (1991). The effects of prototype-based biases on leadership appraisals: A test of leadership categorization theory. *Small Group Research*, 22(3), 360–379.

Open Science Collaboration. (2015). Estimating the reproducibility of psychological science. *Science*, 349(6251), aac4716. Retrieved from http://science.sciencemag.org/content/349/6251/aac4716. Last accessed: January 9, 2018.

Pedula, D. S. (2011). The hidden costs of contingency: Employers' use of contingent workers and standard employees' outcomes. *Center for the Study of Social Organization Working Paper Series*, Working Paper #6. Princeton, NJ: CSSO.

Pfeffer, J. (2015). *Leadership BS: Fixing workplaces and careers one truth at a time*. New York, NY: Harper Collins Publishers.

Tomlinson, P., & Modica, M. (2015, October 28). 'Happy but leaving': Can a new value proposition manage risk of talent drain? *Brink News*. Retrieved from www.brinknews.com/happy-but-leaving-can-a-new-value-proposition-manage-risk-of-talent-drain/. Last accessed: January 9, 2018.

Uhl-Bien, M., Marion, R., & McKelvey, B. (2007). Complexity leadership theory: Shifting leadership from the industrial age to the knowledge era. *The Leadership Quarterly*, 18(4), 298–318.

US Bureau of Labor Statistics. (2015, December 8). Employment projections: 2014–24. Retrieved from www.bls.gov/news.release/pdf/ecopro.pdf. Last accessed: January 9, 2018.

Walker, R. C., & Aritz, J. (2015). Women doing leadership: Leadership styles and organizational culture. *International Journal of Business Communication*, 52(4), 452–478.

Ward, J. (2010, October). The services sector: How best to measure it? *ITA Newsletter*. Washington, DC: Department of Commerce. Retrieved from http://trade.gov/publications/ita-newsletter/1010/services-sector-how-best-to-measure-it.asp. Last accessed: January 9, 2018.

Warren, A. K. (2009). *Cascading gender biases, compounding effects: An assessment of talent management systems*. New York, NY: Catalyst.

Wegner, D. M. (2002). *The illusion of conscious will*. Cambridge, MA: MIT Press.

FIRST INTERLUDE

Pivotal Points in Leadership Development

After surveying 274 women about their leadership experiences (results reported in Chapters Six and Seven) we wanted a more in-depth understanding of the complex views and perspectives we were discovering. To accomplish this, we interviewed 20 women, with each taped interview lasting from 30 to 90 minutes. Collectively these women have over 500 years of experience working and leading in organizations in jobs ranging from airline pilot to federal government executive to stay-at-home parent to library fundraiser. They range in age from 24 to 60. They are black, white, Latino, Asian, gay, straight, married, divorced, some with and some without children. In certain instances they worked for pay; in other instances they worked as volunteers. The Interludes and Chapter Five present excerpts of the transcripts and help make sense of the survey results that follow.

We asked women first to tell us about *the most pivotal points in their leadership development*. Here are some of the compelling stories we heard.

Janet J., attorney, former high level executive with the National Collegiate Athletics Association, now consultant: I certainly believe that attending a girls' school from grade school to high school helped me become a leader. I am a different era than the young women coming up now. But, I think that I was a good student and I think that it was those formative years for me to understand that you can, you know, help people, make things better, take on those kinds of projects. I played a lot of sports and I think that helped me develop as a leader. It helped me with my confidence. I think education—going to law school, as much as I disliked it immensely, it gave me confidence I didn't have before. I was essentially an introvert and going to law school forced me to overcome that. Working with one of my bosses years ago at the NCAA was a pivotal leadership experience. I was really young and in some difficult high pressure roles. I had to make some difficult decisions. I had to analyze a lot of information that was coming at me fast. My boss would ask me how I made that decision, why was it successful? He allowed me to believe they were successful. And they usually were for the most part, but he really instilled in me this notion that I should make decisions, that I could make decisions, and that gave me confidence. It was quiet affirmation, really. He had no problem affirming me. And I didn't get a lot of that elsewhere. It was pivotal in my growth as a leader.

Marla, expert in information technology, now a graduate student: Well the ironic part is, I never thought of myself as a leader, and it wasn't until I started to do research and study public management that I really started to think about it. So, once I delved into how it has been conceptualized theoretically, I thought, maybe I am a leader. And so, I had to do some backtracking and some thinking about how I got to this place. And I now realize that my parents put me on a leadership path. I was socialized with leadership at a very early age. For example, they would emphasize the need to be organized, the need to check my work, look for mistakes, so that was very influential to me in the early days of my life.

And then, actually, going into the workplace and seeing what formal leaders did, just in terms of how they had to manage staff and how they had to contend with maybe not so pleasant employees, was also pivotal in my leadership growth. Even in instances where I saw people behaving badly I learned that's what I do not want to do. I saw the best leaders put their noses to the grindstone. Everything they did, everything they said, sent a message to the organization. Even if they may not have realized, it, they gave me those golden nuggets, I was watching and learning. They taught me by example. I remember one boss in particular who said to me, "Do you. Just do you." And I never forgot that because what she was saying was be authentic, be yourself, and do … what [you are good at]. And that has never left me. I always remember that. So, if you want to talk about significant moments; that was probably the biggest one.

Jan, former United States Air Force (USAF) officer, now a police officer: Well certainly at the air force academy [they] taught us about leadership all the time. That's like everything that you do from the time you get there. At basic training you learn how to be a follower so you can be a better leader. So there's a lot of formalized training with the academic part of it, but then there's also the different ranks and different responsibilities at different levels. So, I had a lot of those opportunities. And then being on the tennis team, that's certainly a leadership opportunity too that's a little more free-flowing. It's more informal, you know. I was the captain in our last year. As a very good athlete [I felt like I had] impact on the team and the direction of the team.

Kirk, former urban planner, founding director of a new federal agency, now a professor of practice: When I think about leadership development, I go back to my mom. Because my mother was a very strong personality—VERY—and she was really creative. She landed in a conservative town in West Virginia where she raised her children and she had an enormous impact on that community.

So, I grew up with a woman who knew how to get the city charter plan passed, became executive director of a very large museum, and before that for many years worked without having a paid job. She was a political activist. As much as I had difficulty with a strong mother, her presence has certainly inspired me and has given me some of my power to not let things stand in my way. Or to not be shy—that's for sure. I certainly never felt that my being a woman was a handicap or got in my way. I went to Princeton, I was in the first woman's class. And even though there was only one tenured woman professor at Princeton at the time, and very few women scientists, I never felt held back or discriminated against at all. If women were held back, I just didn't see it, given the powerful role model my mother was for me early on. Anything was possible.

Dannielle, change management expert and leadership coach, who worked in corporate environments for 20 years before the transition to start her own business: I have two examples. The first concerned the organization I was working for that was going through a lot of changes. I was in a situation where there was a lot being kind of dumped on me in terms of work with very little resources. It was one of those situations where I asked myself, do I hang in there and trudge along as I would have in the past? I did a lot of self-reflection and realized that I had other options at this point in my career ... that I was in a good place reputation and experience-wise. So being brave enough to leave to pursue another leadership experience was a pivotal experience for me. I left mainly because I felt like it was hard to distinguish between my role and the people who were above me and I felt like every time I talked to my manager she could not articulate for me the distinction between her job and my job, and what I needed to do to go to the next level.

The second example is sort of the opposite—it was when I realized you can be a 'leader in place' —that you don't need a senior director position to lead. It was a time when my entire cohort group wanted to be senior directors. They just wanted to be senior directors because it was the next rung on the ladder. And I'm thinking to myself, "Okay, I'm much more concerned about doing meaningful work and whether I can do it in a flexible way." And to try to go for a senior director job would probably have undermined what it was I was trying to do. I want to do the work I love. I have a friend, a woman who works here, and she's a VP, but she's like "Yeah I don't like my job that much. All I wanted to do is be a VP. I don't need to do anything else. And I'm just fine because I don't love this that much: but it was the position that mattered to me." To me it is not the position that counts but the work that counts. You can be a leader without a leadership position. You set your priorities and work to your priorities, right?

Shannon, software development professional, stay-at-home mother, and angel investor: The very first job I had was my most pivotal leadership experience. I was the fourth employee of a defense contract startup, and the three people who formed the company were terrific. They were in their 40s. They had a lot of experience, came from military backgrounds, and they were leaders. They were good business people, but I would not say they were great business people. They encouraged us to write proposals—right out of college. They encouraged us to expand our business profiles, and also to improve our technical skills. They let us be in charge of things. And they were always there to help. They let us do presentations. I mean you're talking about very junior people getting up before a group of senior people and giving presentations and taking questions, knowing that our bosses were there for us if things got tough. They were just really smart and respected in their field. They were willing to mentor and help bring people up through the organization. They were just really amazing people. And they were men who hired a lot of women to work for them, joking that when all the women left, the company would fall apart. They had a lot of young women engineers working for them and their view was 'up or out'. The leadership opportunities they gave me were invaluable.

Anne, Chief Operating Officer for a large health-care NGO: I think the most pivotal leadership growth experiences for me have been the most challenging times I faced in the last 33 years—times of crises at the NGO I helped lead. There have been a number of times where I had to walk around to all of our staff, saying, "Okay, what doesn't kill you makes you stronger. When God closes a door, God opens a window." There have been real critical times when we have stepped out on a limb as we are known for doing in our field. We pioneered [adoption] system reform, system changes that were hard for people and not popular and people fought it. And those are times when I literally had a stomach ache every day and every night for what seems like a long period of time. But I really do think that it is leadership in hard times that is the true test. And I do think that is where I really had to learn how to not let others see me sweat and not let our staff worry and put on my game face. Fake it till you make it. Staying focused on just putting one foot in front of the other, making sure we did good work. You can't take everything personally. You have to have a strong backbone to be a strong leader.

Mary H., 30-year member of the US federal government Senior Executive Service, then an NGO director, now a university professor: I never really thought about being a leader when I was in graduate school eventually earning my doctorate degree. I thought I would teach. Then I got hired by a consulting firm. At the firm, I just did what I always did, which is work really hard and try to figure out what they wanted, needed, and why and how. And at some point, a top level director said, "We have this significant project coming in and we would like you to be the deputy director." And I said, "What?" And then, he didn't train me. He just kind of threw me into it and the guy who was running it hadn't been trained either but he was a systems analyst, so that made him a leader in that setting. So, it was kind of hit and miss. Eventually a pivotal leadership experience came from people who said, "This is what we see in you, and you are really good at this, and you should move up, and you should be a manager now". I was like,

"Okay, what does that mean?" I never did receive any good answers except by watching the leaders in the organization. I saw that the president communicated informally to all of us that if we stayed and really worked hard, we most likely would be promoted. I saw clearly that someday I could be a vice president. But even though I was good at it, I did not like being a Beltway Bandit. I thought we did good work—important work—but I just didn't like 'selling' the work and trying to obtain contracts.

Even though that was not 'my place', that leadership experience really gave me confidence. So I applied to the Government Accountability Office (GAO). I was brought in as a manager, but once again I did not receive any training. That is why I am so passionate about the training today. From that negative experience I learned that my leadership priority is to make sure my staff receive excellent training. Another negative experience that ended up being pivotal to my leadership journey was when I had a boss at GAO who was always trying to manipulate people, and forge their futures for them without them knowing it. It was a horrible experience and I do not think I handled it very well . . . [Eventually] A new Comptroller General came in and put together a big task force of high level people. After asking me to analyze a couple of reports with a sociological bent to them, he picked me to be the staff director. Now, that was God picking this little thing out of the ants on the ground. I ended up leading people who outranked me. The experience stretched me, in only the most positive way.

Marilu, former librarian, former Chief Information Officer, now Vice Provost: My dad was a very task-oriented construction manager who never went to college. I got two things from him: One is industrial engineering systems get stuff done. He loved to work with his daughters on projects and he would lay them out and organize us and teach us skills. We would do these camping vacations but weeks before, we would practice putting up the tent in the driveway. And he would time us—we all had our jobs. I was living in this little industrial engineering world. And my mother was quite organized too so they fit quite well together.

The other thing I learned from my father is that he knew that the only way he could be successful as a manager was for people to know that he cared about them. I would get up at 4 or 5 in the morning and sneak into the living room and listen to him on the phone. He would do these rounds of calls to tell his foreman what kinds of projects they were going to do that day. And every person he called, he would ask some personal thing first. It would be, "Hey how did your daughter's recital go last night?" That taught me that you can be 'system task efficient' and maintain relationships with people at the same time and not sacrifice a whole lot of productivity doing that. And that has been really important for my leadership career.

I did things like that when I first became Chief Information Officer for the university and there was this whole technical segment in that organization that thought, "A librarian woman is my boss? Seriously?" So I spent my first three weeks with them doing their jobs. I had my jeans and T-shirt on and was crawling around in the steam tunnels pulling wire. I was deathly afraid of mice, I wanted to scream every ten seconds. But, after that, the IT installer, Charlie, knew me by my first name and I knew a little bit about him and his kids, and we ended up having a very productive working relationship. I learned that from my dad.

The second person who really influenced my leadership trajectory was my management professor in library school. He said, "There are three types of employees based on your response when they tell you they are leaving. There are 'scotch employees' who are the employees you cannot afford to lose, so you take the bottle of scotch from the drawer and start drinking because you are so depressed that they are leaving. Then there are 'champagne employees' who you are so glad to get rid of that you go buy the bottle of champagne and you celebrate. And then there are 'Post-it note' employees who are good enough that you are kind of sad, but they are not really all that critical. You figure "Oh, I can move this around and I can do this," the same way you move around Post-it notes. That idea had a profound effect on me as to trying to figure out how to think about what was critical within organizations and who was critical within organizations.

And then my teacher-mother taught me that every moment has the possibility of being a teaching/training moment when you help somebody learn and grow. Or you yourself learn and grow. And most opportunities are both. That has been incredibly critical for me in my leadership roles. So my pivotal leadership learning experiences were learning to be organized, know who your key employees are, and every moment counts as a possible learning experience.

Helen, retired Colonel (United States Air Force), professor, and academic administrator: Early on in my Air Force career, I was a squadron action commander, so I worked for the commander and alongside an enlisted top leader. I worked on a lot of personnel and disciplinary issues, and acted on the commander's behalf in those situations. Just getting the sense of leaders' decisions and how they can impact the larger organization was a pivotal leadership experience. I was part of an organization of 200 to 400 people, a diverse organization that was mostly, at one point, composed of officers and more senior personnel. This was in sharp contrast to organizations I worked in later that were more oriented towards younger personnel where there were [large] differences in the skill sets and maturity levels. Understanding, first of all, how those commanders' decisions can affect the overall organization was pivotal to me: How you have to keep some consistency, how important communications is—articulating expectations— and how important it is to follow through. Dealing with the younger folks later not only in a disciplinary way, but also in a motivational way to get them back on track—that is the sort of thing that also taught me some leadership lessons. I learned the importance of leveraging the expertise that's in house, to not be afraid to ask questions, that there is no need to pretend that you know everything; that it is okay and important to collaborate and ask questions.

Kathleen, former stay-at-home mother, founder of publishing company, now director of development for a library: My mother was a good organizer. Her charges were seven kids and she was able to get them organized and get them doing things. She split up the jobs, the responsibilities and then put everybody to work and there were consequences if you didn't do your job. And it was very clear. So, I had that model very early on. Other pivotal leadership lessons came from different school teachers who allowed me to have opportunities to lead a project and guided me along the way. I learned that where you see something that is not right, you fix it. Just do it. Both my parents had an incredible work ethic. I think leaders have to have an incredible work ethic. I really do think that is true. I have worked for people who did not [have a strong work ethic], and as somebody who likes to work hard, I get so frustrated by people when I am the first one in and last one out and they end up getting paid three times more than I do. And they walk out the door with things halfway done. It's like, "Oh my God. That's not fair." So I guess it goes both ways: I have had pivotal leadership learning experiences from people who were really great leaders and people who were terrible leaders.

M'lis, commercial airline pilot, retired United States Air Force (USAF) pilot and former NCAA basketball champion: In addition to playing college basketball and being the first black woman instructor pilot in the Air Force, which were both pivotal leadership experiences for me, I remember very clearly a discussion early on in my military career with a Colonel that influenced how I think of myself as a leader. He said, "I want to give you some advice and I hope you don't take offense." So I said ok sure let's hear it and he said

> There are going to be times in your life, in your career where you're going to apply for a job or a position or a promotion or maybe you're up for an award, and you are not going to get it and the only reason you're not going to get it is because you're a black woman. Then there will be other times that you're going to be up for promotion or you apply for a position or you're up for an award, and you are going to get it and the only reason you will get it is because you are a black woman.

He goes on and says

> The kicker is that you have no control over any of it because you have no control over whether you got it for the right reason or the wrong reason. Or you didn't get it for the right reason or the wrong reason. But you know one thing that you do have control over no matter what . . . is you can always make sure you're qualified because then you can convey that you deserved it if they look at your record.

I always want to be able to say that I deserved it. I'll stack up [favorably] against anybody.

And he was right. I have experienced times ... whether I was black, whether I was a woman or whether it was both, where I didn't get things and there were definitely times where people put me on a pedestal and I'm not so sure that I know why I got those things. But I learned a key leadership lesson, and that is while you can't always control outcomes, you can control your own excellence. Always strive for excellence. That mentality made a complete difference. I never felt bitter when I got passed up for something, nor boastful when I was successful. If anything, I just had more desire to keep trying harder and to be better. That was probably the best piece of leadership advice I ever got.

Heather, managing director, commercial construction company: When I look back at my leadership trajectory, I can see that I had one opportunity after another. But there's one team I worked with in particular that had a tremendous influence on my leadership approach, including my whole approach to business development. I learned that it is all about relationship building. I learned this when I was in the middle of moving from being an office manager to leading a marketing team, I would interface with people—clients and prospective clients—and my manager never talked about what she wanted. Instead she focused on what it took to deliver in terms of trying to get people to trust and respect her, and that carried her so much further than it would have if she had just kept it as a business transaction. It really was with her that I switched gears to really focus on how to develop my relationships at a higher level in a way that would not necessarily be using people, but really trying to be smart about things. It really is not just about the work that you do, it is really about knowing people so you can help each other along the way. She was one individual who taught me a valuable leadership lesson.

Another important person in my leadership trajectory basically changed my whole career just with one decision because it would have taken me a lot longer to get there had he not understood or seen what I was capable of. But he had the vision and he was fantastic [in making me see that I could do the job]. And my current boss at Vistage gives me a lot of professional development opportunities. He understands how challenging the current situation is. I have never had more professional development in my whole career than I've had this year. He sent me to conferences about marketing communication and leadership and he understands the investment in that. He has been a great individual supporter. Those are some of the experiences that have supported my leadership development.

Mary S., former principal of grade school, now classroom teacher: In the early years, when I taught public school, there was a man—our Vice Principal—from whom I learned a tremendous leadership lesson. He is one of the leaders that I admire most because, frankly, he taught me not only how to teach, but how to lead by example as opposed to pulling the students [as well as the teachers] by the nose. I watched him teach and watched him in action outside of the classroom and enjoyed learning from him. He was probably one of the most influential men

I've ever met. He led by example, never really telling anyone to do something, not trying to persuade. He just presented the situation and they jumped right in without even thinking. And that kind of leadership style is what I have always strived to emulate both as a teacher and later as a principal: Your actions matter and send a message through the organization that "this is how we do business."

Lisa, vice-president human resources consulting group: I have done different types of work, from internal consulting, external consulting, HR general type work, and I have done some work outside of the HR field. And I have had good experiences and bad experiences. I have made big mistakes and small mistakes. I have had success and gotten feedback and I feel like all of that is what has come together to make me the leader that I am today . . . I really feel like having life experience and maturity are important . . . Most recently I was promoted to Vice President, a new position that my organization created. There were four of us that were promoted at the same time. And it was pretty vague what that even meant. We sort of knew what our expectations were which were all different for each of the four of us and I went into this spiral of a crisis of confidence where I just, I felt the pressure of being in that position of leadership but not knowing how to apply what I have done before and wondering whether other people [thought that I] deserved to be promoted . . . I went to my leadership [heads of organization] and said that I really felt like I needed some help in getting focused. They agreed that I could work with a coach and that was absolutely so helpful to me. The feedback I got from my peers was so eye opening, even though some of it was negative. This experience was pivotal.

PART II
The Story from Many Voices

4

QUESTIONS OF LEADERSHIP, AND WOMEN

Seeing Those Who Lead in Place

Organization management scholar Stacey (1992), writing about strategy in a complex environment, observed that new insights do not arise when

> discussions are characterized by orderly equilibrium, conformity, and dependence . . . People spark new ideas off each other when they argue and disagree—when they are conflicting, confused, and searching for new meaning—yet remain willing to discuss and listen to each other.
>
> (p. 120)

While we surveyed and interviewed women, what can be learned from a cross section of women's stories is germane to leadership in general. We live in an era of increasing complexity and transforming expectations on virtually every front. Social norms, technology, and demographics have all shifted dramatically in recent decades. (See Box 4.1.)

BOX 4.1 WOMEN, MEN, OR PEOPLE?

A mid-level leader survey respondent, aged 41–50, noted: I am quite concerned that by emphasizing a distinction between the leadership styles of men and women we run the risk of losing sight of the fact that men and women, when managing teams of people, are primarily managers of 'people' and should be treating them in the same (highly humanistic) way. I think that's especially important in our current environment of restraint and uncertainty, when it is all too easy for managers to start to view their staff as 'resources' that can simply be shifted around without much care. To me, this is an issue that goes far beyond gender and to the basics of how we treat people in the workplace.

Perspective-taking constitutes a critical skill for leaders. It requires taking in information from others and applying filters to make sense of that information. It means individuals have to be able to step outside their own heads, and try on different ways of looking at a situation. Seeing something different, or seeing something differently, creates new insight. Insight, in turn, ideally leads to different behaviors, actions, and outcomes. This book is an invitation to try new perspectives on how leadership unfolds in modern practice generally, and on the topic of women and leadership specifically. Women are already leading throughout organizations and communities. This needs to be recognized and valued whether it occurs in the workplace or beyond.

As discussed in Chapter One, we label this phenomenon *leading in place*. Drawing on Nelson Mandela's words and example, Hill (2010) infused the phrase "leading from behind" with the meaning of positional leaders essentially engaging and working collaboratively with their teams. When leading from behind, an individual is enacting a particular leadership style from a designated position. Leading in place, in contrast, is quintessential emergent leadership— a gender-neutral phenomenon. Those who lead in place typically do so without a designated position of leadership, or they lead well beyond the parameters of their position. Beneath the top layer of executives, they materially contribute to motivating and sense-making for teams, collaborative groups, and networks. (See Box 4.2.)

Those who lead in place identify gaps in leadership that compromise organizational health or mission accomplishment. At other times they identify potential organizational enhancements or innovations. In either case they fill gaps in ways that are needed. This might include, for example, prompting sense-making, motivating others, initiating structure, promoting constructive engagement, crafting cross-boundary networks. Leading in place is a spectrum of expressed behaviors,

---

BOX 4.2 LEADING IN PLACE

Leading in place describes a gender-neutral phenomenon of leadership that unfolds beneath the top layer of designated positions (e.g., CEO and top executive team), without positional authority (or over and beyond positional authority), that keeps teams and organizations moving towards mission achievement. Leading in place is a spectrum of behaviors proactively enacted in response to observed need, whether in response to gaps left by those with designated positions of leadership or in response to perceived opportunities beyond existing boundaries and practice. Leading in place is a proactively self-selected activity—for which one should be recognized and rewarded.

BOX 4.3 WHAT ARE OUR LEADERSHIP NORMS?

A front-line leader survey respondent, aged 61+, shared this story of finding her way. "I was newly in a position of management. I was told that I should be staying in my office, directing staff to do tasks, rather than joining with them in doing the work. I had also tried to adjust work schedules to accord as much as possible with the individuals' preferences. I was told that I identified too much with the workers. My response was to decide that I didn't want to be this kind of leader/manager/administrator. Instead, I took a clinical consultant position that used my knowledge and skills while allowing hands-on supervision, teaching and mentoring of staff. This was more personally satisfying to me."

proactively identified and enacted. Both men and women can lead in place. Within traditionally structured, hierarchical organizations, it can either be by choice or by default. It may be the only option available if prevailing prototypes preclude segments of the population from making it into designated leadership positions. (See Box 4.3.)

There is as much need to examine and redefine what we expect of leaders with and without position, across settings, as there is to ensure women are proportionately represented in boardrooms. It is imperative to include diverse perspectives, including those of women, not only in positions of leadership but more fundamentally in defining norms of leadership.

Until very recently, research had missed the power that individuals' internal narratives play in both exhibiting and assessing leadership, and failed to account for the significant contributions of leadership-without-position that keeps organizations functioning in the modern world. Those who find themselves constrained to leading in place by default may find themselves there for any number of reasons: e.g., biased leadership prototypes, flawed leadership development and selection processes, insufficient understanding and systemic undervaluing of emergent leadership outside designated positions. These factors have often combined to disproportionately pare women from formal leadership pipelines. Equally, some intentionally opt to lead in place for any number of reasons. Far too little is known about what motivates individuals to lead in place versus competing for designated, or more senior designated, positions. (See Box 4.4.)

There is every reason to believe that many capable women have been leading in place, but the stories that are told do not reveal this. Too often stories of women and leadership tell of only a skewed sample of the population. Digging deeper into the stories of a cross section of women as we do in this book provides a more thorough understanding of how women might experience leadership

---

BOX 4.4 RELATIVE VALUE-ADD OF LEADING IN PLACE

Little is known about the relative value-add of those who very effectively lead in place versus those who less effectively execute from designated positions. It has not been systematically studied. As intentional experience with leading in place accumulates from holacracies (e.g., Zappos) it will be possible to explore such questions. One hypothesis is that results will vary depending upon whether the frame of analysis is financial (short-run monetary returns) versus economic (longer-term organizational viability).

---

and the varied manner and contexts in which women lead. It contributes to a greater appreciation of the importance of leading in place. In short, what has tended to be invisible, and consequently undervalued, needs to be made explicit in 21st century conceptions and practice of leadership, to position women to proactively define their leadership paths and enable organizations to make the most of available talent.

Stories Shape Our World

The most elemental and obvious stories in any culture are the myths and epics. Our understanding of how modern humans are influenced by more subtle collective and individual narratives has expanded wildly since the mid-20th century. For example, fields such as cultural anthropology and sociology focus on understanding the role and power of stories in human and cultural functioning.[1] The role of stories people tell themselves has even filtered into the most rational of studies—economics. The 2002 awarding of the Nobel prize in economics to Daniel Kahneman and Vernon L. Smith for their work integrating psychological theory and methods (respectively) into economic research brought expanded legitimacy to considering the role of human narrative in both 'serious' social science and real world outcomes—capping a trend initiated by the Nobel prize awarded to Becker (in 1992) for his work on non-market (read 'non-rational') behavior.

At the individual level, our narratives are the sense we make of our experiences and interactions with others. Kahneman (*Thinking fast and thinking slow,* 2011) did a brilliant job of summing up findings from across a vast body of cognitive psychology and neuroscience concerning the importance of stories.

According to one theory, the human brain essentially has two interrelated systems—one of which we're aware (conscious), and one of which we remain largely unaware (unconscious). Conscious experience contributes to layering the unconscious which, in turn, influences the sense we make of conscious experiences. "This is how the remembering self works: it composes stories and keeps them for future reference." (p. 387) Accumulation of retained 'stories' form a sort of reference base, or framework (i.e., our individual narratives) that guides future judgments and sense-making.

Using stories to communicate research is an established practice. Interestingly, it appears to be a particularly popular and/or powerful technique when collecting and communicating evidence counter to the prevailing paradigm. For example, Gilligan's (1982) groundbreaking *In a different voice* applied the approach to studying gender differences in moral reasoning in children. More recently, Bell & Nkomo (2001) used the approach to explore the influence of race on experiences of female managers. Children learn through the stories they're told or read, or the family stories they hear. The power of Grimms' fairytales, Roald Dahl's *Matilda*, and those of countless other children's books, is the implicit message that children can endure and overcome great challenges.[2] Those who study such phenomena tend not to use the word story, but instead use the term narrative: the same thing by different names. Research in the fields of psychology and neuroscience, among others, continues to extend understanding of the extent to which internal narratives that individuals construct to make sense of experience can influence both individual and collective outcomes.

Humans can't think deeply about each and every experience—we just don't have that much brain power. So we layer both learning and stories we make from experience into 'heuristics' or filters that we apply subconsciously to make sense of experiences in the present. (Leadership prototypes, discussed in Chapter Three, are one type or subset of heuristics.) This has upsides and downsides. For example, medical doctors typically have very few moments to spend with each patient, and must take in visual, verbal, and intuitive data about symptoms—and line this up with a vast array of possible diagnoses. For practiced doctors who pick up effectively on all data presented, heuristics work to everyone's advantage.[3] Heuristics can also manifest in much less positive ways—i.e., as negative stereotypes or unconscious biases.

An evolutionary psychology perspective indicates that a certain share of our responses come pre-wired, such as the fight or flight instincts; the rest are acquired as we develop. The process of building filters we use to make sense of the world starts very early in life. For example, a young child who gets bitten by a dog will likely form the heuristic that dogs are dangerous—and possibly carry a lifelong aversion to dogs. A young child given the message "you can do anything" along with opportunities to actually accomplish tasks and goals, is positioned to develop self-efficacy and grow into a confident, capable adult. Conversely, a young child faced with less empowering messages—overt or subtle—may face a much steeper path to confidence and capability.

Myriad factors frame and influence the stories or narratives that individuals create for themselves. These range from highly specific individual differences (e.g., personality characteristics, affect) to environmental conditions (e.g., cultural setting, socio-economic environment).

Notably, while it's generally understood that the sense individuals make of the world is predominantly shaped by the reference banks of 'stories' they compile over their lives, relatively less is known about the malleability of these reference banks. Clearly, some individuals are able to access and modify—or replace—stories they use to make sense of the world. This is a very common reaction to potentially terminal health experiences—e.g., cancer or heart attacks. Survivors often change not only health behaviors, but also their outlook on life. There are notable examples of very public figures who clearly experienced (or at least professed to experience) fundamental shifts in their framing stories. Changes in worldview resulting from an altered internal framework for understanding have been expressed by reformed bigots (e.g., think George Wallace's renunciation of segregation) and chastened policy-makers (e.g., Robert McNamara's (1995) evolution from architect of the Vietnam War to his later admissions of misjudgments in his memoire).

Intentionally provoking shifts in narrative is the realm of positive psychology, mindfulness practices, unconscious bias training, and a variety of specialized coaching practices. Drivers and constraints of individuals' ability to access, reflect upon, and 'edit' or alter their respective stories remains a field of possible discovery. What is known, at a minimum, is that intentional effort is required to edit heuristics we apply and internal narratives that often underlie those heuristics. For example, an adult can overcome a fear of dogs acquired during childhood. Surmounting an ingrained fear response, however, requires intentional effort. An individual has to want to get past such a fear—it won't happen just because someone tells them they shouldn't be afraid.

Constructed narratives have power at the group level as well. We experience these continuously. Overt marketing promotions (e.g., Nike's famous "Just do it;" anti-smoking campaigns) influence worldviews. So do more subtle cultural narratives (e.g., anyone can rise up the US socio-economic ladder, shopping is a form of recreation). A meaningful narrative that served the United States during World War II, and may have been an unwitting precursor to the seismic shift in the female labor force participation rate of the mid to late 20th century, was that of 'Rosie the Riveter'. During 1939–1947, the United States accomplished a profound transformation (Carter, 1970), from a heavily agrarian to industrial economy, relying upon a labor force demographically transformed by war. The mainstay of the labor force, able-bodied men, was a depleted resource in the early years of this transformation. Women stepped into the breach—and the mythological Rosie was born (see US Library of Congress, 2010, for a short review and song lyrics). However, Rosie was implicitly expected to step back in place when the men came home.

Given the importance of narrative in individual sense-making, it stands to reason that examining women's narratives and how these influence their perceptions, expression, and experience of leadership might provide useful insight for both individuals and organizations. Narratives are fascinating because of the two-part dynamic: what happens on the outside, and what sense we, as individuals, make of that experience.

Stories, Women, and Leadership

In some cases women fail to progress through organizational leadership ranks because systems can be implemented (by men and women) in ways that are unconsciously biased. More basically, women may not be recognized as leaders because systems are built upon implicitly male (and increasingly outdated) prototypes of leadership. Do women experience this playing out? How might leader prototypes be adjusted to better serve all? We set out to understand what could be gleaned from a cross section of women's stories.

Our aim was not to develop the next great theory or solve the dilemma of how to get more women into top positions of visible leadership. Our aim was to bring a cross section of women's voices to the table and move conversation past the 'great woman' fixation. The motivation was a desire to influence conversations around leadership, as well as thinking and action around leader selection and development practices, for both individuals and organizations.

For years women have reported publically and privately the costs of attempting to work and thrive in environments in which they are unwelcome, stereotyped, objectified, or worse. Mainstream leadership research has only relatively recently shifted to integrate this into work at any deep level[4] (see, e.g., Hogue & Lord, 2007; Kahneman, Lovallo, & Sibony. 2011; Lord & Dinh, 2014). Reports of real-world evidence and experience alone did not push theory and research in this direction. Rather, findings from other disciplines—cognitive and neuropsychology—around the deep-seated influence of implicit biases on human perceptions and interactions, and the costs these can impose both upon those who are perceived as (or perceive themselves as) belonging to out-groups but also to organizations themselves, could not be ignored.

Most organizations have both formal systems and processes, and also informal norms, practices, and networks by which the organization actually functions. Cleaning formal systems of bias is far easier than ensuring informal systems remain equally fair. Formal systems don't have to be elaborate and process-heavy. They just have to be clear, transparent, and consistently implemented. Startups, family-held businesses, and a share of small businesses tend to be exceptions. These organizations often operate with, at best, thin formal systems; either they don't see the need, or they haven't had the opportunity to thoughtfully invest in talent management practices. Ideally, in any organization, there is a high degree of complementarity between formal systems and informal norms, so that they are mutually re-enforcing and facilitate getting work done. When more distance exists between the two systems, or a formal system hasn't yet been rolled out, the informal can swamp the formal. This can allow the development of environments in which favoritism and being 'in' with the power network determines who is seen as a leader and who makes it into leader positions.

If those with position and power in the organization hold strong male-oriented leader prototypes and/or hold unconscious biases about women, then women are at a significant disadvantage. If women do exhibit leadership without position by effectively influencing others to achieve shared goals, it's unlikely to be recognized. If they seek to be candidates for leadership positions, they are likely to face a steeper access curve than males competing for the same role.

Technology may be a double-edged sword exacerbating associated challenges for workers in the 21st century economy. On the one hand, through remote and alternate work arrangements, technology enables flexibility. However, depending upon organizational culture and norms, reduction in 'face time' may have negative effects in terms of others' perceptions and opportunities for growth and access to designated leadership positions.

More significant and specific to women, the tech industry and the venture capital industry that supports it, continue to struggle to create inclusive workplaces. Women comprise only one-quarter of those employed in computer and mathematical occupations (US Bureau of Labor Statistics, 2016). Widely covered challenges associated with cultures and treatment arise frequently.[5] Facebook very publicly improved parental leave practices but only after the multi-billionaire owner personally experienced first-time parenthood.[6]

Trends and patterns in the venture capital business, which funds most startups, appear even less encouraging, although they do align with popular reports about the realities for women in the financial sector more generally. Not all firms receiving venture capital are tech companies but it is hard to grow a tech company without the level of resources venture capitalists can make available. The share of women partners in venture capital firms declined notably between 1999 and 2014 and only a negligible share of companies receiving venture capital had female CEOs (Brush et al., 2014). So, while a boon from one perspective in that it facilitates flexibility of timing and place of work, as a sector, technology is not currently positioned to perform at the forefront in selecting and developing a robust, inclusive leadership cadre.

Exploring How Women Experience and Value Emergent Leadership

Those who step up and get things done may not always look like what senior leaders and managers expect in a colleague, but they often keep organizations running. While biases built into leader selection and development practices may make it difficult for women to get into the queue, there may be another phenomenon compounding the challenge. Leading in place can be an 'only available default option' in the worst case, but it can also be a choice for some. Leading in place should be recognized, not stigmatized.

A subset of women may prefer not to 'lean in' because they resist an antiquated model that does not correspond to their experience as leaders. These women may be exceedingly capable and willing to lead in positions that are better designed to fit them, their values and priorities. Position and power will always matter in organizations. However, as discussed above, conceptions of positions may well need to adapt and expand to simultaneously satisfy worker expectations, organizational goals, and dynamics of power in complex environments. Better understanding of what really unfolds behind the phenomenon of women who lead in place will promote robust theory and research. More immediately, it can equip organizations to facilitate inclusive, adaptive leadership practices.

Not all women seek formal leadership positions within organizations. Anecdotal reports abound, however, about contributions by those who lead in place. To reiterate, we are *NOT* suggesting that women either want, or ought, to be restricted to leading in place. We are ardent supporters of women in formal positions of leadership. As laid out in the following chapters, however, we have found evidence that appears to support the notion that some have tended to lead in place. This may be partially attributable to personal life-balancing choices. It may be because leadership assessment, development, and selection systems are built on models—and practices—so rife with unintentional and unrecognized bias that women's leadership strengths, capacities, and contributions tend to be either not recognized or implicitly discounted. It may be because a wide swath of organizations fail to create missions, cultures, and results that motivate women to prioritize commitment to those organizations. Or it may be because of other factors.

Until a broad cross section of women's voices and experiences are integrated into the conversation, we won't really know. It's worth exploring whether this is a mere anecdotal artifact, or whether there's really something to this. Why might women choose to lead in place? Are there systematic patterns that would explain this? For example, is it that women haven't had opportunity, is it that they are disaffected by opportunities that are presented, or is it that there is an unexplored calculus at play?

Maybe it's not, as Hewett (2007) suggests, that women take a scenic route. Maybe some women experience competing priorities; maybe other women become disaffected with the prevailing climate and opportunities in their places of work. In response to either driver, women might make value-driven choices about distributing their resources, and in the process take professional risks. In 2014, just under 20% of the female labor force reported working part-time for other than economic reasons; the comparable figure for men was just under 5% (US Department of Labor, 2014).

Instead of starting from the question of how we fit women into existing leadership tracks, why don't we ask how women *see leadership* to explore whether conceptions and implementations are biased? Why don't we ask if there remains a need to counterbalance biased prototypes? The restricted flow of women into

---

BOX 4.5 CONTINGENT WORKERS IN THE ECONOMY

The Bureau of Labor Statistics (BLS) classifies those "who do not have an implicit or explicit contract for ongoing employment" as contingent workers. BLS includes independent contractors, those on call, and those holding temporary positions, but excludes business owners. In 2005, the last year in which BLS reported on this category, 7.1% of all employed were contingent workers, up from an estimate of 2.8% in 1995.

Forbes (May 2015) reported that the Government Accountability Office estimated the level of contingent workers in the US economy at 40 %. Clear definition and reliable statistics remain elusive. Pew reported a lower number—30% of all employed. Those who track labor trends agree that whether described as contingent work arrangements, self-employed, or independent contractors, this category will likely continue to grow as a share of total employment. These trends have garnered particular attention in the higher education sector, where reliance on non-tenure track faculty has expanded.

www.forbes.com/sites/elainepofeldt/2015/05/25/shocker-40-of-workers-now-have-contingent-jobs-says-u-s-government/#68d6fdda2532

www.pewsocialtrends.org/2015/10/22/three-in-ten-u-s-jobs-are-held-by-the-self-employed-and-the-workers-they-hire/

---

senior leadership might be because the leadership behaviors that an appreciable number of women choose to enact are under-identified and undervalued in theory and practice. These are not questions you can ask when looking for the next CEO. By then it's too late: Many of the women have moved on, because they've made calculated choices to pursue what they evaluate as more productive endeavors. (See Box 4.5.)

It is not employing women, or any particular demographic, that contributes to robust and resilient organizations. It is having an organizational culture with aligned talent management practices that successfully support and develop a diversity of talent positioned to meet needs over time that results in resilient organizations. Given the increasingly contingent nature of employment relationships—i.e., the rise in freelance; short-term contract; or other fluid, easily shed, positions—organizations will likely require adaptive systems with leader roles diffused beyond traditional hierarchical structures of first-line supervisors, middle management and senior executives. We predict that organizations will increasingly evolve towards holacracies, requiring significant numbers of adaptive workers who are willing to lead in place. This will require redefining roles and structures to recognize and reward such contributions and behaviors.

This seems a good moment to step back and ask questions about received wisdom on what constitutes leadership, as well as how to develop and select effective leaders. Women like Anne Marie Slaughter and Sheryl Sandberg have provoked a very important conversation but they speak from positions and experience of privilege and access. They have used their respective platforms to benefit all women, but their experiences are not representative of a broader cross section of women. Bringing women's stories to this endeavor can enhance results at two levels. First, it provides data to either validate or challenge assumptions underlying current theory. Second, results can inform the framing of more robust practices. We were curious how a cross section of women's experiences might increase fidelity of theory and improve practice. What are women's experiences of leadership—as leaders, as followers?

Notes

1   Social scientists using this lens to study American politics have a goldmine in sociopolitical terms that unfolded around the 2016 presidential election.
2   It's worth noting that, as a genre, modern books for children in the US appear to have more of an "it's ok to be different" message (e.g., *Tacky the Penguin*) than "you can endure and survive" social narratives, and thus the sense individuals make of the world changes over time.
3   Groopman (2007), who has written extensively about the use of heuristics in medical diagnosis, offers a pithy introduction to the concept—as well as upsides and downsides of application—in a 2007 column in *The New Yorker*.
4   Possible corroborating evidence of a revolution in norms around leadership, the convention that women are supposed to accommodate, and/or go quietly, broke in 2017. Pressure on organizations to act on 'or worse' behavior was very publicly ratcheted up.
5   See Thomas (2015) for a first-hand observation on the challenge. More colloquially, one can also explore the wide and long online trail about 'Gamergate'.
6   Is this leadership? Certainly, there must have been staff at the company who desired, and would have meaningfully benefitted from, such leave before Mark Zuckerberg became a parent.

References

Bell, E. L. J., & Nkomo, S. M. (2001). *Our separate ways*. Boston, MA: Harvard Business School Press.

Brush, C. G., Greene, P. G., Balachandra, L., & Davis, A. E. (2014). *Women entrepreneurs, 2014: Bridging the gender gap in venture capital*. Needham, MA: Arthur M. Blank Center for Entrepreneurship, Babson College.

Carter, A. P. (1970). *Structural change in the American economy*. Cambridge, MA: Harvard University Press.

Gilligan, C. (1982). *In a different voice*. Cambridge, MA: Harvard University Press.

Groopman, J. (2007, January 29). What's the trouble?: How doctors think. *The New Yorker*. Retrieved from www.newyorker.com/magazine/2007/01/29/whats-the-trouble. Last accessed: January 9, 2018.

Hewett, S. A. (2007). Off-ramps and on-ramps. In B. Kellerman & D. L. Rhode (Eds.), *Women & leadership* (pp. 407–430). San Francisco, CA: Jossey-Bass.

Hill, L. (2010). Leading from behind. *Harvard Business Review*. [Web log comment]. Retrieved from https://hbr.org/2010/05/leading-from-behind/. Last accessed: January 9, 2018.

Hogue, M., & Lord, R. G. (2007). A multi-level complexity theory approach to understanding gender bias in leadership. *Leadership Quarterly*, 18(4), 370–390.

Kahneman, D. (2011). *Thinking, fast and slow*. New York, NY: Farrar, Straus and Giroux.

Kahneman, D., Lovallo, D., & Sibony, O. (2011). Before you make that big decision. *Harvard Business Review*, 89(6), 50–60.

Lord, R. G., & Dinh, J. E. (2014). What have we learned that is critical in understanding leadership perceptions and leader-performance relations? *Industrial and Organizational Psychology*, 7(2), 158–177.

McNamara, R. (1995). *In retrospect: The tragedy and lessons of Vietnam*. New York, NY: Random House.

Stacey, R. D. (1992). *Managing the unknowable: Strategic boundaries between order and chaos in organizations*. Hoboken, NJ: John Wiley & Sons.

Thomas, R. (2015, July 27). If you think women in tech is just a pipeline problem, you haven't been paying attention. *Tech Diversity Files*. Retrieved from https://medium.com/tech-diversity-files/if-you-think-women-in-tech-is-just-a-pipeline-problem-you-haven-t-been-paying-attention-cb7a2073b996#.2gu39ctps. Last accessed: January 9, 2018.

US Bureau of Labor Statistics. (2016, December). Table 11, *Current population survey (CPS)*. Retrieved from www.bls.gov/cps/cpsaat11.pdf. Last accessed: January 9, 2018.

US Department of Labor. (2014). Percentage of the labor force that work part-time by sex and reason, 2014 annual averages. Retrieved from www.dol.gov/wb/stats/percentage_lf_work_pt_sex_reason_2014_txt.htm. Last accessed: January 9, 2018.

US Library of Congress. (2010, July 20). *Rosie the Riveter: Real women workers of World War II*. Retrieved from www.loc.gov/rr/program/journey/rosie-transcript.html. Last accessed: January 9, 2018.

5

'HER STORIES' ABOUT LEADING IN PLACE

We started this book by asking the question, "What insight would listening to women's perceptions and experiences of leadership contribute to refreshing thought and practice?" After reviewing (and questioning) the pertinent research, theory, and literature, we moved on to the importance of stories in helping us understand how women's reality concerning leadership is often at odds with prevalent practices.

In this chapter we jump head first into women's stories by listening to women who amplify the idea of leading in place by discussing their own experiences frankly and honestly. We randomly selected survey respondents (17), and then deliberately invited others (3) to ensure a cross section of women with very different leadership experiences. What we heard was that, regardless of path or current position, each of these women had stories of, and diverse reasons for, leading in place. Their stories contribute to a more robust understanding of this phenomenon. This chapter ends with a summary of major take-aways from these stories and then sets the stage for a discussion of our survey of 274 women.

We first asked our interviewees to weigh in on the question of whether leadership resides in the person or the position—is it about behavior or title? Next, we asked them to give us an example of when they led in place without positional authority. Finally, we asked them for their insights about leading in place generally.

We heard these phrases a lot: "You just described me! I have always led in place." "You always have the opportunity to be a leader whether you have the position or not." "It's about living an authentic life." "Not all leaders want to be on top." "There is a lot of room for leadership wherever you are in the organization." "I will always lead in place." "It's about background leadership versus foreground leadership; both are leadership." "If a woman chooses to lead in place and not go after the gold, will she be ridiculed?" "You need to be okay with who you are." "Don't ever stop talking about women and leadership."

Position or Behavior?

We asked the women we interviewed, *Is leadership a position or a behavior? How do you think about leadership—more about the person or position?* The response came through in many voices:

Anne, Chief Operations Officer for a large health-care NGO: While it can be both, I tend to fall back most as thinking about it as behavior.

Terese, city and county engineer: In my view it is definitely a behavior. Obviously, your leadership opportunity might be because of a position too, but you have to have the behavior to really be a leader. You can't just have the title.

Anna F., scientist, entrepreneur, director of product development: Leadership is a behavior. I don't need a formal position to influence and catalyze. In fact, I have been called 'happy hour coordinator' because I have had my greatest leadership impact by setting up social drinks with people and the conversations that ensue.

Lisa, vice president, human resources consulting group: I think it is both, but I think the person is more important than the position. You can have plenty of people in leadership positions who are not good leaders, so position is not enough. And, you can have people who are not in leadership positions who are fantastic peer or informal leaders. But I think that what I have learned being in more of a formal position of leadership is that it does give you authoritative power.

Janet F., former managing partner of an international travel agency, now an executive coach for small businesses: I look at it as a behavior because I believe in personal leadership.

Jan, former United States Air Force (USAF) officer, now a police officer: Well you know, with my background in the military and now as a police officer I have many experiences with positional leadership. You wouldn't see a lower level officer bossing around a higher level officer, for example. But I do think that individual leadership behavior matters, especially as a police officer on a call when your supervisor is not there looking over your shoulder.

Amy, formerly executive track for Heinz Corporation and AT&T, now stay-at-home mother and CEO of her own marketing firm for Catholic schools: I think it is a behavior and would add that it requires specific behaviors: being prepared, being knowledgeable, being assertive, and being humble.

Kirk, former urban planner, founding director of a new federal agency, now a professor of practice: I think definitely it's a behavior. For example, you may be in a leadership position, but if you don't have any credibility or people don't trust you, you won't be able to make things happen to move the organization forward.

Heather, managing director, commercial construction company: Leadership is both behavior and position, but I think behavior—particularly personal character—really matters.

Marilu, former librarian, former Chief Information Officer, now Vice Provost: I agree that it is definitely a behavior. But I think it is very hard to get away from it as a position and as an authoritative component of the organization. But, to me, it's an opportunity in every interaction to move something forward.

Kathleen, former stay-at-home mother, founder of a publishing company, now director of development for a library: I don't think it is that easy to choose behavior or position. The way I operate, it is a behavior because I have never really had the position. But there are so many situations where there is no substitute for the head person—whether they are effective or not. I don't care if you are a mannequin sitting in the chair, there are certain people who only want to deal with you because you are the head guy or gal. So, there, position becomes very important.

Mary S., former principal of grade school, now classroom teacher: Definitely a behavior. I have been offered some lovely teaching positions at a higher salary, but have turned them down because of the behavior of the person at the highest leadership level—the principal.

Janet J., attorney, former high level executive with the National Collegiate Athletic Association, now consultant: I think it is overall a behavior. It's one that's motivating, enthusiastic, and authentic, gets others to have that enthusiasm, and sets the goals—maybe in times of difficulty. Or maybe just when it looks difficult to achieve goals and helps the group get there somehow. I would say it is easier to be, in some ways, a leader if you also have the formal position. Positional leadership is a great place to be because you have access to resources—not only the staff, the people with whom you are working—but also you have access to power and other things necessary to help you get things done. But true leadership is a behavior.

Marla, expert in information technology, now a graduate student: It's both, but I think the most important thing is the behavior. I think we have all seen cases where you have people in leadership positions who are not great. They do more harm than good. So, the most important thing is the behavior. I think that is what separates a good leader from a bad leader because you can have someone in a leadership position, but if they are not about making places and people better, then they are not leading.

M'lis, commercial airline pilot, retired USAF pilot, and former NCAA basketball champion: Both, but behavior is most important.

Helen, retired USAF Colonel, professor, and academic administrator: Like most of you, I do think of it in terms of behaviors, so that it's not necessarily a position. I would see it more as a set of behaviors that emerge at times rather than something that has to do with the organization chart or organization structure.

Shannon, software development professional, stay-at-home mother, and angel investor: I never think of it in terms of position. Your ability to lead is something that you project to people. So I think it's definitely more behavioral based than positional. The beauty of position, however, is that you have legitimacy. If you have a good position, a high, in-charge position, then you have the ability to make things happen a little easier than if you are just a cog in the wheel. Honestly though, just a cog in the wheel can have the ability to lead and organize people.

Tish, director of large social services non-profit organization: It is definitely a behavior. I have never pursued a leadership position. To me the question has always been, "how can I best serve?" And leaders are servants. That perspective has taken me down the path to many leadership/service opportunities that I felt I had been called to fulfill. I learned that leadership is not a four-letter word but rather it is a way to serve. My approach is service, full service leadership.

Mary H., 30-year member of the US government Senior Executive Service, then an NGO director, now a university professor: Well I think that it is more than what everyone in the group has been saying. Leadership comprises beliefs, values, and behaviors.

Dannielle, change management expert and leadership coach who worked in corporate environments for 20 years before transitioning to start her own business: Leadership is a behavior. I say this based on looking back over the past 20 years, and seeing how the workplace and organizations are evolving. If I had to do a breakdown, I'd say it's 80% behavior and 20% position. It's different, depending upon the work and industry, and upon key drivers and objectives. If you're talking about the armed forces or police, it's more position because of direct command and control. It's definitely evolving to be more of a behavior.

Let me share why I think that way. There are people who are able to not only manage themselves well, but they're able to engage people in a way that builds collaboration, creates synergy, and both minimizes and manages conflict. There are things converging: factors, elements, and situations. One is the fact that taking a grass-roots approach creates much more momentum and ownership. It's felt across the organization when it can come from the bottom. That whole top-down approach has been ineffective and doesn't work well. There's understanding of the power of the grass-roots approach. It doesn't have to come from the person at the top. Oftentimes it can be rejected from the person at the top. You see it in different parts of our society, not just business. Generational imbalance [also plays a role]: baby boomers, lots of those folks; gen-Xers; gen-Ys; and millennials. You have all of that in the workforce. Baby boomers have stuck around a lot longer, but you have these gen-Xers who are senior now. They may not be able to have the title because the baby boomers are still in place. Millennials are right on the heels: People can leverage and use their knowledge and experience to position themselves as leaders, even if they don't have a title. I see it evolving for different reasons, in different ways. Even in the leadership development research and literature, there continues to be the conversation about personal leadership, exhibiting leadership even when you don't have reports.

Stories of Leading in Place

Women constantly are urged to step up to leadership positions, yet each of the women we interviewed told us that leadership is a *behavior*, not a position. Sure, position helps because of access to resources—not only the staff—but also power and access to funds to help get things done. The beauty of position is that you have legitimacy, they told us. If one has a good position, a high, 'in charge' position, then one has the ability to make things happen a little easier than if one is behind the scenes. But in the end, leadership is about behavior, and anyone can lead, regardless of position. To this end, we asked women to *tell us about a time you led without having positional authority.*

Anne, Chief Operations Officer for a large health-care NGO: I was given very early on some positional authority. But, right before getting that, I was the new part-time teacher in a meeting at our non-profit with the psychiatrist and psychologist and social workers as well as the CEO. They all very clearly had more clout and experience than I. I was definitely out of my league, but after listening for a while, I asked a lot of questions. Others in the room gave a lot of deference to these people because of their positions. We were talking about a 6-year-old boy and they were all talking about the child having enuresis—involuntary urination. The discussion focused on what kind of meds to give him for enuresis and I, as a young mother (and out of the field), asked, "Does anybody know how much water he is drinking at night before bed? Is it really a medication issue and enuresis?" I am sure I asked many naïve questions, but, in time, when we built the new facility, I was then asked more and more to participate and ask questions. And then I was asked to be the administrator for the facility and I was floored. And then I was promoted to chief operations officer. Our CEO said it was "because you routinely challenge the status quo. You just don't accept how it's always been and you ask questions." You know, I was floored when he said he wanted me to be the administrator. I was thinking, "What?"

Anna F., scientist, entrepreneur, director of product development: I think about that [leading in place] a lot because I am typically the number two person in the company or even in my own volunteer work. My job is usually to support the president, the director or other staff. My role is the catalyst, building the energy around the number one position and creating deputies along the way, facilitating the full vision and strategy. But I haven't gone for the CEO spot myself. Part of the reason that I enjoy leading from second place is you have the opportunity to recruit the rest of the team. So, it is much more, for me, hands-on than the director, or the number one spot which sometimes needs to be isolated from day-to-day operations in order to be able to set the tone and get the cash. The CEO or the number one can't do everything. They also need help with delegating. And that is what I am really good at: delegating. And so delegation works better for me in the second spot than the first spot. To be clear, I wouldn't say that I 'stay in my place'. I actively select roles where I can support the leader and lead in place.

Mary H., 30-year member of the US federal government Senior Executive Service, then an NGO director, now a university professor: My example occurred after I left the Senior Executive Service, in my capacity as a professor of practice. I helped put together an Academy for school superintendents. The person I was working with had been a superintendent of schools for 20 years and was a faculty member in our College of Education. He was a wonderful guy. He and I were like partners on this and he had all of the knowledge about education and I was helping create the leadership part of the curriculum which he had a good bit of knowledge about too. I knew that "she who holds the pen can make things happen that wouldn't otherwise." And so I deliberately did a lot of the writing on the proposal and I think that it came out more my way than his way even though we weren't really struggling. We were partners, it wasn't like he was the boss, but he outranked me because he knew the education system so well . . . I do that a lot these days because I don't want that top leadership position anymore. I am very good at organizing ideas and writing them up, and then turning it over to the decision maker. I make sure that I am real clear about how I see it, which direction we should go, and how we should get there.

Janet F., former managing partner of an international travel agency, now an executive coach for small businesses: Well, when I look back, I actually think that I rose to be a leader even though I did never shoot for it. My earliest experience of ever feeling like a leader was when I was 21 years old in college. It was such an 'aha' moment it shifted everything in my life. Up to then I had existed in a 'pack' of friends or family members my whole life. But I found myself at a town hall meeting at my university without my 'pack' and I remember standing up and talking. People listened to me and were persuaded by what I said. It was the first time I had ever been able to do that. It was the first time I ever got noticed. I felt alone and okay with it. It was a defining moment. And all of a sudden, I emerged in my individuality then, instead of being part of a group. From then on, I started speaking up and I became an 'influencer' whether I was in a position of authority or not.

Jan, former United States Air Force (USAF) officer, now a police officer: As a junior police officer, I was assigned to a new unit where there was not much supervision. There was no boss right there. It was just me and my partner . . . working with a couple more officers. I would say, "We're going to do this today," or "We need to see if there are things we need to check off." I ended up being the informal leader, and my boss treated me like I was the leader, even though I did not have the rank or the pay. Technically I was just one of the other junior officers but I ended up leading in place.

Amy, former executive track for Heinz Corporation and AT&T, now stay-at-home mother and CEO of her own marketing firm for Catholic schools: At AT&T, I was in marketing management and I was a project manager. Sitting around me at meetings were high level managers and directors who were in charge of their own departments. Some were from customer service, some from engineering, some from finance and some from marketing. And they didn't report to me, but I had to work with these people, not as their manager, but as the person who connected everyone to move a project—a new technology—forward. I led without positional authority using data and the calendar. I am also a person who is driven by profits, and I kept reporting back profit information to them. I am by nature very collaborative and people call me a 'connector'. So, I connected group members with each other, while also connecting myself individually with commit-tee members. I have that Midwestern ability to befriend people who I don't have a lot in common with. For example, I would ask them about their kids and their families. And I think that goes a long way. I used a combination of fierce project management and people skills.

Kirk, former urban planner, founding director of a new federal agency, now a professor of practice at a university: Well, I can say that for the first several years of working at the Institute—a completely new and unusual federal organization in the making—there was no credibility, there was no track record. There was no predecessor organization, you know, so I would say that even though I had the position as director of this small entity, I didn't have any authority. So I had to figure out how to work with numerous interest groups, politicians, environ-mental advocates, federal workers, and seasoned mediators to build a whole new organization. My strategy consciously was realizing that we had no track record and no one really knew who I was either. I really had to demonstrate that I was listening. I had to demonstrate that we were looking for ways to fill gaps, create value, and that we were not competing with them. I had to show that we wanted to build the field for both the private sector practitioners as well as with the sev-eral federal agencies and stakeholders. So I had a whole lot of stuff to balance and I led by striving to be neutral and impartial with all the different stakeholders, strategically, hoping things would go our way of course. I had to earn their trust bit by bit, little by little.

Heather, managing director, commercial construction company: In the commercial construction industry, the 'rainmakers'—those who bring in the most money—are considered leaders, whether they have a position of authority or not. I am not a rainmaker, so it has been difficult for me to lead. But there was one inci-dent where a very toxic rainmaker was engaging in unprofessional behavior. I called him out for his behavior, even though I am not his boss. I told him he was acting unprofessionally. "I can't have you packing up your toys and leaving the sandbox just because of X, Y, or Z," I told him. "I need you to meet me halfway. I need you to work with me. You have to help me help you." I was very professional and very cordial and very honest. That solved the problem, but not in the way I anticipated: He hired someone to be the intermediary or shock absorber between us! The person he hired was highly professional and we worked well together.

Lisa, vice president, human resources consulting group: Consulting, which I do every day, is the perfect example of leading without having positional authority. You may not be a supervisor and you may not be able to direct your client, but at the same time you are leading a project or initiative down a path where you need people to do certain things. You need to demonstrate credibility, deliver on expectations, be reliable, and build relationships, with the fundamental goal being having the other person know that you are really there to help them be successful and help them solve their problems.

Dannielle, change management expert and leadership coach, who worked in corporate environments for 20 years before transitioning to start her own business: A large portion of my career [at a global corporation] was in that space where you don't have control over people; the team that you're working with are not reporting to you, but they're working on a team that you're leading. This is how I leapt out [in the company]: I was on a team for a change-management work stream. There was an external consultant, a couple of internal trainers, and a couple of internal business analysts. What's challenging about that type of situation is ensuring that roles are clear and making sure people understand what lane they're playing in, and understanding interdependencies. From a leadership perspective, I always want to value people's expertise and their experience. So, when you're leading without authority you have to do that even more. You are really depending on those individuals to show up strong, to be able to lend expertise in a way that's needed, in a way that's adaptable. That doesn't always happen, and so you do get into these difficult conversations. Those are not comfortable situations or conversations. When you're working on a project like that—it's an initiative, an effort—and oftentimes team members are still doing their 'regular' jobs. They have another component/tasks that they're responsible for. Your initiative isn't at the top of their mind, isn't always priority. So, it requires a lot of communication, a lot of clarifying what the deliverables are, what you're trying to achieve, and what's critical and necessary to get to that point. If you're working in a large program with many moving parts, that's extremely difficult. I wasn't the only one that was challenged in that way.

Looking back on it, I probably would have brought top leadership into the conversation earlier. But you expect professionals not to throw up unreasonable resistance. There was one guy, on the operations side: A key [. . .] person with the knowledge and expertise around the work stream (being addressed). He was well-known; people started referring to him as 'the talent' in a sarcastic way. He was a high-maintenance prima donna from beginning to end. You're working around this person, you're doing things to make them happy. You don't have a hammer.

I did not get much support from leadership in the situation, because his leader was weak. There was an email exchange that got ugly. In the last response I copied the manager, listing out all the efforts that had been made to accommodate the individual. I got a little more pleasant conversation out of him after that. It's a classic example of where you're leading the effort, no matter how grand or big the scale, but others choose the level at which they're going to play. As a leader, you have to manage around that.

Terese, city and county engineer: As the only woman engineer in my (city and county) departments for years, I was always in charge of my own area. My instances of leading without position would be when I was on committees over the years where I wasn't the in-charge person, but I had a huge amount of influence in the outcome. One example is when one of our professional organizations started a scholarship program for engineering students in college. I wasn't the person who started it. But I was one of a handful of people who initially worked to implement the idea. And I think it was all just about, you know, being a positive voice for the scholarship and we created an auction to support the scholarship. So, after leading without being in charge on this committee for years, I became chair and worked in that capacity for ten more years.

Marilu, former librarian, former Chief Information Officer, now Vice Provost: When I was Chief Information Officer for a university, we had a really bad relationship between the technology department and the faculty who wanted to use technology in the classroom. We tried to solve that problem in lots of different ways and we weren't being successful at getting it solved. So I said to my number two employee, "you are going to run the organization for the next four months and I am going to form a team of our best and brightest across the university and we are going to work on this problem." And so I stepped out of my role as CIO, with the permission of the Provost, of course. I chose a time when not a lot was going on. I created teams of faculty, librarians, and IT people. We got together and wrote vision statements of how things could be. The teams went off and did their work and I had reserved ahead of time a part of the budget to implement their recommendations. I told them at the beginning, "We are going to implement whatever you come up with. There is no authority approval process here. We are going to do it." I wanted them to feel empowered. We called it HVC2 for 'High Velocity Change through High Volume Collaboration.' The only parameter around the work I gave the groups was "You must get it done in three months" because that was the amount of time I had off from my job. And we came up with all these projects, we implemented all of the projects, and in that whole process, I was just a member of all these teams. I sat there; we had these teams which we all professionally facilitated. I trained a whole group of facilitators to lead the groups and then I deliberately became merely one of the group members as we worked through all the issues. So I guess I was a positional leader in the beginning, but then led without positional authority by empowering the groups. To this day, I have faculty who were on these teams who come to me and say, "You know, that was the only time I have been on a taskforce where something actually happened."

Kathleen, former stay-at-home mother, founder of a publishing company, now director of development for a library: Much of my career has been leading without positional authority, mostly just to move an organization forward. Usually it was because the person who was in the position of authority wouldn't do it. One example has to do with our town's library. There are two organizations, the library itself, and the library foundation which raises money. The library had a director who was shy and retiring and not very effective. He liked to hide out in his office. Nothing was done. But the organization was bursting at the seams with employees with creative ideas. So because we at the foundation had the money behind us, we kind of had a little bit of say in things and so our board and I sort of took it and ran with it because, frankly, I don't think it would have happened without that board. It was a huge group effort. So I became this weird person from outside the library who was collaborating to lead this revolt against the library director. I call that 'sneaky leadership'. I led by providing information and facilitating the free flow of ideas. I was behind the scenes, but it was the board that was pushing, pushing, pushing. And I was right there with them doing it. And we kind of shoved changes through. Eventually we got a bond passed to build a new library, and got the director to retire. While I was a leader in the coup, there was so much help from a city commissioner who we had lobbied behind the scenes to be on our side. I mean, it wouldn't have happened without him. It wouldn't have happened without the woman who handled the library campaign. It wouldn't have happened without the library board of trustees. There were a lot of community people who worked behind the scenes. Eventually a new director came on board who was much stronger in terms of . . . he was just much more comfortable in the community limelight. And now the library is thriving.

Mary S., former principal of grade school, now classroom teacher: I have not been a principal for years (I stepped down to return to the classroom), but I feel like I lead in place every day when I mentor new teachers. And I love the lack of constraints that come with that leadership behavior not being dictated by a job description. I can mold it the way I think it should work best. I feel more like a leader now that I have returned to the classroom than I ever did as principal. I feel like people listen to me more, that they are more responsive to anything that I have to say or offer when I observe and mentor without positional authority. And that is exciting, fun, and satisfying.

Janet J., attorney, former high level executive with the National Collegiate Athletic Association, now consultant: After my work with the NCAA, then my work with a law firm, I decided to slow down and was hired to work under an athletic director of a mid-sized university. I wanted a change of pace. I was not interested in being 'in charge'. I did not have positional authority over him and yet I think I had influence. And that was influence I had through my leadership skills as well as my NCAA knowledge. That's an obvious example. I think that also, outside of organizations, volunteering on many boards has taught me how to influence without having positional authority. I actually think it is easier to lead without positional authority as a volunteer than it is as a member of a highly structured organization.

Marla, expert in information technology, now a graduate student: When I was at the EPA interning, my boss kind of put me in charge, so to speak, of revamping the Region 5 intranet for employees. It was very old technology. She really wanted to create it as a safe portal so that employees could be more productive, share information, and become more efficient with their work. It was a big communication tool, it was a working tool. I was in charge of making that happen. I was dealing and working with individuals who a) had a LONG tenure at the EPA, and b) were quite a bit older than I was. They had their ways of doing things and their ways of thinking. But my boss gave me, not official position, but she gave me the okay to go ahead and start pushing this initiative. So, for me, I not only had to do the visionary work, but I had to do the nitty-gritty work as well. It wasn't just about coming up with the vision concerning what the new intranet site would be like, it was about getting people on board. And it was about making sense of this tool and being able to market it, thinking about what kind of value it might add to our work. I was able to totally revamp the intranet, all without a formal position of authority.

M'lis, commercial airline pilot, retired USAF pilot and former NCAA basketball champion: After I played college basketball, I coached basketball. One of my first jobs was as a varsity assistant at a high school. The head coach was a very polarizing type of a person. Some of the girls really liked him. Some of the girls really did not like him. A lot of the parents were split along that line, and it was controversial how the previous coach left in the first place. So there was a lot of drama when I entered this scene. We came to a point in a game where there was a clash between the head coach and one of the star players, and it was really completely unnecessary, because we were winning the game by 30 points in the third quarter, and the discussion could have happened in practice about what was going on. The head coach said something very derogatory and mean-spirited to the star player, and then benched her for the rest of the game. She was truly the leader of the team, and you could see that his actions affected everyone negatively.

And so here I am as the assistant not trying to go against the head coach. However, I thought it was really important to make sure that individual spirits weren't broken, and we didn't have a mutiny on our hands. So I remember at some point of time in the game I went over to that player just quickly and bent my head over, tapped her on the shoulder, and said, "Hey, keep your head up!" And the next day, at practice, I talked with the six seniors and asked, "Hey, is everybody okay?" And they're all like, "No, we're not okay." So I gathered those girls together, and

I said, "Look, being a senior and getting a new head coach is terrible. It sucks. It's awful. It's not the thing you would want to happen in your senior year. You want the coach that you've worked with for three years . . . I totally get that . . . and you want your senior year to turn out a certain way. And unfortunately that didn't happen to you. And those are the facts. Here is the better side: You're a senior and this is your senior year. And no matter who the coaching staff is, and no matter what play we call, when you get inside the line, it's your game. And you own it. You have to do what you want to do with that senior experience . . . no matter what the external factors are." I remember the next game, we went out and we won against the toughest team with a 3-point shot at the buzzer. It was really a spirit-high moment. The star of the team came to me after that game, and she said, "I would've quit if you weren't here. You're a guide to this team. I don't know how you ended up here, because when you look at it, there's no way we could win a championship, but I think you were brought here for a reason. And I'm speaking for all the seniors and all the girls on the team, we would've quit if you weren't here." I made them not quit; I made them hang in there. And that team went on to the final eight in the state. The head coach finally did get fired, and things changed during that year. I really felt like me being there, and supporting those girls, was the right thing to do at the right time. I was a leader even when I did not have that role. You always have to be leader. It doesn't matter if you've got the title or not.

Tish, director of large social services non-profit organization: A Catholic nun who ran a non-profit spiritual and religious education center where I lived would book speaking engagements for a small group of us. Oftentimes she was very busy and would say to us, "I'll meet you there. I have to take care of something else. Just go. I'll be there." Well, she wouldn't get there. And then it would be like everybody would be like, "oh well I guess Tish you have to do this," because I was at the time one of the older ones. And I think that sometimes they did look to me when she was not around as the next person in line, you know, the leader. I hated her for not showing up because I was like, "I can't believe she did this again! I just can't believe it." But, in the meantime, I was taking on the leadership role without having the position, and getting confidence. Eventually I was like, "oh well, if she doesn't show up, I guess I can do this." Or sometimes she would schedule meetings, and again, would just not show up. And then I would have to take over. I would say, "Well, somebody has to lead this meeting." So, I learned a lot of hands-on leadership skills because she either intentionally or unintentionally made me the leader, without the position. Looking back, I think she trusted enough that I could handle it. If she didn't, I think she would have definitely shown up.

How Prevalent Is Leading in Place?

We followed up with the women we interviewed, thanked them for their stories, and told them that we call leading without having positional authority 'leading in place'. Sometimes the women who lead in place do not want—for whatever reason—senior leadership positions or 'the top spot'. Sometimes these are women who are blocked from 'in charge' positions for a multitude of reasons. These women choose instead to lead in other ways, from being a stand-out team member and collaborator, to leading without position by stepping up to assist a superior. We asked our interviewees one last question: Based on your experiences, *how prevalent is leading in place?*

Anne, Chief Operations Officer for a large health-care NGO: You know, I in some ways fall into this category which is kind of odd because I have been in a senior leadership position within our organization for the last 28 years. I have had a high level position (COO), but have never been CEO. At the same time, I often do CEO jobs such as fundraising, and board development. But because I just don't enjoy those tasks—and I am not as good at them as much as my COO tasks—I do not want to be the number one person at the helm of the organization. Now that our CEO has turned 70 and has started talking about retirement, I found myself thinking again that I could be effective in his spot in a different way, but I don't think I would enjoy doing what the job entails as much as I absolutely enjoy all aspects of my job right now. So part of this is the job description and what you enjoy the most. Another aspect of this concerns our staff and the feedback we give them. As Jim Collins (author of *From good to great*) writes, we need to have the right people in the right seat on the bus. I don't think that everyone is suited for every seat. Sometimes I find myself counseling people that they are a hugely important part of our organization, but they are in the right place, right now. To myself I might be thinking that they might not be a great fit for the next highest position of leadership, but they are doing a good job leading in place right where they are.

Mary H., 30-year member of the US federal government Senior Executive Service, then an NGO director, now a university professor: Absolutely I have seen it, people—largely women—leading in place in most organizations I've worked. I might not have noticed these people right away sometimes because they are often behind the scenes. I think probably it happens because women in some instances have not been told that they should go after a position of leadership. They have not been told that they would be a good (positional) leader, and that they should think about throwing their name in for consideration for a top spot. In other instances that may just be the most comfortable place for them to be—behind the scenes and helping and being invaluable to somebody who may or may not be a good leader. And because most of us as women have grown up wanting to be appreciated for how helpful we are, that is pretty gratifying for a lot of women. It has been a big part of the US culture, as well as other cultures. I certainly have seen it, but no one really talked about it. I am hearing more about it now. But we are hearing that some of the younger generation—those in their 20s, 30s, and even 40s—are not wanting to move up into the positions their bosses hold, if, for example, their boss is getting ready to retire, because they have watched the bosses go through hell. I heard this recently from a city official who is going to be retiring soon, and he has been grooming people to come up the ladder after him. He is saying that many of his best people are not interested. "They watch me get beat up by the politicians and they don't want to have a life full of conflict" he told me. Which makes a whole lot of sense. And then, a non-profit CEO recently told me that the person she was hoping would fill her position didn't want it because she had seen her boss work so hard and such long hours. She did not want that.

Lisa, vice president, human resources consulting group: Leading in place is very prevalent in the workplace, but not explored much in the literature. That was one of the biggest problems that I had with the book, *Lean in.* The author's whole focus is on how many women CEOs there are. I don't think you have to be a CEO to be a successful leader. I do think that women can lead and do lead in lots of ways and it goes back to trust. You can be someone who can help the organization be successful without being in a formal leadership position if people trust you and have faith in you. For example, the most powerful person in an organization might be an administrative assistant.

If you make yourself irreplaceable, that is being a leader. You are a go-to person. You are someone who others can rely on whether they are a peer, above you, or below you on the organization chart. But you are leading in some way because people are turning to you and looking to you and respecting what you have to add. I think that if you are in a situation where you have a say in what matters, you are a leader whether you are in a positional leadership role or not.

Terese, city and county engineer: I think leading in place is prevalent. For example, when I took the position of engineering division manager for the county, I had a boss who supposedly was the leader of the group, but he didn't do anything. His superiors would give him a task to be done and he would never respond back for, like, nine months. It was just ridiculous. So eventually the female engineer who acted as his assistant decided she would bypass him. Because if she asked him a question, he wouldn't give her an answer, so she ended up just bypassing him and talking to me, asking me directly. He became a non-functioning person so she was able to bypass him and get the technicians to keep working and they would get stuff done without his guidance and sometimes without his knowledge. One story was that he went on vacation for two weeks and, while he was gone, she completed several projects that were just hanging out there that would have taken months or maybe years to accomplish had he been involved. When he returned, he walked around joking "Maybe I should go on vacation more often!" And I was thinking, "Yeah, you just need to get out of here." Firing someone who works for the county is very difficult, so we were never able to get him fired, despite his poor annual reviews. His assistant basically did all his work for him until he finally left for another job.

Janet F., former managing partner of an international travel agency, now an executive coach for small businesses: If you live the authentic life and lead with values, once people get clear about what they stand for, speaking up in a way that allows others to not be wrong, they will demonstrate leadership skills in whatever they do. Whether you are a mom leading the neighborhood association or a worker in an organization who sees a team going off in the wrong direction and steers them back on track, if you speak up and say your truth, still allowing others to influence you, you are a leader with or without positional authority. To me the perfect example is leadership on a jury in a court of law. It is the person who can describe reality without laying blame who emerges as a leader whether they are designated or not. It is the person who is listened to: the one who is calm and not one-sided, not closed-minded, not "my way or the highway." They are authentic yet they are accurate. So it is a very high level of conversation, of communicating, of interacting. Some call it "bringing people to the intersection," some say it is more collaboration. It is synergizing the ideas and brains of others instead of dividing the ideas and brains. Leaders are people who work from intersections instead of opposite views and ask, "Where do we all agree? Now, what are we trying to achieve? Okay, now how can we all work together to get this done?" And it can be done whether you are in a position of authority or not. This is the way I view people who lead in place.

Jan, former United States Air Force (USAF) officer, now a police officer: I think leading in place is prevalent. Personally, I don't want to have my phone ringing every night at 2:00 a.m. That does not appeal to me. So I feel fulfilled in my informal leadership role as a junior police officer, making my boss look good, even if I am not the executive. I do not think I am unique in being an informal leader, but not wanting or seeking a formal position of leadership.

Amy, former executive track for Heinz Corporation and AT&T, now stay-at-home mother and CEO of her own marketing firm for Catholic schools: I have always loved being the number two person in the private sector corporations I worked for. Because being the number two person allows you to do everything you have always done, but you have that error coverage of the number one person. It feels safer. But now that I have my own consulting firm, I have no error coverage. I think that was the hardest thing for me. I can't 'lead in place' behind the scenes anymore. I am always having to be in the limelight. I think in some cases you are allowed to lead in place and in other situations you just can't. In other situations you are forced to lead in place. At H. J. Heinz where I used to work, the rule is you are either promoted to a positional leadership role after a couple years, or you are out. My friend who is vice president at Enterprise car rentals has never led in place—she has always been the visible positional leader. But then almost all my other women friends have chosen not to advance because of personal family situations or lifestyle choices. They stayed in place because of their situation. Another example to show how complicated the idea of leading in place is: I work with a lot of principals of Catholic schools in my consulting business and they are all underneath the parish priest. But they are number one in the school. Are they leading in place or are they positional leaders ... or both?

Anna F., scientist, entrepreneur, director of product development: Like Amy, I have always preferred the number two position. And while I know there has been a lot of literature on followership, I don't consider myself to necessarily be following the leader, nor do I consider those who lead in place to be following the leader. I do think leading in place is prevalent, but rather than blindly following, I see it as facilitating and catalyzing around the vision and the mission of a common goal. We train our staff that they need to make sure that they align goals and objectives, the short term and longer term, so that everyone is going the same direction. And with that alignment and that alignment creation, I have seen in the last several years the incredible power in being able to mobilize the team and the company, working together whether someone has a formal position of authority or not.

Kirk, former urban planner, founding director of a new federal agency, now a professor of practice at a university: I would include myself in the category of women who have 'led in place'. I think it is different in private and public and non-profit spheres. I would say, behind every male private sector executive, there is a female doing all the work. I am not sure that is entirely true in other sectors. You really need to reward these women who are leading in place, but don't have the top positions. I am thinking of a woman who runs our financial office and she is extremely competent and knows everything. And she is a gatekeeper in the best sense. She is really essential to the School and she's had that job for a long time. I don't think she has the ambition to go to the next level to the Provost's office and join the administration. And I think that we should be careful assuming that leaders want to be on the top all the time.

There is lots of space for leadership. There are lots of ways in which one can be a leader. One can lead by example. One can lead informally, like a student who works in a department who is really functional. She doesn't have formal power or authority, but everybody—students and faculty—come to her. She is in a very good place to resolve problems and to advise other co-workers on how to make something happen and get something done. I think there is a lot of that. And I probably do think that it is more of something that women do. So, because of their tendency to work in networks, or laterally, they know a lot about the organization and, at the same time, they are willing to help people figure out how to operate within the organization informally. I think that some women really like to close up shop and shut the door at night and go home and not have to have the burden of the bottom line and take it all home with them. And that doesn't mean that they aren't leaders.

Marilu, former librarian, former Chief Information Officer, now Vice Provost: I, too, think it (leading in place) is pervasive. I have seen a lot of it. I have done a lot of it. I think it is very underappreciated. I think that it goes unnoticed because we tend to focus on the formal organization—the work chart and the titles—instead of the informal organization. I think 'leading in place' gets noticed a little bit more in team-based environments where people can lead for a short period of time and get recognized for that. I think recognition is important. And I think we often don't see women leading in place, don't recognize them and don't reward the behavior. I think there are a hell of a lot of women who have led from where they are and made very incompetent men successful—and I have seen teams back up incompetent women in positions of power too. I have done that myself because it advanced my career. It was a conscious decision. Maybe some people do it not so much consciously, but for me it was a conscious decision.

Kathleen, former stay-at-home mother, founder of a publishing company, now director of development for a library: There are a lot of women who lead in place, and I think that is okay. I go back and forth on this topic because the bottom line is—do you want to be in that top spot? And you know, there is a whole thing that I am sure you have read, like in the book *Lean in* where women look at a job and they feel like they have to be able to meet all of the qualifications whereas a guy looks at the same job and says, "Oh, I can do most of that." Or maybe even just half of that and they will go for it. For example, I feel like I have the political skills and the networking skills to be the library director, but I don't feel like I have the personnel and financial skills for it, and I'd have to go back to library school before I would have the credentials for a position of leadership. I don't want to do that because I think going back to school at my stage in life would be a waste of time. So I will never have the number one position—which means if I stay here I will always lead in place.

Shannon, software development professional, stay-at-home mother, and angel investor: I have been in lots of situations where my position was low or not at the top, never been at that top, but where I lead none the less. People in charge, they know who their leaders are in the room, even if they're five rows down or ten rows down. They know who's motivating people, who's leading people; who people go to, to make things happen. These are the people who lead in place.

Janet J., attorney, former high level executive with the National Collegiate Athletic Association, now consultant: I see a lot of people leading in place in organizations; it is usually unrewarded, particularly for women. One of the things that I thought about over the years is when I had ideas and I shared those ideas and my ideas would be taken and somebody else would get credit for them—particularly when I was not in a position of power for that setting. That is something that happens when you are not in that top leadership position. I think of this issue as 'background leadership versus foreground leadership'. Not everybody can be a CEO. There are only so many senior leadership positions. I think part of the struggle for women is that there is this push that all women can be leaders and that all women can have it all and that all women can make a lot of money. I think that is a lot of pressure put on women. Particularly if they have families and work outside the home, because it is still a fact that women do most of the child-rearing in this country. I think there is certainly a role that needs to be validated and supported in organizations for background leadership. You can be a leader even if you are not in the top position, but you might not have all the opportunities that a CEO has and you might not get all the credit.

Women who lead in place need to make sure that they are known and that is where some women also have a hard time: letting people know what they have done. Men oftentimes are better at tooting their own horns. You've got to let those who hand out the rewards know what you are doing and show what you have contributed, show why you are valuable. And I think that we have to validate that kind of position, that kind of role—leading in place. Fact is, not everybody can be in those 'limelight' positions, nor should they be. And with those so-called CEO positions —senior management positions—there is a lot of stress and it's often not what it is cut out to be. I think a lot of women see that and realize that and walk away from those CEO positions. If we had more opportunities that were spread around collaborative, group kind of team-making, where people feel like they have contributed and are validated for it, it would be a good thing for women who lead in place.

Kathleen, former stay-at-home mother, founder of a publishing company, now director of development for a library: I agree. Women sometimes have this idea that if you work your butt off and you do really well, someone will notice you. And you will be appointed a leader, you know what I mean? You work hard and lead in place, therefore you think you will get you are chosen for the promotion. And in my case, that has sometimes worked. But, that wasn't always the case.

M'lis, commercial airline pilot, retired USAF pilot and former NCAA basketball champion: I have an example of this from my work experience. As a pilot, I'm one of those people who may be visible to the other pilots, but I'm definitely invisible to the management. We have a quarterly award that's given to employees who are recognized for doing a good job and nominated by fellow workers. I was nominated by someone I don't even know very well for revising 10,000 items in our safety handbook. It took me five years to do it! I figured I had a pretty good chance of being one of the 400 people chosen for the award that year. But I was not chosen.

As I read who was chosen and why, I was shocked to read about a guy who was heralded for the way he greets first-class passengers! I was incredibly disappointed but I know being a good leader is not about being recognized; my goal was to do that job correctly and well. My goal wasn't to be a quarterly award winner, but it still hurt. I applaud anybody who puts out leadership effort anywhere whether it's recognized or not. You're still a leader—the leader of your Girl Scout troop, or the leader of the running club. It doesn't matter. Just do something for someone else and make everybody else around you better. That's being a great leader at any level anywhere.

Marla, expert in information technology, now a graduate student: Honestly, leading in place IS me. I am totally fine not having a formal leadership position, not being a senior executive or not having that title. I think, for me, that is where I can be my best, if I lead in place, but it is really a weird tightrope. As much as I want to see women in these high level authority positions, I am okay with not doing that myself, because I am comfortable with my strength being behind the scenes, kind of being that amicable hand. And that is probably more of a personality trait as opposed to any social construction of what being a woman is about. The challenge is that if a woman wants to lead in place—if she does not want to go after the gold—will she be ridiculed or criticized? This comes back to one of my boss's advice: to "do you." Just be who you are. And if who you are is to take the bull by the horns and be that formal authority figure, great. But, if it's not, that's okay too, because the reality is that not everyone is going to be or should be in a senior level executive spot.

We need leaders everywhere. If you think of an organization as a body, not everyone can be the brain. You have to have the hands, you know, you have to have the foot, you have to have the shoulder, you have to have some eyes, you have to have some elbows, you have to have some heart in order for the entire body to function. As long as you are exhibiting leadership behavior, then you are fine. I think it is a personal choice to a certain extent, if you decide that you want to aim for a formal executive leadership position. And sometimes, it is not just about making a political statement, it can be time or context dependent. Especially for women of color, we are all on these paths that many consider diversity initiatives. That is great and needed, but at the same time, you can't ignore the fact there might be great sacrifice involved and the reward just might not be there.

Tish, director of large social services non-profit organization: In women's religious orders, leading in place is very prevalent. I just think there are some people who, by their nature, by their personality, by their caring attitude, by their work ethic, are looked up to. And they may not be the designated leader, but they are leading by example and everybody is listening. And sometimes, I believe people are listening more maybe to that person than they are to the positional leader.

For example, imagine that I am a worker and I haven't had very positive experiences in my past with supervisors or positional leaders, and I've got kind of a negative attitude, and the current leader or supervisor is just okay. I am not attracted to really spending time with them or listening to them. But imagine that I've got a co-worker who I really like and admire, someone who I watch what they do and I hear what they say and they are always positive and always encouraging everybody else, and they get things done and move the organization forward. I might pick up on, and be inspired by, that form of leadership, more so than I might the so-called leader's behavior. Likely, that is happening everywhere today.

M'lis, commercial airline pilot, retired USAF pilot and former NCAA basketball champion: I too think you have to do what you feel most comfortable doing and be the best at it. Not everyone is meant to be the focal point or the trailblazer. Not everyone should be a Hillary Clinton. It takes a lot of talent and a lot of sacrifice to lead from a high level position. It comes back to that whole basketball team analogy: it takes every player on the team to have a great attitude and to work hard every day. And even though we only play five people on the court at a time, we need all ten people on the team rooting towards that goal. I applaud the women who say "you know I'm going to do my leadership thing but I'll do it as a support person", like getting your candidate elected to Congress. I applaud that perspective because it isn't just about the visible person and you know for those people who are truly talented and truly selfless to go out there and actually be in that position and to take that risk to run for office, for example, if we don't have good leaders in the background supporting them, they'll never be successful. It takes a village you know.

Janet J., attorney, former high level executive with the National Collegiate Athletic Association, now consultant: The bottom line is that the world needs more people leading in place. And the people who lead in place should be rewarded for their leadership.

Dannielle, change management expert and leadership coach, who worked in corporate environments for 20 years before transitioning to start her own business: I think leading in place can be something that just happens. In my observation I don't think it's associated with a certain demographic. I do think people who have energy around the work that they are doing and whose work is well-respected can find themselves in the right circumstances, in the right environment, where someone will give them gateway experiences to lead visibly without position. Let me share an example [of my own experience]. I was doing org design/effectiveness work, working with senior leaders, helping them to figure how many people they needed and why.

What I was noticing was that the people I was working with at the VP level, sometimes they really weren't effective at knowing who they needed to bring along, weren't effective at managing the resistance and push-back. This is not uncommon in a large, big organization. It's a challenge having to socialize the idea that managers have to understand what people are feeling and thinking. [The group of leaders who were my direct customers in the global corporation] weren't really that strong in that area; they weren't effective. I went to the head of leadership development and said "Hey, this is what I'm noticing about those leaders that I'm working with. There seem to be gaps in their ability to lead change."

I proposed going and talking to people in the organization about what it's like to lead change in that environment. I took that initiative, I took that on. It wasn't my department; I did that, and took the findings to different people in the organization. That's a long way of sharing [that it's hard to know whether leading in place] is about passion, or is it about demographics? Sometimes it just happens. I saw a need, a gap; nobody really had time to think about it, nobody had energy or passion around it to address it. It's funny. I remember one of the executives I interviewed—I interviewed change management folks, I interviewed executives, I interviewed those who had change efforts [in their business area], HR folks. I remember one of the change management consultants said: "so where's this coming from?" I gave her the spiel [about my observations] and she said "Oh. You didn't ask for permission, you just did it?"

M'lis, commercial airline pilot, retired USAF pilot and former NCAA basketball champion: I think the important thing is, don't ever stop talking about it. The conversation has to be had. Some people are like, "Yeah, women leadership, we've heard about it. We've read about it, and nothing's changed." But it's the conversation that we need to have all the time. Every single day, every single year. Every girl, woman, needs to experience that and share it and be pushed, because that's the only way everything gets better, that we keep moving forward and that we keep motivating youngsters and keep telling them they can do anything, because they can. And the subject never gets old, and I think that's really important.

Conclusion

The women profiled in this chapter all felt comfortable with the notion of leading in place. These women do not only lead in place, several have significant positions of leadership. However, they all had stories of leading in place, and described a range of reasons for doing so. From the examples they shared, a spectrum of leading in place behaviors emerged, as well as gaps targeted when they led in place. Many behaviors they reported deploying while leading in place align with behaviors often expected of leaders; others vary. Leading in place clearly was not a wholesale substitute for positional leadership; rather it was a complement.

In this exchange, a spectrum of behaviors used while leading in place (without or beyond position) were discussed, including:

- Prompting vision and sense-making by: challenging the status quo, speaking truth to power, bringing in objective data to change the conversation, pushing change, helping others make sense of complexities, reframing a situation;
- Promoting effectiveness by: strategically building relationships, volunteering to write a report in order to influence outcomes, pinning down exact dates to promote better project management, managing around problem managers or working networks to influence strategic conversation and get poor leadership replaced, catalyzing clear communication including clarifying what is needed to get the job done;

- calling out inappropriate behavior, describing reality without laying blame, having difficult conversations, seeking out the perspectives of a wide variety of stakeholders in order to build trust, energizing others, asking "where do we all agree?"; and
- Getting the best out of diverse teams by: being a positive voice, advocating for and empowering others, providing information and the free flow of ideas, supporting others in need, and facilitating around a common goal.

It is important to note that these are examples, not an exhaustive list.

Also evident were concrete examples of some gaps targeted by those we interviewed who led in place, including:

- Failure of those in leadership positions, evidenced by: poor judgment, insufficient supervision, lack of vision, a leader who turns people off.
- Dysfunctional team behavior manifested by: lack of trust, unprofessional behavior of colleagues, need to compensate for others' lack of knowledge.
- Potential missed opportunities created by: clients who did not know what to do, need to fill gaps in an inter-organizational task where colleagues have other 'regular' jobs pulling them in multiple directions, and operating in environments when no one is in charge.

Again, this is not an exhaustive list.

The reasons for leading in place articulated by those we interviewed included:

- A high comfort level with being a behind-the-scenes player;
- A high energy or dedication concerning the work they are doing/passion;
- Trying to right a wrong;
- Getting the work done that someone else is supposed to be doing;
- Wanting to influence direction;
- Attempting to catalyze teamwork;
- Desiring to make oneself irreplaceable;
- Hoping to be noticed;
- Seeking work-life balance;
- Personal family situations;
- Not wanting the stress of the top position;
- Not wanting to be isolated as one might be in a CEO slot;
- Not wanting the spotlight;
- Not wanting the burden of the bottom line;
- Lifestyle choices; and
- Not being promoted into a position of leadership.

Based on our interviews with women, as well as our survey discussed in the next two chapters, our analysis of the literature offered at the beginning of this book, and our own life experiences, we believe that it is out-dated and fundamentally wrong to conceive of leadership as predominantly positional, just as it is fundamentally wrong to conceive of leadership coming from the top of hierarchy. Yes, we want women in positions of leadership, but women have been and are leading. The challenge is that it is not always in a way that mimics the stereotypic prototype, and so it often goes unnoticed and unrewarded.

Leadership thinking needs to change to adapt to modern phenomena. Moving in this direction will specifically increase understanding of the under-representation of women in top positions of leadership, and generally result in greater recognition of the multitude of ways in which women and others lead in the modern world. The next two chapters take us out of individual cases and into a larger survey to examine women's leadership views and experiences.

SECOND INTERLUDE

What Does Leadership Success Look Like?

We asked 20 women leaders *what does leadership success look like?* We found their responses to be fascinating reflections on their own leadership journeys as well as insightful suggestions for future leaders.

Mary S., former principal of grade school, now classroom teacher: In many ways, it looks like it is through somebody else's eyes when you see someone begin to flourish from the help that you have assisted them with—that's where I see leadership success. They can go out on their own and do X, Y, or Z.

Tish, director of large social services non-profit organization: Number one, there is a vision and a mission. Those can be intertwined. You are saying, "This is what we hope to do." You are accomplishing that vision. Number two, you are growing the people who are working with you whether that is employees or whether that is other group members. And then number three is that it is a team effort. It is not like the leader is the one who is making it happen and takes the credit for that success, but really a team together is accomplishing that vision and they are working together and they feel that they are accomplishing it together. The leader is constantly developing new leaders.

Lisa, vice president, human resources consulting group: It is when you have a group or a team or person and they are working with you and feeling motivated to work towards a goal put out by your organization or you. And that it is a two-way street, I think of leadership as a relationship, not something you do to somebody ... My role models for leadership and women in leadership have been extremely positive. The common thread among all of them and what I thought made most of them strong was that they were very clear that they cared about my success and they were very supportive of me taking chances and stretching and

I knew that they had my back. I knew that if I made a mistake or failed they would have my back and that they wanted me to be successful.

Heather, managing director, commercial construction company: It is making sure that you are empowering your people to be strong at what they are doing. It is making sure that there is continuous learning and that you are at the top of your game and that you are continuing to cultivate yourself and other people. And you are going above and beyond to try to engage other organizations to help contribute the time and success and energy of your skills and your expertise.

Anna F., scientist, entrepreneur, director of product development: Leadership success is enabling followership. Which sounds kind of vague, but what happens when a leader is being successful is that it is not about the leader, but the group. The group tends to get its own life and grow around whatever the subject that is being explored.

Janet J., attorney, former high level executive with the National Collegiate Athletic Association, now consultant: Leadership success can be a result or a process. I have looked at it both ways. As a result, I think it is changing the status quo by using groups or individuals and using their various processes. Effective leadership is influential, creative, collegial, and transparent. It is a sharing process. I think it is something that has to be top down. It can go across lines. And it has to be connected with good leadership across the group. Leadership success is really changing the status quo.

M'lis, commercial airline pilot, retired USAF pilot, and former NCAA basketball champion: One of the things that makes me a really good leader is the fact that I have a lot of compassion and a great sense of honor. I think that people do much better in their jobs when they're relaxed and feel confident and comfortable. My job is to evaluate them, and I want to do that at their best not at their worst. You know I have to evaluate them in some of the worst weather and aircraft conditions but not necessarily their worst condition. So I really feel like, one of the best things that I ever learned about being a good leader has nothing to do with how well you do. It really has more to do with what kind of environment you create for those around you to do their best. So I think that's the most important thing I've learned about being a leader. It really is about trying to make those around you better. And sometimes I think people forget that.

Marla, expert in information technology, now a graduate student: I can look at this from a professional and a personal standpoint, because in my opinion, workplace leaders don't just affect organization function, they also affect people. Successful leaders get to people at their core. They speak to them mentally, emotionally, spiritually even. And so, for me overall, success to me is when the people and places are better as a result of a leader's guidance and commitment and hard work, talent, humility, and relationship building. Have they reached their goals?

Do they see themselves more positively? Has their self-efficacy improved? Have they learned more? Have they opened their perspective and how they see the world, and how they see themselves? In terms of places, has the environment gotten better, has the culture become more innovative or accepting, have processes improved, have behaviors improved? Is it easier to get things done? And ultimately, are the organizations and people meeting the goals that have been set out for them?

Kathleen, former stay-at-home mother, founder of a publishing company, now director of development for a library: To me, it is having someone who has a clear vision of what needs to happen. It is like they have it all sort of formulated. What the future needs to hold, where you need to go, where you need to get, and then they can articulate a clear path to get there.

Marilu, former librarian, former Chief Information Officer, now Vice Provost: Leadership success is absolutely, totally, related to accomplishing a vision. It is all about where you are trying to go. I think the first part is vision, and the second part is helping everybody else who is in the milieu become better at what they want to be in that process. So, in all the leadership projects and jobs I have had, I have always had that dual objective: I am trying to accomplish a vision and I am trying to help people become who they truly want to be.

Helen, retired Colonel (USAF), professor, and academic administrator: One, it is developing your people, and having them reach their goals and aspirations. Two, it is meeting the overall organizational goals or outcomes. And three, it is building relationships, or having a team, creating a good environment so they're enjoying what they're doing and moving the team forward.

Shannon, software development professional, stay-at-home mother, and angel investor: I don't think it's important to be liked as a leader; I think it's important to be respected as a leader, so I would say success is when you are respected by your peers as well as the people who work for you, as well as your boss. People know that you operate in a certain way and that's where the respect comes from. Obviously success is measured in lots of different ways, but I think on balance, if you're known and respected, then you have the ability to be successful because you have the ability to lead people down the path you need to be on to have the organization be successful.

Anne, Chief Operating Officer for a large health-care NGO: I put a tremendous emphasis on positive outcomes and results. I think there are many faces of leadership. I think ideally, someone who can create a response in others that creates trust and confidence and passion and a shared vision. But I still tend to come back to the number one for me: Positive results. I think I have found that I could probably follow an obnoxious arrogant leader if they achieved the results that were important to me, that I had bought into.

Mary H., 30-year member of the US federal government Senior Executive Service, then an NGO director, now a university professor: A group of people accomplishing goals together that they understand and believe in … and they think is the right thing do. Their skills and knowledge are being used well and they trust and feel safe to raise issues and say things they need to. And this is happening because the person leading is making sure that the environment is set up so that they are able to do all of that together and feel appreciated for doing it and have fun.

Terese, city and county engineer: Leadership success is about accomplishing goals and projects. In my situation [as a city and county engineer] it is usually completing projects on time and on budget that are good projects. As the leader, you are trying to bring everybody together to do that. Whether it is the designer or surveyor, or the contractor. You are all working towards that goal of achieving a project.

Janet F., former managing partner of an international travel agency, now an executive coach for small businesses: 'Leading' can be a verb, adverb, adjective, or noun. Leadership success means people living an authentic life. Being true. Leading with values. So leadership in an organization would be one where they model that and demonstrate that and give other people courage to do that. I know that sounds like 'whoo-whoo', but I am idealistic in that belief. And I really do stand by that. The culture is defined either formally or informally by the person at the top. The top person is leading the organization whether they know it or not. Some advocate from the throne and don't really offer solutions with intention and authenticity and the right moves, but they are leading by their example. But, whether they know it or not, there is no trivial act or comment by a leader. And that is just something that we pound into people … [T]hey don't realize sometimes that their fingerprints are all over it. So, I believe true leadership success is being intentional about that. And to mean it.

Amy, former executive track for Heinz Corporation and AT&T, now stay-at-home mother and CEO of her own marketing firm for Catholic schools: A leader is prepared. A leader is knowledgeable. A leader is assertive. A leader manages, and from an action standpoint, manages up and down. And a leader most importantly, when needed, is humble. Because if we can't be humble when we screw up—which we all do—if you can't admit to your mistakes, then you are not a good leader. The term I use with my kids— and this should be on my tombstone—"success is defined as where preparedness meets opportunity." You will never be successful unless your ducks are in a row. Because once that opportunity comes, you need to be prepared to jump on it.

Kirk, former urban planner, founding director of a new federal agency, now a professor of practice at a university: I think you have to look at their passions over time and how they connect with their staff, other leaders, and externally. Some leaders are given opportunities to rise to some occasion and really take the forum. And as a result of their leadership, significant decisions or policies come about that can be attributed to that person ... or the leadership team, which can be considered leadership success. But it couldn't happen without the effort of that person leading.

6

WOMEN'S PERCEPTIONS

Men almost always believe they are meant to be leaders, many women have to be convinced of this.

(Survey respondent aged 21–30, experience working mostly for male leaders)

You may be presented with many leadership 'opportunities' and you should weigh these carefully . . . not all opportunities are beneficial for your short-term and long-term goals. In fact, taking on too many opportunities, or the wrong kind of opportunities, can sometimes be more harmful than helpful. Don't be afraid to be yourself. Think about who you want to be in the future and plan a path to get there. That journey starts with understanding who you are today and what you need to do to reach your potential. Take care of yourself first: no one else can do that for you. You will be your best self, and able to do the most good, when you prioritize self-care.

(Survey respondent aged 31–40, experience working equally with male and female leaders)

Introduction to the Survey

Since "what comes to constitute knowledge, as well as those who are deemed to be knowledgeable subjects, are inextricably wrapped up with power" (Ainsworth & Hardy, 2012, p. 1695) research and conversation about women and leadership should be informed by a cross section of women's voices. We set out to gather stories to contribute towards this end. We knew that we would want to interview women in depth, but equally wanted to hear from a broader cross section than one-on-one interviewing would allow. We opted for a two-part approach.

First, invite as many women as possible to share stories (to the extent possible in an electronic survey). Second, use this rich resource as a starting point for in-depth interviews with a smaller sample of women.

This and the next chapter summarize the stories women shared through a survey that included demographic questions, scaled response items, and open-ended questions. We found some anticipated patterns and others that were unexpected.[1] In this chapter we describe broad characteristics of the cross section from whom we heard. We also present results on perceptions of leadership by exploring three themes: satisfaction with professional role; perceptions of what constitutes leadership; and experience of others as leaders. In the next chapter we turn to respondents' experience _as_ leaders.

Who We Heard From

Women were asked to share the survey with others in their own networks. Only one listserve was used. All other contacts were direct invitation, with a request that the survey be shared. A total of 274 women shared their stories, with 203 reporting residing in the United States, and 15 reporting living in other countries: New Zealand, Australia, and selected European countries.[2] Responses from within the United States clustered relatively heavily east of the Mississippi, but did have some geographic distribution. Respondents reported locations in 21 states (142 unique zip codes) spread from the west coast (Washington, Oregon, California) across the country (Arizona, Colorado, South Dakota, Texas, Kansas, Missouri, Illinois, Michigan, Indiana, Ohio, Tennessee, West Virginia, Alabama, Georgia, New York, Pennsylvania, Delaware, Virginia). Around 85% indicated their age range. Figure 6.1 indicates the share of respondents across five age ranges—from 21 to over 60. The racial diversity of the samples was more limited, but it is hard to indicate exactly to what extent. Only 68% of respondents

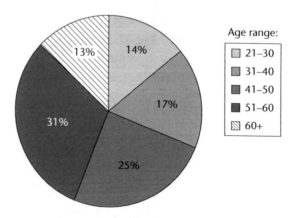

FIGURE 6.1 Distribution of Survey Participants by Age Range

indicated ethnic origin—of this pool, 87% reported European origin with the remaining 13% distributed between Hispanic (4.8), African American (3.8), Middle-Eastern (0.5), and Asian (3.8). Comparable figures for the US population[3] are 72% White, 18% Hispanic, 13% Black/African American, and 6% Asian (with Middle-Eastern not reported).

A snapshot of those who shared their stories indicates variety both in types of activity in which they're engaged and personal situations.

- Of the 213 women who reported work status, 91% work outside the home (full or part-time).
- Just over half (51%) of the women work in the public sector (federal and state/local), just under a third in the private sector (29%), and the balance in the non-profit sector.
- Over half (52%) are employed in professional services roles (e.g., consulting, financial, law) and just under a third (29%) in education. The balance work in direct services (e.g., medical) and 'other' sectors.

Responses to questions about domestic status (80% provided answers) paint a picture of women in family systems. There wasn't a strong relationship[4] between the leadership level at which women report operating and whether they reported being parents. Only 6% of those under 30 reported having children. However, for any given leadership level, roughly half of the women are parents and roughly half aren't, which lines up with census data indicating that roughly 48% of US women aged 15–44 do not have children. Taken in aggregate, reports of these women appear to indicate that parental status does not have to constrain leadership attainment. Four-fifths are either in a committed relationship or widowed (79%). While slightly higher than the national rate of 'family households' which was 66% in 2012 (Vespa, Lewis, & Kreider, 2013), there is reason to believe that the sample is roughly in line with the overall US population on this dimension. We did not ask respondents whether they were *living* with partners, only if they had them. Essentially the same percent (80%) have at least one living parent; this is in line with current life expectancies, given that 44% of our sample is 51 or older. This *may* be an indication of the relative socio-economic status of respondents, as there tends to be a positive correlation between socio-economic status and longevity.[5] Finally, almost half (45%) of our respondents reported having children. The figure is slightly higher (i.e., 55%) if adjusted to include only those respondents who actually answered the question. In sum, we are not pretending that we accessed the average or quintessential 'everywoman'; she doesn't exist.[6] It is fair to say, though, that a range of voices was captured. Perspectives shared in the survey provide a window into how a cross section of primarily US-based women perceive and have experienced leadership; how they have faced trade-offs. (See Table 6.1.)

TABLE 6.1 Survey Respondents' Family Demographics

Characteristic	Percentage of respondents
In a committed relationship or widowed:	79%
With at least one living parent:	80%
Have children:	45%

Perceptions of Leadership

We had certain expectations about patterns we would find. Key among these, we anticipated identifiable generational differences. The world of work has changed, is changing. Experience *and* expectations of those born before about 1980 differ substantially from those born later. We heard some of what we anticipated: there is generational variation. At the same time, some surprising messages came through.

In aggregate, responses to the question "What three qualities do you believe are essential in a good leader?" covered virtually all dimensions that researchers and practitioners might propose. The word cloud in Figure 6.2 displays graphically the top 50 words or phrases used by respondents; the more mentions, the larger the font. While 'vision' appears to come out as most important in this simple exercise of 'count the occurrences' it actually recedes slightly in importance on second glance. The complementarity across other characteristics that show up strongly tends to overshadow vision. Behaviors of listening, communication, and the personal quality of integrity appear to be more commonly valued as necessary to good leadership since related characteristics or capacities of empathy, honesty, and compassion also show up strongly. Respondents appreciated the importance of vision as essential to leadership, and maybe even more importantly, that effective leaders must care about and engage those around them in order to *implement* vision. This result is validated when using all respondents' input, but restricting results to the ten most common responses. This generates a cloud clearly dominated by characteristics of: vision, listening, communication, and integrity.

Disaggregating responses by reported age reveals clear and intriguing differences across age groups. (See Figure 6.3.) Confidence appears more essential from the perspective of those under 40 than it does to those 41 and older. This could reflect normal differences by age. For example, a positive correlation between experience and confidence might be expected. Alternatively, this difference may reflect a generational shift in women's perceptions towards seeing themselves as leaders. This simple result is consistent with research on generational differences and a greater sense of self-efficacy and expectations among millennials generally. Whether results seen in our sample are attributable to social messages or to greater opportunities at younger ages (or both), it's encouraging. Maybe a generational shift will mean that women as a group are becoming less inclined to wait to be asked to see themselves as leaders.

FIGURE 6.2 All Survey Respondents: Top Three Qualities of a Good Leader (Top 50 Words)

Top Ten Responses For Those Under 40 . . .   *Top Ten Responses For Those 41 and Over . . .*

FIGURE 6.3 Top Three Qualities of a Good Leader: Survey Responses Disaggregated by Age Group

Professional Satisfaction

We asked women about satisfaction with professional roles for two reasons. Conceptually it's a relevant question. How individuals feel about their circumstances influences how they interpret and assess past experience and future options. More importantly, responses serve as a check that the sample we pulled from did not implicitly have an axe to grind on the topic of leadership. Over two-thirds of respondents (68%) indicated satisfaction. Predictably, there was a linear relation between age and level of satisfaction. Two drivers are likely at play. First, the older an individual, the further they've traveled in professional journeys; by definition, they've had more time to reach goals and personal acceptance. Second, there is some evidence that older individuals tend to hold more positive outlooks[7]; a given individual is likely to respond to identical situations in a more positive manner at age 60 than they would have at age 30 or 40.

Counterintuitively, the results appear unrelated to parental status. Of the women who responded to a question about parental status (80%) over half (55%) reported having children. Based on popular and scholarly writing about 'over-stressed' parents and the challenges of 'work-life balance' for those with family obligations, one might expect women with children to feel less satisfied with their professional roles than women without parental obligations. That was not borne out by the reports of the women from whom we heard.[8]

While other research has indicated millennials have high expectations, it's slightly troubling that 27% of those aged 21–30 indicated specific dissatisfaction with their current professional roles. This is substantially higher than the 15% rate for the 31–40 age group. A certain amount of dissatisfaction can be productive, but too much undermines motivation and achievement. It's possible that the higher rate among the younger age group is consistent with similarly situated males, an artifact of a recovering economy, or a flag for individuals and organizations—or all three. Generally, though, those who took the survey felt positively towards their professional experience and standing. This question served as an important check on the mindset from which survey respondents provided feedback on their experience of leaders.

Experience of Leaders

Individuals' experience of others as leaders inevitably influences both their own ambitions and development as leaders. For example, if the male prototype of leadership prevails in a given setting, that organization may not tend to either see or develop women as leaders. A corollary is that if women have negative experiences with leaders, or cannot 'see' themselves in leaders with whom they interact, it likely influences their interest in taking on leadership positions. Such experience might spur women on towards seeking positions in order to 'do it differently' or 'do it better.' Typically, though, if organizational culture primarily promotes and recognizes a male prototype of leadership, women will be, consciously or unconsciously, dissuaded from pursuing participation in that leadership structure. The end result is diversion of women away from pipelines, and consequently, senior positions.

Mix of Leaders Worked For

Women reported experiences of having worked with a fairly even mix of male and female leaders. Close to half (46%) had worked with as many men as women leaders; just over one-third had worked exclusively for male leaders. A minority of respondents (18%) had worked only with female leaders. As illustrated in Figure 6.4, results by age group generally reflect an expected pattern—younger women have had the experience of working for a more balanced mix of male and female leaders.

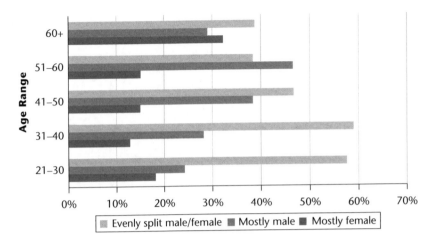

FIGURE 6.4 Gender of Leaders for Whom Survey Respondents Have Worked

Women 61 and older indicated a noticeably higher rate of having worked only for female leaders. This is not necessarily surprising as they also reported a much higher concentration of effort in the non-profit sector than other age groups. More than one-third (36%) of respondents 61+ work in the non-profit sector. The non-profit sector has historically employed a very high proportion of women. What does seem a little surprising is that these women worked for female leaders in a sector that until only recently was, as a whole, notorious for a thick glass ceiling. Selection bias likely plays a role here. For example, this result may reflect the fact that one population we tapped into in distributing the survey was women working in, or leading, non-profit organizations focused on delivering social services for women and families.

Perceived Effectiveness of Leaders

Women were asked to indicate their level of agreement with the statement "Leaders I have worked with have been high-quality and effective." Overall, responses were moderately positive. Just over half (56%) indicated either agreement or strong agreement with the statement. The balance of responses were fairly evenly split between a non-committal 'neutral' (23%) and specific disagreement (21%) indicating negative perceptions of leaders experienced. There was a marked difference in responses between generations. Those under 30 gave higher marks (70% positive) to their experience of leaders than those 61 and older (53% positive). Possible explanations and drivers are myriad. Many of these came out in the narratives (reported in the interludes and boxes below).

Consistent with prevailing concerns about maintaining engagement in today's workplace, those in the 41–50 age group appeared to be least positive about their perceptions of leaders with whom they've worked. Less than half (48%) indicated any level of agreement with the statement. Whether this is reflective of economic environment, respondents' life-cycle status, or other factors, the result is troubling. This is the pool from which the next wave of leaders will be drawn. How might the fact that they appear to not have generally positive perceptions of leaders influence their engagement and own development as leaders?

Leading in Place

Leadership in organizations (government, commercial, non-profit, community/volunteer) can be uneven. Myriad drivers contribute to poor (or inadequate) leadership, ranging from capacities and behaviors of those holding positions, through insufficient resources, through churn and/or inattentiveness at the top, or a host of other explanations. Regardless of the reason, if an individual holding a position of leadership fails to fulfill the requirements of that role, but is left in position, several outcomes are possible. The worst end of the spectrum may be if the problem is the capacity or poor behaviors of the position incumbent. If the individual is not removed the team/unit becomes seriously dysfunctional (e.g., manifesting significant disengagement, conflict, and/or attrition) and significantly underperforms. The least-worst end of the spectrum (for the organization) may be when insufficient resources or vacuums (intentional or otherwise) in an organization create such demands that an assigned incumbent cannot possibly fulfill all the requirements of a leadership role.

In either condition,[9] employees committed to the mission of the organization (or with other positive motivation) may well step up to lead in place. Whether as a proactive move to support a respected leader/cause, or whether as instinctive behavior to ensure achievement of shared objectives, most in today's world face opportunities to lead in place; women have been doing it without recognition for some time.

This can be a formative leader development experience. Under the best of circumstances it can also present an opportunity to be recognized by others, whether peers or leaders elsewhere in the organization, as a leader. Almost three-fourths of respondents (73%) reported experience of filling leadership gaps. Distinct patterns showed up within the stories shared. Even if there is some degree of self-report bias in this number, it is still high.

More interesting were responses to a related question about recognition of women's efforts to support and compensate for leadership gaps.[10] In aggregate, only 20% felt that they received credit for such efforts. This low rate of perceived recognition caught our attention. We looked for an underlying, nuanced story. Might there be systematic variation across the women themselves (i.e., age, level of effort) or the environments in which they've worked (e.g., gender of leaders, sector) that explain these troubling results? Whether the women are in fact not getting credit for exercising leadership in the breach, or even if they simply *perceive* that their efforts are unrecognized, it could influence both willingness to stay with an organization and willingness to step into leadership positions in the future.

Looking deeper, patterns emerged. Differences became evident along four dimensions: age of respondents, gender mix of leaders for whom they've worked, nature of effort, and sector.

Age: Women 31–50 were most likely to agree (28% for each age cohort) that they get credit when compensating for leadership gaps. The rate fell significantly for the 21–30 and 51–60 age cohorts (15% and 16%, respectively). Dramatically, only 3% of those 61 and over perceived that they were credited when leading in place. There are many possible explanations for the variation. It is impossible to say whether this pattern is a function of natural variation in perceptions and attitudes over the life cycle, an indication that older women were systematically overlooked as leaders in earlier years, or evidence of ageism.

Gender of leaders: Women who have worked for both men and women are most likely to report that they get credit when leading in place, with the rate not that different for those that have worked mostly with men. Those who've worked mostly with female leaders report that they are least likely to get credit when compensating for leadership gaps. We anticipated that this might be age-related, but the data did not support this interpretation: the same pattern held within age cohorts. (See Figure 6.5.)

Two alternate explanations pop to mind. Maybe the so-called queen-bee syndrome[11], women being harder on other women than they are on men, plays out for this subset. Or context may influence the degree of recognition they receive for emergent leadership. It comes across pretty clearly, in personal stories that our respondents shared, that something more structural likely unfolds. Fairly stark patterns emerge by both effort and sector of work.

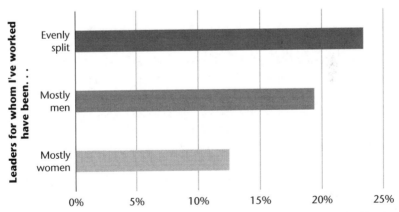

FIGURE 6.5 Survey Respondents' Experience Compensating for Leadership Gaps

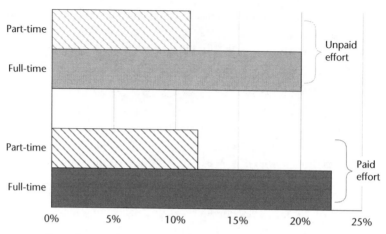

Share of respondents reporting they receive credit for filling leadership gaps

FIGURE 6.6 Recognition for Compensatory Behaviors Reported by Survey Respondents, by Type of Effort

Nature of effort: We expected differences between paid and unpaid effort. Volunteer effort is often 'invisible', more a labor of love than for personal recognition. The challenges of getting volunteers to engage with a consistent level of effort are well known. One expects at some level to fill in gaps that others leave.

As illustrated in Figure 6.6, the real fault line, though, for these women runs between full-time and part-time effort. Those who are engaged full-time are almost twice as likely as those engaged part-time to perceive that they receive due credit when filling leadership gaps. This has dramatic implications for women and the organizations that employ them.

A share of women choose to work part-time at some point in their careers. It raises questions about whether women's emergent leadership is being recognized for value added. Do women working part-time gain positive reinforcement for leadership behaviors that helps them see themselves as leaders, or are these contributions (and implicitly the women) undervalued? Implications for individuals and organizations are significant and long-lasting.

Systematic bias against recognizing women's emergent leadership in non-paid work poses a problem for society. One can make an argument that that is a price to be paid for personal choice: women choose to pay that price in pursuit of other priorities. At the same time, there is every reason to flip this, and explore what it means if this narrow thinking contributes to undervaluing women's leadership contributions and capacities. If biases against recognizing women's emergent leadership in *paid* effort (even if that effort is part-time) are pervasive, the effects would include the undermining of both economic value and equity issues. And it appears that certain sectors may have further to go on this front than others.

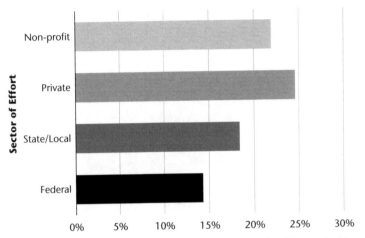

FIGURE 6.7   Recognition for Compensatory Behaviors Reported by Survey Respondents, by Sector of Effort

Sector of effort: Over three-fourths of the women (76%) who took the survey reported their primary sector of effort as: federal, state/local, private, or non-profit. Using this information to look more closely at recognition of emergent leadership draws a clear picture (see Figure 6.7). Those working in the private sector are most likely to perceive that they receive credit for emergent leadership (i.e., 25%). The rate is slightly lower for those working in the non-profit sector (22%). It drops noticeably for the public sector, with women working in the federal sector reporting the least positive experience.

A high percentage of women experience themselves as leading in place, but a low percentage reported perceiving that these efforts were recognized. If women develop and contribute as leaders but either do not receive or do not perceive that they receive positive feedback or remuneration for this effort, both individuals and organizations lose. There is a risk of disengagement at the individual level. Organizations can lose by failing to leverage the benefits of leader development unfolding in practice, and may artificially constrain the flow of women in the leadership pipeline. In aggregate, the story of the experiences shared by these women indicates that organizations have some distance to go in recognizing women's leadership that unfolds in place, especially in the public sector.

Encounters with and Influence of Stereotypes

We asked two specific questions designed to elicit information about perceptions and experience of stereotypes. We were interested in whether respondents believed there are gender-based differences in leadership style between men and women. We asked specifically and also indirectly in order to probe for perceptions and

observations on the operation of prototypes. Respondents also had the opportunity to share stories of direct experience of stereotypes in action. The intent was
to understand common filters and biases, both those that women encounter and
those they may hold. Respondents had a lot to share on these questions.

Less than half (42%) indicated they have been advised by leaders or peers to
change their style in the workplace at some point. Only one-third of those who
got such advice attributed the motivation for this advice to gender-based stereotypes. Many provided vignettes of these experiences. Some advice came from
females, some from males. Several shared that the feedback to change style,
whether motivated by gender stereotypes or not, increased self-awareness and
contributed to effectiveness—one way or the other—either in the moment or over
time (See Box 6.1).

BOX 6.1 GENDER-BASED ADVICE TO CHANGE STYLE

Selected verbatim responses to open-ended survey question

- *I was coached early on in my career to channel my emotions in other ways so
  that I developed a thicker skin in the workplace. That advice guided me and
  served me well,* recorded respondent 247, aged 51–60, having experienced a fairly even gender mix of leaders and currently working full-time.
- *I was encouraged to change my approach to certain contentious situations
  (either people or issues) to a more direct approach. In the past, I had been
  somewhat passive. I embraced the advice and worked with my 'leader' and
  others she recommended, but my 'style change' led to greater success and
  actually diffused contention,* stated respondent 490, aged 61+, having
  experienced mostly female leaders with current work status not reported.
- *I was by nature laid back and bit overly sensitive. Though I had many male
  bosses, the women made an impact on me by showing me there is nothing
  wrong with being stern and making direct contact, that it builds your self-
  confidence and shows you are not a pushover,* observed respondent 881,
  aged 41–50, having experienced a fairly even gender mix of leaders,
  and currently full-time in the workplace.
- *In the 90s, a corporate boss suggested I be more assertive and dress more
  professionally. I was an issue manager, working with a variety of colleagues, so I pushed back and said if I wasn't who I was, which included
  being an inclusive person who got along with a variety of people (without
  table pounding), I wouldn't be as successful in my coordinating role and
  wouldn't be able to develop consensus on issues as well. He amended my
  evaluation. On the dress front, I did the corporate thing and wore suits
  more consistently. I continue to dress well and professionally (even styl-
  ishly!). Suits are no longer as prevalent in the office place, which gives*

women more options. I strongly advise against dressing at work in a manner that could be considered provocative, and worry that many young women are not differentiating between work and non-work attire, said respondent 152, aged 51–60, having experienced a fairly even gender mix of leaders, and currently working full-time.

- *It was very early in my career and I was encouraged to be a bit more outspoken. It was a message I needed to hear and I am grateful for it,* noted respondent 187, aged 31–40, having experienced a fairly even gender mix of leaders, and currently part-time in the workplace.

- *I conformed as I was told. Looking back I should have remained with my own style, but to succeed in that setting I conformed. After seeing how it changed me, I left that position and couldn't be happier now that I am no longer there,* explained respondent 847, aged 21–30, having experienced a fairly even gender mix of leaders, and currently full-time in the workplace.

- *I'm in the legal field. I am a trial lawyer, and my field of practice is highly emotional, stressful, and fast-paced since it's child welfare. As a result, many people burn out due to the high stress and from the emotional pull. I am passionate about my field, and ensuring that children are protected. I was approached (by a male attorney not in my office) that I should calm down and not take my cases so seriously. I was new in the field, and I was startled that I should be told to 'settle down' considering the cases. I wondered if I was alienating others, and causing judges not to listen to me due to my passion. I did pull back but felt like I was only doing a half job. I reached out to my supervisor who told me to be myself, and if the situation called for a louder voice, do it. If someone is wrong, with all respect to the court, point it out. I went back to court and went back to my way that was how I wanted to be. The quality of your words, not the volume, carries the greatest weight, and I do not regret disregarding a throwaway comment from someone who was burning out. I'm still here, and I'm still going,* stated respondent 812, aged 31–40, having experienced a fairly even gender mix of leaders, and currently full-time in the workplace.

- *I have been told that my communication style is sometimes 'too direct' or 'too honest' and that I need to learn to be softer and more tactful. I accept there is some truth to this, and have made a lot of effort to communicate differently. But I also think that I would be less likely to have been given this feedback if I was a man,* said respondent 195, aged 41–50, having experienced mostly male leaders, and currently part-time in the workplace.

Deeper messages, primarily about interaction styles based on female stereotypes were also encountered. These tended to be less positive messages and experiences (see Box 6.2). While reported by a minority of respondents (11%), an unfortunate picture still emerged of women either diverted and/or discouraged by a destructive focus on stereotypes as opposed to results. They included messages

BOX 6.2 COUNTERPRODUCTIVE GENDER-BASED MESSAGES AND EXPERIENCES

Selected verbatim responses to open-ended survey question

- *As a young Latina woman my colleagues seemed to have a view that I should stay fairly quiet when in meetings and decision-making in my department after graduate school. A senior, white male chair told me that I did not fit what he was expecting and thought that it would be easier for me if I did not try to take on any leadership roles and just went along with the view that he and another white male colleague had for our department. This was rather inconsistent with what he told my peer male colleagues, who he encouraged to speak at meetings and said that he wanted to have an environment where everyone was contributing,* recorded respondent 423, aged 21–30, having experienced a fairly even gender mix of leaders, and currently full-time in the workplace.

- *I expressed my concern over changes in policy that impacted the unit's ability to function operationally. My superior officer suggested that I get more in line with the big picture and to stop 'mother henning'. I continued to disagree with the changes and expressed my opinion, to the superior officer only. I have since been transferred, by request,* stated respondent 298, aged 31–40, having experienced mostly male leaders, and currently full-time in the workplace.

- *When I was first hired into my department as an advanced assistant professor, I was told before the first faculty meeting to be like untenured Male Colleague X and not like untenured Female Colleague Y in meetings. X never opened his mouth in meetings and never tipped his hand as to how he might be leaning and would often abstain from public votes. Y was very vocal, voted readily on all matters . . . and ended up not being renewed at Year 3, even though she had a research and teaching record that were commensurate with X at that point. I responded at first with anger about this (because my opinion as an untenured colleague HAD been valued by my department at my previous institution), but senior colleagues explained that this was the culture and to just bide my time until I was senior, too. They saw this as an issue of seniority and that children are to be seen and not heard. However, many of the issues that Y was raising related to work/life imbalances and were explicitly aimed at unmasking patriarchy as an element of the cultural dynamic in our department. Their advice was to wait until I had tenure and then start to reform the culture,* observed respondent 200, aged 51–60, having experienced mostly male leaders, and currently full-time in the workplace.

- *I have been encouraged by male colleagues to not be such a 'go getter'. This message made me mad. At first I stepped back but now I am moving forward with full force,* explained respondent 370, aged 31–40, having experienced a fairly even gender mix of leaders, and currently full-time in the workplace.

- *[I was told] to be less motherly to staff and later (when I made that change) to try and be more motherly,* noted respondent 176, aged 41–50, having experienced mostly male leaders, and currently full-time in the workplace.
- *After I graduated from my Master's program I returned to my country. The professor who had encouraged me to go to graduate school in the US discussed high ranked job opportunities at my country's national university. I was excited with the prospects and began telling him things that I could do to contribute to the university. He then slowed me down and told me I needed to change my self-confident demeanor because "Women who know more than men are very threatening and not well-received at our university." I then thanked my professor for reminding me why I did not want to repatriate. I never did, and instead went to law school in the US,* said respondent 398, aged 51–60, having experienced a fairly even gender mix of leaders, and currently full-time in the workplace.

that, in a variety of ways, appear to have all been intended to communicate that women should not enact behaviors consistent with the 'male' prototype of leaders, and that male sensitivities should be the constraint of concern. Messages were reflective of different expectations of males and females in the workplace, but most boiled down to the message that female colleagues should be seen and not heard. Respondents reported being encouraged to be quiet and subservient.

Whether because of social change over time or because more time lived simply equates with more experiences accumulated, we anticipated that experiences of gender-stereotyped, non-productive style advice would be more prevalent among those who have been in the workplace the longest. Using the arbitrary cut-off of 50, we tested this hypothesis. We didn't find what we expected. Rates were virtually identical. Overall, women under 50 reported vignettes of essentially negative experiences motivated by what they perceived as gender-based stereotypes at a rate of 34%. This compared with a rate of 33% among those 51 and over. There was no pattern of concentration by sector for either age group.

We found this result surprising so we looked at the rates by each age group. While 35% of women over 61 believed that stereotype biases motivated advice they received about changing style, the share was 47% for women in the 41–50 age range. It fell to 14% for the under-30 age group. (See Figure 6.8 for an illustration of anticipated versus observed relation.) This pattern could be explained in a number of ways. For example, women in the 41–50 age range may have encountered more resistance in attempting to migrate into positions of leadership as they bumped up against the baby-boomer generation. Alternatively, social norms may have changed sufficiently over the years that fewer leaders and peers feel free to dispense gender-biased advice to women 40 and under; or, these women may be less inclined to hear it. Regardless of the driver, at least within the pool of women

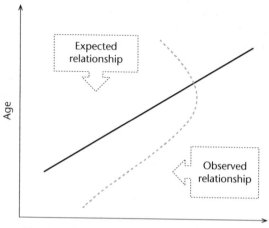

FIGURE 6.8   Indicative Relation between Survey Respondents' Age and Perception That Gender Bias Motivated Advice on Workplace Style

we heard from, dramatic shifts in experience and/or perception appear across generations but the message from those in the 41–50 age group, the pool from which tomorrow's top leaders most likely will be drawn, raises concerns about their reported experience of gender-based biases.

Some don't believe there are gender-based differences in leadership style:

> *Honestly, I'm not sure if the differences fall along gender lines. The best leaders I've worked for are gay men because they had this ability to balance making difficult decisions while considering, and actually addressing, the impact on the workforce (from a cultural and emotional impact level as well as productivity). Female leaders tend to incorporate the emotional intelligence part of leading better than straight men, who, in my experience, just care about their own reputations and the bottom business line.*
>
> (Survey respondent, 31–40, experienced an equal mix of male and female leaders, current mid-level leader.)

> *I have seen both styles and there are more similarities than differences. Leading people means being a person of influence. Men may be more direct in their approach but that is not always the case. Women tend to be more empathetic in their leadership but I would not use a broad brush to paint that picture. Leadership is a wide topic and there are many who have been successful with a multitude of personalities. Steve Jobs was an emotional micro-manager as was my previous employer who happens to be female. There are cultural differences, social differences, race differences, gender . . . and the list goes on and on.*
>
> (Survey respondent, 41–50, experienced an equal mix of male and female leaders, current executive)

However, at an overwhelming rate of more than 3 to 1, independent of whether they report having been advised to change their style, the women we surveyed believe that there are gender-based differences in how men and women lead. Three-fourths (76%) responded affirmatively to the question "Based on your experience do you believe men and women tend to lead differently (e.g. 'have distinct styles')?" This was remarkably consistent across age groups, contrary to our expectation. We thought it likely that younger women would be less inclined to believe in gender-based differences in leadership style. As one respondent working in STEM eloquently pointed out, gender-based differences may be *becoming* less prevalent:

> *Actually—it may be a generational male style—older males were more stand-offish to women and disdainful. I am an engineer and older men are just not used to having women around at all, much less being knowledgeable and capable. I have not felt that from younger men. I have felt that there is no difference. Both younger men and women expect people to work hard and contribute.*
>
> (Survey respondent, 41–50, experienced an equal mix of male and female leaders, current executive)

A retired mid-level manager implied that a more fundamental issue than style was relevant, noting "*I think men have more opportunities to lead.*" Another woman, a current executive (who did not provide her age), shared a specific story illustrating such an experience.

> *Told I was not 'hungry' enough for a management promotion which went to a younger man. I think it was because I wasn't sufficiently overt about wanting the promotion, but rather assumed my actions to speak for themselves (e.g., I'd played a very active part in the management team and played a significantly greater role in managing some difficult 'people' issues than the younger man, as well as successfully leading a complex and very political cross-agency policy project which people didn't think could be done). I don't think I was 'seen' by the male manager responsible for the promotion, in the way he 'saw' himself in the young man.*

Fundamentally different leader prototypes collide in this vignette: the stereotypical male leader prototype of an individual posturing for power, and a more stereotypical female prototype of relational behavior. Approaching two decades after publication of Fletcher's (2001) detailed exploration of this collision[12], women continue to report encountering it.

It rarely works out well for women; believing others will recognize and appropriately reward results achieved via collaboration remains a fool's errand in most organizations. It is a misfit of perceptions that can prove to be a critical juncture in women's leadership journeys. If the onus is implicitly placed on women to fit the male prototype, it is an unsurprising outcome that gender ratios are skewed in top leader positions. Many women will not opt in if access to leadership roles requires conforming to a prevailing male-prototype. The cost to self is often perceived to be too high.

Do males and females tend to lead differently? This is a complex issue with no firm conclusions. Those respondents who reported perceptions of gender-based differences expressed the importance of not using a 'broad brush' to label or categorize. Instead, the theme of recognizing nuance and dealing with individuals, males and females, as opposed to stereotype expectations comes across strongly. (See Box 6.3.)

BOX 6.3 ARE THERE GENDER-BASED DIFFERENCES IN LEADERSHIP STYLES?

Selected verbatim responses to open-ended survey question

- *If all things were equal, I'm not sure that men and women would have different leadership styles. However, female and male leaders often have different expectations placed upon them from people within organizations and publicly. For example, when a woman is expressing authority she may be termed a 'bitch' while a man exercising the same behavior may be considered a leader. As a response, a woman may incorporate more traditionally feminine characteristics in her leadership style,* remarked respondent 423, aged 21–30, having experienced a fairly even gender mix of leaders, and currently full-time in the workplace.

- *I think there are gendered styles of leadership but that often women in leadership positions have learned to operate according to stereotypically 'male' norms. Since I haven't worked under very many women leaders, I don't have a lot of direct evidence,* indicated respondent 167, aged 51–60, having experienced mostly male leaders, and currently full-time in the workplace.

- *I would like to note that all of these are general observations and don't necessarily hold true for all male or female leaders. I've personally encountered many male leaders who did a tremendous job of empowering their employees and helping everyone feel valued, and I've run into some female leaders who didn't,* according to respondent 804, aged 41–50, having experienced a fairly even gender mix of leaders, and currently full-time in the workplace.

- *I think that women more frequently have self-doubt than men. I think that men generally think in terms of a hierarchy or vertical structure . . . Conflict is a necessary part of leadership from time to time. Do men and women handle conflict the same or differently?* asked respondent 303, aged 41–50, having experienced mostly male leaders, and c urrently full-time in the workplace.

- *For most men, the style is 'the great man theory of leadership'. It is all about them. For most women, the style is collaborative . . . It is not about them, but about the group and the organization,* noted respondent 304, aged 51–60, having experienced mostly male leaders, and currently full-time in the workplace.

- *Men talk about seeking consensus but if it doesn't come immediately, will make a decision without. Women tend to take longer to abandon consensus-seeking,* remarked respondent 451, aged 41–50, having experienced a fairly even gender mix of leaders, and currently full-time in the workplace.

- *Women tend to be better at leading a team by collaborating and communicating with people. They are also often more committed to achieving something that is meaningful to them. They inspire others to also want to achieve that goal. Men tend to be better at leading by excelling at what they do and inspiring people to want to be in their position,* stated respondent 134, aged 31–40, having experienced a fairly even gender mix of leaders, and currently full-time in the workplace.

- *Women want to be fully informed and educated first before assuming a leadership role. Women tend to lead through collaboration more than men. Many women preferred to be liked rather than feared,* said respondent 318, aged 31–40, having experienced mostly male leaders, and currently full-time in the workplace.

- *Women generally make more of an effort to recognize their subordinates' efforts. Women generally communicate and share information more frequently. Women are generally more collaborative,* observed respondent 488, aged 41–50, having experienced mostly male leaders, and currently full-time in the workplace.

Even among those who reported believing there are gender-based differences in leadership style, many made thoughtful cautionary observations about checking biases (including one's own) in perceiving and assessing others' behaviors. This corresponds with a related result. In response to the question "What three insights or 'words of advice' do you believe a wise advisor/mentor should share with a young woman starting her leadership journey?" less than 1% of respondents cast their response in terms of gender. (See Appendix for all verbatim responses.)

Taken together, the respondents' reported experience of leaders and perceived gender-based differences in leadership align strikingly with the growing body of findings on the pervasiveness of unconscious biases. We all have them—whether actively instilled or whether simply the effects of broader social norms. Women can experience downsides of this phenomenon, but are not immune from carrying their own biases. Many women provided self-aware responses, implicitly highlighting that we do *not* have to remain captive to unconscious biases. For example, a respondent in the 41–50 year-old age range who has worked for a fairly even mix of men and women indicated: *"No, I don't think they have different styles of leadership, but in my experience their similar styles are interpreted and characterized differently by others."*

Those who attributed observed leadership style differences to gender identified a variety of contrasts. Unequivocal agreement came through on only one dimension. According to these women, men are more inclined to mentally frame leadership as individual competition while women are more likely to apply a collaborative framing; 35 respondents specifically used the word competition to refer to male styles, 69 used some form of the word 'collaborative' to refer to female styles. By far the majority of gender-based leadership style differences suggested referred to differences in how men and women tend to treat others, even when the nominal topic was communication, or decision-making. Some respondents explicitly extended this, referring to deeper, perceived significant gender-based differences in decision-making styles and willingness to seek input and take others' perspectives on board.

Summary

The cross section of women surveyed hold a strong sense of what it takes to be an effective leader. Providing vision and the characteristic of integrity (both personal and interpersonal) stand out. The perceptions reflect variation by age range. The younger women reported confidence as a characteristic of leadership at a higher rate than the older women. The older women reported lower perceptions of gender-motivated bias than did women in their 40s and 50s.

The women's experience of leaders varies not only by age, but substantially by sector and level of employment. Taken as a sample, the respondents offered nuanced reflections on biases operating in leadership dynamics, including their own. A handful shared stories of encountering—but not being stopped by—explicit, destructive bias. Many more had stories of encountering subtle, unconscious biases associated with leader prototypes held by individuals and organizations.

Notably, characteristics and behaviors that fall outside the 'great man' or 'great woman' prototype of leadership, but align with collaborative leadership and leading in place in complex realities, pervade the stories the women shared. Yet the stories also indicate that the paradox of post-heroic leadership continues to prevail for a majority of women; they may provide needed leadership, but the systems in which they operate often fail to recognize these contributions. This is particularly true for women providing part-time effort. The private sector appears to have made more progress than the public sector on this front.

Notes

1   We also asked demographic questions in order to gain a sense of the representativeness of the sample achieved. All non-demographic questions were randomized, and the survey was piloted with a small group before being widely distributed.

2 The remainder did not respond to the question.

3 As estimated for 2015 by the Census Bureau. US Census Bureau. (2015). *Quick facts.* Retrieved from www.census.gov/quickfacts/table/PST045215/00#headnote-js-a

4 Pearson's correlation coefficient of 0.55.

5 For recent analysis correlating socio-economic and life expectancy trend data in the US, see Wang et al. (2013).

6 One caveat is important. While we did not collect data on educational level, there is every reason to believe, due to the starting point and snowball nature of the survey, that virtually all respondents had at least a college degree. This differentiates the respondent pool from the national average of just slightly over 30%. Clearly, the subset of women that are college-educated is not the only group either interested in, exercising, or capable of exercising, leadership in the workplace or society. This is the group, however, most likely to be activity engaging in conversations about how women lead and why they are not more proportionally represented as a category in senior positions.

7 Kennedy, Mather, & Carstensen (2004) gathered that older individuals may have a positivity bias in recalling past experience. An intriguing line of research has followed this early work.

8 Responses to the satisfaction and parental status questions reflect no correlation (0.02).

9 We hypothesize this is most likely to occur if the organization is otherwise functional, if the position incumbent is a good (but simply overwhelmed) leader, and/or if the subject employees have either a professional accomplishment objective or extreme commitment to mission. However, this is a question for future research.

10 Questions in this part of the survey were randomized, so the question did not 'follow', strictly speaking.

11 Evidence on how and when this effect plays out in the workplace is inconclusive, but there is an interesting line of research kicked off decades ago. See Staines, Tavris, & Jayaratne (1974).

12 Fletcher (2001) conducted an in-depth study of female design engineers in the workplace—and how relational behavior actually disadvantaged them in the workplace.

References

Ainsworth, S., & Hardy, C. (2012). Subjects of inquiry: Statistics, stories, and the production of knowledge. *Organization Studies*, 33(12), 1693–1714.

Fletcher, J. K. (2001). *Disappearing acts: Gender, power, and relational practice at work.* Boston, MA: MIT Press.

Kennedy, Q., Mather, M., & Carstensen, L. L. (2004). The role of motivation in the age-related positivity effect in autobiographical memory. *Psychological Science*, 15(3), 208–214.

Staines, G., Tavris, C., & Jayaratne, T. E. (1974). The queen bee syndrome. *Psychology Today*, 7(8), 55–60.

Vespa, J., Lewis, J. M., & Kreider, R. M. (2013, August). America's families and living arrangements: 2012. *United States Census Bureau.* Retrieved from www.census.gov/prod/2013pubs/p20-570.pdf. Last accessed: January 9, 2018.

Wang, H., Schumacher, A. E., Levitz, C. E., Mokdad, A. H., & Murray, C. J. (2013). Left behind: widening disparities for males and females in US county life expectancy, 1985–2010. *Population Health Metrics*, 11(1), 8. Retrieved from http://pophealthmetrics. biomedcentral.com/articles/10.1186/1478-7954-11-8. Last accessed: January 9, 2018.

7

WOMEN'S EXPERIENCES

As a woman who is younger, just beginning her career, I feel there is great pressure to even choose now between seeking marriage, children, and family life or a career. If you choose family you're seen as not willing to pursue a career or make strides for women. However, if you don't choose family you're seen negatively as well, that you don't value family or love and compassion; that you're self-centered and would rather focus on your career.

(Observation of front-line supervisor survey respondent, aged 21–30 who has worked mostly for women.)

My greatest challenge is watching incredibly capable women wait to be asked to lead. I find it so frustrating that this talent base is lost. I have one friend in particular who told me she did not take something on because she was not asked. Most people don't even know what they need let alone know who to ask. It is not that we should insist on being a part, but waiting to be asked instead of stepping up renders an entire group of talent lost. Why might you be timid about stepping into leadership positions? That might be the question ...

(Observation of an executive survey respondent, aged 41–50, who has worked for a fairly even mix of men and women.)

In addition to having a clear understanding of leadership and experience with a diversity of leaders, women who responded to our survey reported both broad leadership experience and habits of investing in themselves as leaders. They have made choices about which leadership roles to step into—or to step away from. Trade-offs between priorities and goals have been factored into employment and leadership decisions.

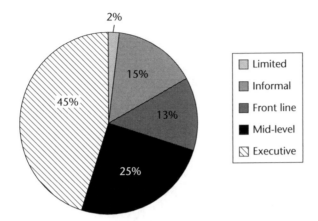

FIGURE 7.1   Survey Respondents' Reported Highest Level of Leadership Experience

Experience as Leaders

Survey questions about respondents' experiences as leaders covered a range of topics, from level of experience, leadership aspirations, leader self-development practices, to identifying the biggest leadership challenges encountered. The women who responded to the survey invest in themselves as leaders, and reported clear views of their leadership successes and challenges. Much of what these women expressed might well have come from any sample of leaders, regardless of gender. At the same time, some perspectives and themes that emerge appear to be strongly associated with gender.

We asked about the level of leadership experience attained—across both employment and non-employment settings, including volunteerism and professional membership. A majority (83%) answered the question. Of these, close to three-fourths (73%) reported experience in leader positions: front line through executive. As a group, the respondents represent a relatively high achieving pool. This result is predictable. Women responding to a survey about leadership are likely to have an interest in the topic. Those who forwarded the survey to those in their network likely tapped into populations with similar experience. (See Figure 7.1.)

Aspirations and Learning

More than two-thirds (68%) of respondents indicated that they were satisfied with the professional role they currently fill. Satisfaction doesn't mean stagnation. These women are looking towards future opportunities: Table 7.1 summarizes the responses to questions we asked about leadership aspirations. A strong majority (72%) hold a clear view of the role to which they aspire. Just under two-thirds

TABLE 7.1 Survey Respondents' Leadership Aspirations

Percent of respondents who 'agreed' or 'strongly agreed'

Age Group	21–30	31–40	41–50	51–60	61 +	ALL
I anticipate my future leadership aspirations will be easily realized	64	31	33	37	32	40
I have a clear sense of the role to which I aspire	76	69	72	75	74	72
I aspire to a visible position of leadership	85	69	63	53	36	61

(61%) indicate that they aspire to a visible position of leadership. No variation in the degree of clarity about desired role shows up across age groups.

However, a distinct inverse relation between age and expressed interest in a visible position of leadership shows up. Of the 21–30 age group, 85% aspire to visible positions of leadership. Only 63% of those 41–50 have such aspirations; the rate drops to 36% for those over 60. It's impossible to know whether this pattern reflects life-cycle effects (e.g., older individuals may tend to have arrived exactly where they wish to be), or whether it reflects generational and societal shifts that result in younger women being more motivated to achieve 'top spots'. A difference of more than 20 percentage points between the 21–30 and 41–50 age groups causes a pause. These are women who *are* leading, who are interested in leadership; what is it that potentially deters them from top *positions* of leadership?

While 40% anticipated that professional aspirations will be relatively easily accomplished in the future, complementary responses not detailed above also tell a story: 32% expressed ambiguity (i.e., responded 'neutral') about accomplishing professional aspirations. Rates of negative response were highest among those 31–50. This could be reflective of gender-neutral challenges faced by all in this age range. Women may have been expressing skepticism based on anticipation of barriers (either generic or gender-specific), assessment of their respective abilities, or disagreeing with the modifier 'easy'. However, since belief in the likelihood of one's success (i.e., self-efficacy) is strongly related to actual accomplishment, it's concerning that those in what are considered to be prime work years (i.e., 31–50) do not feel confident about their likelihood of realizing their leadership aspirations. Despite this reported ambivalence, women who answered the survey are investing in themselves as leaders. This would appear to indicate that perceived external barriers influence expectations of achievement.

Respondents reported engaging in a range of leader development practices widely recommended in the leader development literature. They engage in social learning and learn from challenges. On the social learning front, mentoring and transfer of experience between domains (e.g., volunteer work) come through clearly.

Mentoring Relations Are Important

This group is paying it back; an overwhelming majority (87%) reported that they make an active effort to mentor others. A majority (70%) also agreed that mentors have been instrumental in their success. Younger women benefitted from mentors at a slightly higher rate than older women (85% for those 21–30, but only 67% for those over 60). See Box 7.1.

Engaging with Others Promotes Learning

Complementary to mentoring relationships, these women engaged in outside paid work. Discussing leadership challenges with peers and picking up insights from others' stories (66% and 68%, respectively) were techniques used for gaining insight and improving their own leadership skills. Transfer between domains came across as an important mode of learning; 80% reported applying leadership skills gained in one domain (e.g., work to volunteer context).

Getting tips from social media (e.g., blogs, LinkedIn) appears the least used mode for gaining insight about leadership. Notably, little fluctuation by age group

---

BOX 7.1 WORDS OF ADVICE FROM MENTORS TO YOUNG WOMEN

Survey respondents provided pithy advice in responding to the question "What three insights or 'words of advice' do you believe a wise advisor/ mentor should share with a young woman starting her leadership journey?"

- *Watch the leaders around you. Watch each level of management and leadership to get a sense of the organizational style and culture. Begin to understand what you are comfortable with and what you are not and why. Communicate with others and learn from them. Become the person that others talk to and trust. Give the organization a break; try to understand what the organization does, why they do it, how you can contribute to its success.*
- *1) Learn to compromise without becoming compromised. 2) Learning is an ongoing process and can come from unlikely sources. Be open to new people and ideas. 3) Give yourself and others a break. Mistakes are to be learned from, not dwelled upon.*

appears (range was from 2–6%). Younger generations may, as a cohort, be more inclined to use social media than older generations, but the story we get from women who responded to our survey is that the deluge of pieces out there on social media does not constitute a significant resource when women wish to develop leadership ability and skills. Direct engagement trumps media consumption as a preferred mechanism.

Successes and Challenges

Women clearly do experience themselves as leaders. Narratives about the two most positive experiences and two greatest challenges encountered as leaders generated an interesting picture. In terms of what respondents found to be their most positive experiences, there is remarkable consistency in the core message. Greater variability comes through when the question is about the greatest challenges faced—but interestingly, it comes through in terms of lessons distilled from the experience of having navigated those challenges.

These women told similar stories in terms of the rewards of leadership (see Box 7.2). They all have to do with observable impact. Most positive experiences included: being able to develop others, leading teams to accomplish ambitious goals, and making others' lives better. In a few cases, respondents also highlighted the satisfaction of being recognized individually, either as an expert or for some other characteristic. Broadly, however, the language used is strikingly consistent and in line with conceptions of effective leadership as influencing and empowering others. Women talked about 1) promoting others' success and 2) achieving goals (often beyond expectations). Notably, these themes can be cast either as behaviors of good leadership or as behaviors consistent with the gendered stereotype of women being collectively oriented. We opt for the former.

Greater variation arises in the stories of leadership challenges faced. This result is to be expected given the interpersonal nature of leadership and the influence of context on human interactions. A few shared vignettes of operational challenges (e.g., closing a company, motivating disengaged employees). Others focused on personal growth as leaders. While details vary, four themes run through the responses: developing a leadership persona, maintaining balance, getting recognition while mitigating for ineffective senior leadership or 'managing up', and grappling with effects of bias.

Developing a Leader Persona That Fits

Respondents talked about the challenges of intentionally considering how they come across as leaders (see Box 7.3). This is a reality for any effective leader; how you present influences what others perceive and consequently how they engage. At least for these women, overcoming gender-related expectations (their own and others') arose frequently as a challenge faced in creating a leader persona.

BOX 7.2 POSITIVE EXPERIENCES AND CHALLENGES AS LEADERS

Selected verbatim responses to open-ended survey questions

Positive experiences exhibit similarity . . . **Challenges reflect more variation . . .**

An executive, aged 31–40, employed in the non-profit sector, observed:

Beginning to see my decisions helping an organization become more successful. Seeing the success of my team members when I've empowered them to make decisions and use their skills. *Maintaining confidence in my decision-making ability and resolving to stick with my decisions while a few individuals tried to sabotage my success. Implementing change in an organization that had become somewhat stagnant.*

Another executive, aged 31–40, employed in the public sector shared:

Having my projects picked up as best practices and shared with peers across the country. Receiving praise in front of others for stepping up when other leaders did not. *Work-family balance. Figuring out what motivates people, but once that happens it makes a world of difference to productivity and a happier work environment!*

Experience of a slightly older mid-level leader, aged 41–50, who did not report sector of work:

Significantly shifting two organizations' strategies and operating models. Hearing from former staff who tell me that they are still doing/thinking about things that they learnt from me a long time ago (often little things that I didn't realize would have such an impact). *Working for a micro-managing senior executive who expected me to micro-manage the managers reporting to me. Conveying a calm, positive demeanor and staying constructive even when I'm feeling frustrated, stressed or unhappy.*

An executive of the same age (41–50), who did not report sector of work:

1) The opportunity to be part of the development and growth of others. 2) Allowing myself to grow and develop as I do the work. *1) Getting my head around the work of leadership as mainly adaptive—it's very easy to be distracted by interesting stuff that's not key to the work. 2) Allowing myself to grow and develop as I do the work (as opposed to being perfect first!)*

BOX 7.3 HURDLES WOMEN SURMOUNT TO BE SEEN AS A LEADER

Selected verbatim responses to open-ended survey question

- *Controlling my tendency to over-apologize, even when something is not entirely my fault. I do it to smooth over rough edges immediately, but I am wary of how it can betray a lack of confidence and put me in a weak position.* (Individual contributor, aged 21–30.)
- *Having others feel threatened by me (a black woman with a law degree). I'm sensitive, so feeling hurt by harsh people with poor emotional intelligence.* (Mid-level leader, aged 41–50.)
- *Not being free to be my authentic self. Internal sub-group behavioral policing by gender (other women) and race (other African Americans).* (An executive working part-time, aged 41–50, who has worked mostly for women.)
- *Making my voice heard over male counterparts. A few (thankfully) males who tend to dismiss me as whining when I push back on their ideas.* (An individual contributor, aged 41–50.)
- *Finding my voice among co-workers (clients/customers not a problem). And, being a balanced leader that's assertive.* (Front-line leader, aged 21–30.)
- *Maintaining a leadership presence—I am a very informal, open person and am sometimes too jocular and collegial when I should be radiating calm and wisdom.* (An executive, aged 41–50, who has worked mostly for women.)
- *Working in what are often male-dominant topic areas like energy and biofuels makes it more difficult to take a stance that is different to the mainstream. Not sure why. I think it's just that you feel that there is less support.* (Front-line leader working part-time, aged 41–50.)
- *Wondering how I got here—not thinking that I was up to the job.* (Mid-level leader, aged 41–50.)
- *Asserting authority without being regarded as a bitch. Making peace with difficult decisions when I feel there is no perfect course.* (Individual contributor, aged 41–50, who has worked mostly for men.)
- *Self-confidence. Reluctance to lead from the front and be visible—strong preference to lead from 'behind'.* (Executive, aged 51–60, who has worked mostly for women.)
- *Toughening up. Not over-empathizing with people.* (Executive, aged 51–60, who has worked mostly for men.)

Preserving confidence and growing a 'thick skin' or 'game face' clearly constitute common challenges. Some women reported experiencing challenges maintaining confidence while in leadership positions—but also when considering whether to accept and/or pursue leadership positions. The stories for this subset appear to line up with the work of Shipman & Kay (2014), who focused attention on the topic of women and confidence, providing insights from some high-profile women's stories. The extent to which references to confidence came up offers a certain reality check. While younger women understand confidence as an essential ingredient of leadership, there may be a distance to go in ensuring that women naturally see themselves as fits for stepping into leadership positions. Clearly this is a two-part equation, though. It's not just about women seeing themselves as leaders; it's also about organizations updating implicit prototypes so that all productive varieties of emergent leadership that promote results and organizational objectives gain sufficient recognition.

Maintaining Balance

Creating and sustaining a personally acceptable balance between professional and personal spheres poses a gender-neutral challenge (see Box 7.4). Some face the challenges of meeting family (child or eldercare) responsibilities while fulfilling paid or volunteer roles. Others face the challenge of maintaining healthy personal lives

---

BOX 7.4 CHALLENGES BALANCING 'WORK AND LIFE'

Selected verbatim responses to open-ended survey question

- *Maintaining my health and fitness while working full time.* (Executive, non-parent aged 31–40, who has worked mostly for men.)
- *I think this is conflating age with leadership position (they tend to go together, I think) but my challenge is younger colleagues who have a different sensibility than I. For example, as I was 'coming up', the culture of my field was such that junior people did all the extra work. Now that I'm senior, the culture has shifted such that junior people tend to be protected (and do a good job of protecting themselves), which is great. But now it means that senior people do all the work. That may be fair. But the timing for me has been horrible. Had to do the extra work while junior. And have to do it now while senior. Sigh.* (Front-line leader, parent aged 41–50, who has worked mostly for women.)
- *The other challenge was just balancing kids and work . . . those frenetic early years when all of life is like playing tennis at the net.* (Mid-level leader, parent aged 41–50, who has worked mostly for men.)
- *Time—not having enough to be able to attend to all that is needed in a situation. Realizing that some changes made as a leader are not durable— they require constant cultivation and care to thrive, particularly in inhospitable environments.* (Executive, parent aged 41–50, who has worked mostly for men.)
- *The biggest challenges have been time management and balancing volunteer/ paid staff responsibilities.* (Executive, non-parent aged 51–60.)

despite potentially all-consuming paid and/or volunteer roles. Women who either bear a majority of family care responsibilities, or face the expectation that they provide limitless effort because they do not have family care responsibilities, can experience significant pressure. One-fourth of those who provided a response to the open-ended question about challenges (54 respondents, or 20% of the full sample) identified finding time and preserving balance as one of their two biggest challenges as a leader. Finding time and ensuring balance came up with respect to maintaining personal health, fulfilling a family role, and leadership accomplishment.

Managing Up

Sustaining a good relationship with one's boss, or presiding leader in a volunteer organization, despite differences and stresses, typically requires conscious effort. It constitutes a key competency for successful progress in organizations. Respondents pointed to this as one of their greatest leadership challenges. Managing up requires attending to both task-related expectations and interpersonal perceptions. Individuals have to accomplish tasks so that they and their manager or group contribute to mission achievement and demonstrate results in the organization. Cultural norms in many organizational contexts also require that individuals essentially self-promote as a part of managing up. One has to get great 'stories' about oneself out there. One has to have a 'brand' that others recognize and value; this is often as much about careful self-presentation (or promotion) as it is about real contribution.

We heard from many women that this can be an uphill battle, which ties directly back to prototype-associated challenges women face. First, there are questions of what prototypes organizations implicitly promote and apply in assessing and recognizing leadership. Second, women's own prototypes, confidence level, and sense of self come into play. For more team-oriented or introverted individuals, self-promotion can be both difficult and stress-inducing. Several women noted that they found it unnatural to work against their personal collectively oriented mindset in managing up. From an organizational performance perspective, this insight ought to give pause. Effective communication should be expected of leaders. However, it takes distinct types of effort to both project a good 'image' up and collaborate effectively laterally. Studies have yet to determine which distribution of effort and skills between the two behaviors adds greatest value to organizations.

Our results are consistent with contemporaneous work. For example, in a contribution to Huffington Post's June 2013 Third Metric Conference, Padmasree Warrior noted that when hiring and promoting employees, bosses are more likely to look for candidates with stereotypically male attributes. She made the point "We never say we want people who are empathetic, who are creative, who are good listeners. And I think we need to change that." (Huffington, 2013) A survey that same year of LinkedIn members (see Bahadur, 2013) found that women and men tended to describe themselves differently. Men were more likely than women to refer to themselves as confident, ambitious and family-oriented. Women were more likely to describe themselves as good listeners, loyal, collaborative, detail-oriented and happy.

Grappling with Effects of Bias

Overcoming effects of biases—whether individual or organizational, intentional or unconscious—can constitute a necessary part of managing up, simply managing perceptions, and preserving engagement. Reports of dealing with explicit stereotyped and/or negative expectations were the exception among our respondents. But the thread is unmistakable, and sadly not restricted to older women. Roughly 12% reported dealing with some type of bias (gender, age, race, leader prototype) as one of their two most significant challenges as a leader. Several identified challenges associated with being accepted as a leader because of being 'a young female'. Others highlighted challenges associated with "*having personality traits that are seen as positive, natural leadership qualities, but when expressed by a female are seen as negatives.*" In a similar vein of being hampered by male-centric prototypes, one woman called out "*males who tend to dismiss me as whining when I push back on their ideas.*"

While a relatively small share of our respondents identified as being ethnic minorities, the responses reflect complex perceptions of challenges surrounding racial bias. One woman in the 41–50 age range, working as an individual contributor, simply shared "*Racial bias against me*" as her greatest leadership challenge.[1] In contrast, a mid-level leader of the same age range indicated that "*Dealing with individuals who frame every setback as an unfair barrier based on their gender, race, or ethnicity rather than accepting responsibility for their performance shortcomings*" posed a significant leadership challenge for her. Bell & Nkomo's (2001) book *Our separate ways: Black and white women and the struggle for professional identity* elucidates in depth the ways in which women of ethnic minorities face particularly complex challenges in gaining comfort and recognition in workplaces in which they are a very visible minority. While Bell and Nkomo focus exclusively on Americans of African descent, and the specific complexities and experiences certainly vary by ethnic minority (e.g., Latina, Asian), the fact is that women of ethnic minorities can face unique challenges gaining recognition and opportunities as leaders.

Women who shared their stories were almost uniformly clear about one of the greatest dangers of stereotypes: we *all* have them, and are all affected by the consequences of their unconscious application. This is simply human. It can particularly impact those that fall outside any 'expected' stereotype, though. On the front end, it requires extra effort to overcome or deal with effects of others' biases. On the back end, it can have a lasting impact on how an individual approaches all future interactions. So, in the context of women and leadership, if a female experiences bias, whether race or gender-based (or both), it can become part of her narrative. It can form a filter with which she approaches and interprets all future interactions. Guarding against such lasting effects requires energy and attention. If females in, or aspiring to, leadership positions experience strong and/or continuing bias, it not only affects them as individuals but can also compromise an organization's leadership pipeline.

Choices and Trade-Offs

Most people, female or male, succeeding in a demanding job and fulfilling significant responsibilities outside work chuckle (or sigh) when confronted with the phrase 'work-life balance'. Commitments in either work or life can defeat the best planning. In reality, most people make 'in the moment' choices across competing priorities every day. In the modern economy of '24 x 7' accessibility, credibility requires asking what and how individuals make trade-offs between work and other aspects of their lives.

We explicitly asked about only one competing demand: family (i.e., child and/or eldercare responsibilities). This is by no means the only possible demand beyond the workplace. Certainly women face other trade-offs; and men may increasingly be consciously making trade-offs in how they distribute time and effort between work and family. Many women actually commented with displeasure that the survey honed in on family, pointing out that they make trade-offs between effort at work and non-family priorities.

We asked only about family care demands due to the reality of prevailing socio-economic patterns. While social norms continue to evolve, many women continue to bear the greatest burden of family care responsibilities. Whether actually executing or outsourcing tasks, such as cleaning, women tend to devote more time and effort to managing households and care of family members than do men.[2] Pressures on families to balance competing demands will likely continue for some time given the aging of the US population. As a percent of the US population, the share of those 65 years and older has been increasing at the fastest rate; it was estimated at 13.7% in 2012 and is estimated to rise to 16.8% by 2020 (Ortman, Velkoff, & Hogan, 2014). Not all women have children, but all do have parents. To the extent that women provide eldercare services, and they currently provide more than half—i.e., 57% (US Bureau of Labor Statistics, 2015)—women developing and serving as leaders will continue to face challenges in balancing obligations for some time.

A high percentage (86%) of respondents answered questions about trade-offs and choices they've either made or anticipate making in relation to balancing employment, leadership roles/opportunities, and competing obligations. By a significant margin, respondents appeared to indicate that they have clear decision-making criteria, as they expressed a high rate of agreement (70%) with the statement "I am comfortable making trade-offs between work and other responsibilities."

Family needs have been, and will be in the future, factored into trade-offs for the respondents who answered this question; 63% indicated they have in the past "made employment choices" to accommodate family needs (e.g., worked part-time, changed jobs, bypassed opportunities).

Counter to our expectation, generation didn't have any effect here. We anticipated that there might be lower predisposition to accommodating family demands among women under 30—if only because they might not yet have faced the need. However, results were similar between the full sample and the subset of those 31 and under. Those 31–40 reported the lowest rate (i.e., 56%). Nor did this vary significantly by sector of employment. Women make trade-offs to meet personal and family demands as needed, independent of the sector in which they're working. Women's stories vary— there is no one way.

More significantly, however, responses to a follow-up question about factors likely to influence future employment decisions revealed clearly that family care obligations do not constitute the only driver out there. (See Figure 7.2.) Of those responding that they anticipated making accommodation in future, 39% anticipated childcare as a possible driver. 'Personal passion/Other' came in not that far behind (i.e., 29%), trumping eldercare.

We also asked about factors influencing past choices around leadership roles/opportunities specifically. People decline, or move on from, leadership roles all the time. Reasons vary. Success is a function of quality of fit between an individual, the requirements of a role, and the organizational context. It can take more self-awareness and strength to decline a poor-fit opportunity than it does to step into an attractive but poor-fit position. We asked women to tell us whether they'd ever turned down or walked away from a leadership position. This was a discrete question, unrelated to questions around family and trade-offs. Close to two-thirds (63%) indicated that they've made such choices. This is unrelated to whether women reported being parents. In other words, the dated stereotype that women

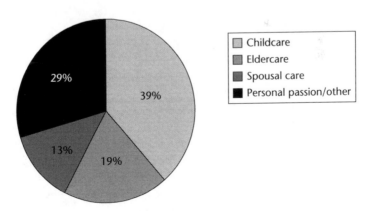

FIGURE 7.2 Survey Respondents' Anticipated Drivers of Future Accommodations in Effort

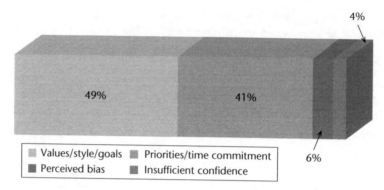

4%

49%

41%

Values/style/goals   Priorities/time commitment

Perceived bias   Insufficient confidence

6%

FIGURE 7.3 Survey Respondents' Reason for Walking Away From or Turning Down a Leadership Position

are poor bets for leadership positions because of family is not borne out by our pool of respondents.

Anticipating that the story might be complex, we also asked about the reasons for such choices. Reported reasons fell into four broad categories: conflict with other priorities, perceived lack of fit with strengths/interests/values, insufficient self-confidence, and gender bias factors. As illustrated in Figure 7.3, lack of fit with values/style/goals accounted for close to one-half of decisions to walk away from or turn down a leadership position. This, together with perceived bias, drove over half (i.e., 55%) of these respondents' choices to move on or refuse a role. Conflict with other priorities and/or time commitments came in second. That such a high percentage reported concerns about perceived fit and bias brings us back to the same question with which we started: is the challenge of increasing representation of women in visible positions of leadership a challenge of women adjusting their behavior, or is it (at least equally) a challenge of addressing and adjusting the way roles are structured and operative leadership prototypes?

Most who elaborated on their choices discussed fit of opportunities with their values, style, and/or goals. Several respondents provided clear articulations of calculations made in choosing whether to move into positions (see Box 7.5). Women exercise leadership; many who shared their stories either hold or aim to step into leadership roles. What we heard, though, is that most establish a clear and high bar in terms of what they're willing to give up in order to take on positions. The story of the majority of these women is that positions of leadership that have been available to them are not sufficiently valued in themselves to entice women to adjust and/or deviate from their values and priorities. Women make savvy calculations about fit and likelihood of success in choosing whether, when, and where to step into leadership positions. These women, as a population, understand and value leadership. By and large, however, when deciding whether to fill a position they appear to calculate carefully what they will take on against their values, goals, and desired quality of life.

BOX 7.5 REASONS FOR WALKING AWAY OR DECLINING LEADERSHIP POSITIONS

Selected verbatim responses to open-ended survey question

- *The type of leadership expected of the position was hierarchical, not sensitive to the staff as individuals, and less interactive than my preferred mode of leading by example, personal connection and egalitarian communication, as well as by demonstrating/sharing knowledge and expertise.* (Front-line leader, non-parent aged over 61, has worked mostly for women.)
- *I really did not believe that I was a good fit for the position. The politics of the institution were divisive and demoralizing.* (Executive, non-parent aged over 61, has worked mostly for men.)
- *I left a very lucrative business career to become a high school teacher. Now I run a cooperative education program for high school seniors that is recognized as the strongest program in the county. I was able to bring my business experience into the classroom and the district let me build the program of my vision. I made the decision to leave the big money and prestige of a marketing career in order to 'make a difference' and now I can say with confidence that I am making a difference every day in my classroom.* (Executive, non-parent aged 51–60.)
- *It was a good job but not the right one for me. Could I have done the job? Yep. Did I want to in the end? Nope. The good news: I was wise enough to see that although I could do the job, I would not be happy, which means others would not have been happy either.* (Executive, non-parent aged 51–60, has worked mostly for men.)
- *The hard work is being a middle-level manager (with direct staff responsibilities), and the sacrifices one makes for taking on those jobs is the future opportunity to move to a more strategic, more well-paid management job of managing the managers. In my most recent management roles, there appeared to be limited opportunity as a female to make it to that next step, with the top tier jobs favoring male managers even though they constituted a smaller proportion of the management pool. Given the limited opportunities for moving up the management hierarchy, I chose to move to an independent consulting role instead, where I can significantly make more money and have a wider variety of work and provide leadership via an analytical role than direct leadership via a management role.* (Mid-level leader, parent aged 51–60.)
- *I had two options, one had the potential to lead me farther down the path I wanted to go down. There were more connections to be had in this position. The position I turned down was, on paper, exactly what I wanted, but there was nowhere to go from that position. I chose a lesser role and title that led me towards more options for the future I wanted. It was a difficult decision but, as I have a more significant leadership role now, I believe it was the right one.* (Mid-level leader, non-parent aged 21–30, has worked mostly for men.)

Limitations and Questions Begging for Exploration

The women who responded to our survey, independent of whether they reported aspiring to senior leadership positions, reported experiencing themselves as adept at exercising non-positional leadership. Many are motivated and willing to step into leadership roles; many in fact are already leading in place. Many are motivated towards positions of higher leadership. Others are not interested in taking up such *positions*—or have stepped away because of a misfit between the organization/position with individual values and priorities.

A disturbingly significant minority of our respondents perceived that organizations are biased against recognizing women's emergent leadership *and* providing opportunities. What we heard from a broad cross section of women reveals a clear disconnect. Many women have stories of organizations failing to recognize or develop them as leaders if they display collaborative behaviors such as promoting team over individual (i.e., promoting results not personal profile), encouraging information-sharing, structuring processes that welcome broad input, and emphasizing constructive communication. Ironically, if well-executed and consistent with organizational objectives, all of these behaviors contribute to engaged workforces and effective organizations.

While contributing a perspective composed from a cross section of women independent of organizations, an approach as yet unplumbed, the survey had limitations that gave rise to a range of questions. For one, are the effects of the snowball sample approach significant, or would a random survey generate similar results? If we had been able to get a higher rate of responses from women choosing not to engage in paid work, would we have found similar perceptions of leadership? In the same vein, what could be gleaned from a larger sample that would highlight difference across industries, regions, and cultures? Clearly there are also questions of how results from a complementary survey including males might line up with the single-gender approach.

Compelling specific questions also arose, around leading in place. We had not anticipated hearing quite so many stories about the limitations of leadership and position, of opting to lead without or beyond position.

Notes

1   This is only one response. Even though we cannot speak to this particular challenge in any detail, given the relatively limited ethnic diversity of our respondents, we do not want to gloss over the unique set of challenges faced by women not of the majority race.

2   Even looking only at unemployed individuals—theoretically those with the most discretionary time available—women spend more time caring for others than men. See, for example, Katz (2015).

References

Bahadur, N. (2013, October 30). Survey reveals 6 important truths about men, women and success. *The Huffington Post*. Retrieved from www.huffingtonpost.com/2013/10/30/truths-men-women-success_n_4164851.html. Last accessed: January 9, 2018.

Bell, E. L. J., & Nkomo, S. M. (2001). *Our separate ways*. Boston, MA: Harvard Business School Press.

Huffington, A. (2013, June 14). Redefining success: Takeaways from our third metric conference. *The Huffington Post*. Retrieved from www.huffingtonpost.com/arianna-huffington/redefining-success-takeaway_b_3444007.html. Last accessed: January 9, 2018.

Katz, J. (2015, January 6). How non-employed Americans spend their weekdays: Men vs. women. *The New York Times*. Retrieved from www.nytimes.com/interactive/2015/01/06/upshot/how-nonemployed-americans-spend-their-weekdays-men-vs-women.html?hp&action=click&pgtype=Homepage&module=second-column-region&region=top-news&WT.nav=top-news&_r=1&abt=0002&abg=1. Last accessed: January 9, 2018.

Ortman, J. M., Velkoff, V. A., & Hogan, H. (2014, May). *An aging nation: The older population in the United States*. Washington, DC: US Census Current Population Reports. Retrieved from www.census.gov/prod/2014pubs/p25-1140.pdf. Last accessed: January 9, 2018.

Shipman, C., & Kay, K. (2014). *The confidence code: The science and art of self-assurance—what women should know*. New York, NY: Harper Collins Publishers.

US Bureau of Labor Statistics. (2015, September 23). Unpaid eldercare in the United States 2013–2014 [American time use survey]. Retrieved from www.bls.gov/news.release/pdf/elcare.pdf. Last accessed: January 9, 2018.

THIRD INTERLUDE

What Development Experiences Would Be Beneficial?

We asked 20 women leaders *"What development experience would you want to provide for women in the future?"* Here are some of their best ideas:

Janet F., former managing partner of an international travel agency, now an executive coach for small businesses: We need to focus on the basics of emotional intelligence, self-awareness, awareness of others, self-management, and influencing others . . . we need to focus on relationships. So, all of the skill-building you could do for emotional intelligence is important. Women are stronger in empathy than men, but maybe less so in assertiveness. So, maybe working on that to make sure there isn't an effectiveness drag. Reality testing, which is one of the ten emotional intelligence skill sets. Problem solving; someone working with any leader on those would help with their effectiveness and their influence, their ripple effect. It could be anything from a course delivered by a university to an online offering to workshops and seminars, where people learn what emotional skills look like. Most effectively though, in the organization the person is in, skill training coupled with coaching and feedback would be ideal. People who have evolved emotional intelligence skills become the better leaders. I come from the world of coaching, feedback-rich, growing, so to me that is just naturally the way people get better. You don't learn how to ride a bike in a seminar, right? So, after introducing the concepts in a seminar format, we meet every single month for up to 90 minutes with every executive individual. This works no matter what business they are in . . . More self-awareness, more awareness of others, all of those skills, and then in the group environment they get feedback from each other and learn how to give each other feedback in a neutral, safe environment. They have to be invested and committed to helping each other. Those are two of our three main values and the other one is challenge: You have to be able to be called on and be able to take it when you are told what your blindside is or questioned when you are not doing what you said you wanted to do, and that's where the growth takes place. Those are our values: trust, caring, commitment, and challenge. And then growth happens. So, our model is set up exactly for what your question is asking. Is there another way to do that? Yeah, we have other ways, but to us, it is creating a safe place to hear what you need to hear and then support while you are dealing with it.

Tish, Director of large social services non-profit organization: I would go back to [helping women develop] self-esteem as the critical piece. Also important is self-reflection. Every woman needs to be true to who she is. Don't compromise who you are to get where you want to be or you will never be happy. Everyone, and not just women, but everyone needs to be exposed to good leaders. If you have not been exposed to good leaders, then you are going to have a really tough time being a good leader. Mentoring—multiple mentors—is very important.

Mary S., former principal of grade school, now classroom teacher: I would like to see communities of women that can support each other as they move up [into leadership positions]. When I was a principal, it was pretty lonely because so many of them were men. Even though they were very nice men and very willing to help, it was lonely being the only woman principal. I lost my confidence. It would have been nice to have a support group to bounce ideas off of.

Heather, managing director, commercial construction company: I think that every woman should have an opportunity to be part of the *Lean in* group. Or something close to that. So that, beyond your company and beyond your friend group, you are able to have very intimate conversations with other women to be able to provide you with guidance, not just one person, but a group of people at different ages and different markets, different points in their careers. They all really should be able to provide a unique and true lesson and to share that insight. Unless you are getting your MBA or you are focused on corporate leadership, a lot of the issues that women face are not necessarily talked about in the workplace and they are not necessarily talked about at school, but that doesn't mean that we are not trying to figure out how to deal with it. And I know that has been instrumental for me so at least you are part of a community and you are not alone.

Janet J., attorney, former high level executive with the National Collegiate Athletic Association, now consultant: What I would provide to women, first and foremost, is the opportunity to really try to understand themselves and understand the specifics of what they want, whatever that is. At the same time, I agree with the standard advice to insert yourself in opportunities to gain leadership, volunteer for that difficult assignment, make sure you get your organization to give you leadership opportunities, go to seminars—those kinds of things. Any way you can become more comfortable as a leader within an organization will be helpful. Oftentimes it is difficult to learn to maneuver in the political landscape of an organization. It is a bunch of politics—so much of it is. All of this is important, but you don't want to lose yourself. I think it is a very tricky thing. I think organizations are difficult. So self-reflection and self-understanding become of paramount importance to leaders.

M'lis, commercial airline pilot, retired USAF pilot, and former NCAA basketball champion: Well, you know, I think the leadership development opportunities need to start at a very young age ... certainly by the high school level. Community service, doing things for others as well as for yourself ... early on. And then we need ... opportunities with seminars and classes so that women can see what's available to them and they can begin to build strategies and obtain tools to compete and succeed for what they want.

Marla, expert in information technology, now a graduate student: You can't do better unless you know better. So, I would want to provide women access to as much knowledge as they can obtain about being a leader, both formally and informally. In particular, I want them to know about the landmines that they may encounter as they are going into career advancement, even if it means stating the obvious. We have heard so many times about how women don't self-promote and we seem to know that, but for whatever reason, it hasn't translated into action. I would like women to have resources that tell them 'here are the challenges and here is how you might address them'. I think they have to know how their gender matters for leadership advancement both consciously and unconsciously, for example.

Kathleen, former stay-at-home mother, founder of a publishing company, now director of development for a library: Seminars on how to deal with difficult people and assertiveness. I guess part of my issue is that I am a people pleaser which is why I am good at development and fundraising because all you do is ... perform back handsprings trying to make people happy. Also important would be lessons about how to self-promote in a professional way. For example, there is a woman who works in my department who works so hard and she is so good at what she does and she is so underpaid. No one notices and she is stuck, unless she wants to leave. It would be great to learn how to work the system, ask for a raise, and self-promote.

Jan, former United States Air Force (USAF) officer, now a police officer: A mentoring program would be good. There should be more men mentoring women and more women mentoring men. I also think some kind of organization where women support each other as they become leaders is needed. Sometimes in a male-dominated field those women-only ... [groups] raise suspicions ... but I think you need to have the opportunity to talk about your common experiences ... to bounce things off of others and to get feedback.

Marilu, former librarian, former Chief Information Officer, now Vice Provost: If I ruled the world, everybody would have a career mentor, counselor, and network that would help them take the next step for wherever they wanted to go. I think it has to be person-driven. I think you have to drive your own career. But I would surround everybody with this tool to help them think about it and then a whole network of mentors and coaches and teachers to help them move forward with educational opportunities. It can't be one size fits all.

Kirk, former urban planner, founding director of a new federal agency, now a professor of practice at a university: Teaching and training for both women and men in collaborative skills is essential. In addition, women leaders need coaching and mentoring, as well as a social network to talk through issues and get support. There are many leadership programs around the country and at the local level that encourage the next generation of leaders to develop there. We have a group in town that supports women candidates: They recruit women for political office and they are very much trying to build a network of women to support political careers. Learning from one's peers in these groups can be quite powerful.

Amy, former executive track for Heinz Corporation and AT&T, now stay-at-home mother and CEO of her own marketing firm for Catholic schools: I would love to mentor women on starting their own businesses. Starting your own business is like studying abroad: It is simultaneously the hardest and best thing you will ever do, because it expands who you are. Starting my own business expanded who I was. You jump off the diving board and then ask "Oh my God, what did I get myself into?" You are on your own. You are totally on your own.

Helen, retired Colonel (USAF), professor, and academic administrator: I would make sure that you're exposing women to leadership positions earlier in their developmental trajectory. The selection for those opportunities needs to be open and transparent, not relying solely on old networking groups. Early experience ideally usually yields learning and some sort of success that should make them more qualified for more senior level positions, and also to lead in place.

Anne, Chief Operations Officer for a large health-care NGO: [When we train people for leadership (either in formal positions or 'in place')] we try internally to make sure that we challenge them on all levels to step up in different ways. It might be asking them to become a member of a committee or to become trainers of a certain skill, for example. We have invested in some leadership fellowships, we have had a couple of people be part of the leadership training where they work in another organization for 18 months and they are traveling and exposed to different organizations nationally and others. We have encouraged women to go for the National Hispanic Women in Leadership Fellowship, for example. In addition, we just created multiple simulation rooms, and we have a woman in our institute going back for training at Mayo Clinic this week about the use of simulation rooms. The practical experience of role playing is challenging and a great learning experience that the participants never forget. I would like to create more simulations, little role plays where staff are observed and trained and given feedback, and helped to develop in some of the areas in which they are challenged.

Mary H., 30-year member of the US federal government Senior Executive Service, then an NGO director, now a university professor: As someone who never received any training, I would certainly want to provide basic leadership training, with an additional piece that would say, you are a woman and you are likely going to be in a male environment: What are some strategies to thrive in this environment? I would like development opportunities where we really talk about this diversity stuff and how you fit in and how you help make the organization more inclusive. As a 'seasoned' federal government leader, I talk to a lot of women who want advice. I usually try to just get them to be themselves and speak up when they really think something is wrong, at a minimum. How to do that assertively without being angry or being accusatory is a teachable skill.

Lisa, vice-president, human resources consulting group: I am trying to pay it forward, so I am trying to give (and this isn't just specific to women, but I do happen to have mostly women working for me) my employees the same opportunities for leadership growth that I received: Letting them lead, letting them take risks, letting them make mistakes. I do want to let them know that they can do more than they think they can. Conflict management is another development skill that we should be offering: I think that when there is conflict the best learning happens, when you go towards a conflict and you don't shy away from it. But because I am an introvert and I'm not someone who likes conflict, I have had to learn that. This is a teachable skill and one where coaching really works.

PART III

What to Make of It

8

FINDINGS AND INSIGHTS ON LEADING IN PLACE

The research presented in this book demonstrates that women hold clear understandings of leadership and do in fact lead, in various ways across a range of settings. Women step up to lead, but frequently the behavior is not recognized or rewarded by organizations. Our goal in writing this book was to bring to light the leadership experiences of a cross section of women in order to inform post-20th century understandings and practices. What we realized is that there is a pressing need to explore the phenomenon of leading in place. It is to the benefit of the workplace itself to be mindful of, and reward, this form of leadership. While perceptions and experience of women served as our entry point to the topic of leadership, leading in place is a gender-neutral phenomenon essential to resilient organizations. We believe integrating recognition of the phenomenon into thinking and practice—while simultaneously shedding unexamined prototype biases from the 20th century—can be deployed to further both women's careers and healthier attitudes about women's contributions to organizations and communities—whether paid or unpaid.

In this chapter we review a number of findings and paradoxes that surfaced from our research. We then present feedback on our findings offered by six executive leaders with extensive human resources experience. In validation interviews, these executives were asked whether our findings on leading in place resonated with their experience. The bulk of the interviews, however, focused on insights and observations on what can be done to improve opportunity for, and recognition of, women leaders. Two of the commentators have run both private and public sector organizations: Sean O'Keefe (currently Professor and Phanstiel Chair at Syracuse University, former NASA Administrator, Secretary of the Navy, and Airbus CEO) and Ambassador Susan Schwab (currently Professor at University of Maryland who also serves on corporate boards and as a strategic advisor in international trade, former US Trade Representative, foundation CEO, and dean of a public policy school). The other four, who asked to remain anonymous, have extensive executive experience. Three are women: one currently serves as the top human resources executive for a global manufacturing enterprise headquartered in the US; one recently retired as human resources director for a federal agency; and the other served as senior talent management executive for a public-private corporation before leaving to start a leadership consulting company serving both private and public sectors. One is male, a successful serial entrepreneur who worked in Silicon Valley for years and currently owns a software startup. We close with a letter to our 20-something daughters about leadership.

The Leadership Literature

We opened this book noting that, in abstract, leadership can be thought of as a three-dimensional puzzle; a complex, dynamic set of simultaneous equations addressing dimensions of the individual(s) leading, those being led (i.e., the followers), and a broad span of contextual (internal to organizations) and environmental (socio-political-economic) factors within which the first two unfold. The review of the leadership literature and the research that supports it, addressed in Chapters Two through Four, reveals a deep and broad enterprise addressing these dimensions that continues to evolve. The review also highlights that many of the assumptions underlying current leadership theory and practice are biased, culturally bound, and incomplete. A certain heterogeneity of findings concerning leadership is inevitable. However, knowledge in the field results largely from accretion, and much of the research over time has derived from homogeneous samples or case studies of the great (straight, white) male leader, and implicitly assumes hierarchical organizations. Consequently, findings are at best imperfectly generalizable to 21st century realities. The results, although they strongly influence attitudes and practice in the workplace, do not adequately capture the diversity of leadership experiences or options. Unexamined implications of the 20th century biases, combined with lack of clear specification as to how findings interact with the dimension of contextual and environmental complexity, compromise understanding.

Few widely accepted, declarative findings have emerged that unquestionably stand the test of practice and time. The bulk of academic research is undertaken from within schools of either psychology or business/management. Psychologists tend to focus on within-person psychological differences or between-person dynamics of leaders and followers. While often drawing heavily upon psychological theories and research, the business/management genre tends towards focusing on how individuals behave to attain desired organizational outcomes, usually in the form of case studies that often do not explore typical leaders, nor do they explore specific hard questions of how interaction between the person, context, and environment are (or are not) generalizable. Taken as a whole, many of the findings in the leadership literature either do not apply to women, or do not capture the reality of women who lead in place. We call for a refreshed understanding of what it means to be a leader as well as the fault lines underlying traditionally defined ideas of leadership.

A range of themes run through research on leadership. We highlighted five: self-efficacy, self-awareness, affect, emotional intelligence (essentially adept practice and deployment of self-awareness and affect), and prototypes. Each of these came through in distinct ways not only via the survey and interviews with women leaders. They also came through clearly in the validation interviews with experienced executives.

Our Findings

Chapters Five through Seven presented some results from the in-depth interviews (Chapter Five) and covered the findings (Chapters Six and Seven) of our survey of 274 women. Our survey tapped into the perspectives and experiences of working women age 21 and older, with diverse ethnicities and family situations, some straight, some not. We heard from women in Australia, New Zealand, and Europe, although by far the greatest number reside (geographically distributed) in the United States. When asked about the three qualities they believe are essential in a good leader, the top three responses to our survey were *listening, communication* and *honesty. Empathy* and *compassion* also showed up strongly. Taken together these describe leadership capacities and behaviors in sharp contrast to the traditional male prototype characteristics espoused for leaders such as charisma or 'strength'. It is notable that the confidence of a leader appears more essential from the perspective of those 40 and under, than it does for those over 40.

We were surprised by the extent to which the women we surveyed reported extensive experience of compensating for leadership gaps. Seventy-three percent indicated that they had done so. Yet only 20% indicated that they are recognized or compensated when they step in to compensate for gaps. The fact that those who are engaged full-time are almost twice as likely as those engaged part-time to perceive that they receive due credit has potentially disturbing implications, not only for women but also for contingent workers in the 21st century. It would appear to substantiate our starting point that the voices of those who lead in place have not been adequately represented in prototypes driving leadership research and practice.

Most respondents indicated that people do not notice when they go the extra mile to compensate for gaps. Women aged 31–50 were most likely to say that they get credit when compensating for poor leadership; only 3% of those women 61 and over perceived that they have been credited when stepping in to lead in place. We were surprised that women who work for the federal government are least likely to report that they get credit when compensating for leadership gaps. While not all respondents working at the federal level were from the US, the great majority were. Given a stated commitment to ensuring an inclusive workforce, along with the extensive controls and practices around selection, promotion, and performance management that the OPM (Office of Personnel Management) insists on across federal agencies, we expected better results.

On the topic of counterproductive gender-based messages and experiences on the job, we were surprised that the percentages of women who reported receiving negative gender-based comments were about the same across age groups. Differences emerged in making sense of such comments. Far fewer women under 30 perceived gender-based advice as bias against women than did women above the age of 40. Susan Schwab validated this sentiment, saying that when men had a problem with her gender, it was early in her career and likely because of her age at the time.

A full 87% of respondents reported that they mentor other women. In light of this commitment, an interesting take on navigating organizations and environments was reflected by the fact that when asked what advice a wise mentor/advisor should share with a young woman starting her leadership journey, less than 1% said the advice should be about gender. Women may perceive that men and women tend to have distinct leadership styles, but they are not blinded by gender in pursuing leadership and success.

When we discussed our findings with her, Susan Schwab presented an alternate face of mentoring: a pattern of very successful, powerful, wealthy, older men 'taking on' and grooming the next generation of male economic/government leaders. But she's only seen this happen between men: "The bright young man being taken under a wing by older, privileged white males." Smart, successful, rich older guys (CEOs, entrepreneurs) identify younger guys (who look like them) and virtually professionally adopt them. We want to know why women do not get the same treatment, and hypothesize that the problem is 'similarity bias': We are most comfortable with those with whom we identify similarities. As Schwab puts it, "there is a system of privilege and access. How do you get diversity into that stream? There is not enough of a pipeline . . . " Interestingly, Schwab says, "women don't differentiate between sponsoring younger women and men [in the same way that] men do" and will mentor all genders equally.

Women as a category are just like everyone else: they don't all agree. Three-fourths of the women we surveyed (i.e., 76%) responded affirmatively to the question, "Based on your experience do you believe men and women tend to lead differently (e.g., 'have distinct styles')?" This response was consistent across age groups, counter to our expectation. A theme running through respondents' observations was that men are more apt to think of leadership as individual competition while women are more likely to look at it in terms of collaboration and interpersonal integrity, raising important hypotheses for future research. On this point also, the views of our validation experts suggested a more complex picture.

The former head of HR for a federal agency reviewed our findings and commented that "culture also plays a role." In her particular organization, male counterparts displayed a tendency to see their role as protecting women in their midst, rather than allowing women to take a leadership role. This influences the perceptions of others concerning women and leadership. In looking at gender differences and leadership styles, she felt that our survey respondents' characterization of women as collaborative leaders is probably more appropriate than the idea of men tending to have a more competitive style of leadership:

> In terms of the way you characterize women as prioritizing team and organizational interests, I think that is something women probably do. Women more generally speaking go in that direction. In terms of men, the best male leaders I have seen emphasize the team. Sometimes there's an appearance that they emphasize their own profile. This could be part of the leadership culture. But the most effective leaders are strongly organizationally focused. It is difficult to lead people around them if they're self-focused.
>
> However, looking a layer or two down, then [the characterizations are] absolutely consistent. Environment has to matter here, and it may well be in some environments women who make it to the top visible positions have taken on the more stereotypical male characteristics in order to progress.

The male software entrepreneur who reviewed our findings did not see the competition versus collaboration style of leadership as a gendered phenomenon, but rather a cultured stereotype. He put it this way:

> You have two things. In the workplace you have people that lead by more of what we typically believe is the 'traditional ideal leader'. What I mean by that is type A: They make decisions; time is of the essence. And then there are people who are more inclined to generate consensus and collaboration. In companies you tend to find those two types of people. With men, you kind of expect them to be the 'traditional ideal leader' type [male prototype]. But I have several guys that are definitely consensus builders; and then I have other guys that are inclined to make a [unilateral] decision and move on. They're sensitive to time. Typically where they have conflict is with people that want to think it through—are more quality-oriented. It's a classic trade-off between deadlines and quality. The people that are consensus-oriented tend to have more of a focus on get it done right. The 'traditional ideal leader' is more inclined towards 'let's just get it done, whatever happens, happens.'
>
> I see this with both men and women. I have several women that are definitely the more 'traditional ideal leader' category and I have several women that are in the consensus category. What's interesting about that is that with men in the consensus category, you tend to see them as a good fit and as

doing what's needed. But when the women are in the more 'traditional ideal leader' category and make decisions, at first it's a little surprising. And they're so effective at it. They are as effective at thriving in the 'traditional ideal leader' style as men are. It's just that it's surprising when they do it.

When I started off [with the current startup] all projects were 'time to market'. My company was full of 'traditional ideal leader'-style people who just got things done. Quality suffered, but we were able to get things out the door. We got business going and got customers. But as you get customers you discover they want quality. Then you end up bringing in these consensus-builders. The consensus-building people are more focused on quality: getting people together and doing it right. So as a company grows, the type of leader style you need changes . . . As far as women go, I think that men and women are equally capable of filling either role. I think though there are a lot of cultural biases in schools and elsewhere that result in people thinking men make the 'traditional ideal leader' and women make the ideal collaboration, leading-in-place people. I think that's more of a social norm; I think it's trained, not inherent in genders.

Susan Schwab weighed in on this issue based on her experience on Capitol Hill: "There are two groups of people on Capitol Hill: the elected and everybody else," she said

> If you're one of the 'everybody else', then collaborative leadership is the single best way [to get things done]. So women's leadership styles are so much more effective on Capitol Hill when you're working with other staffs. The way you get things done on Capitol Hill when you're working with other staffers is the collaborative leadership approach. Make sure this person gets credit, that person's boss gets credit; let them get their provision in. And women are so much better at that than men are, that women do very well, and will work harder.

The HR executive for a global manufacturing company agreed with Susan Schwab, commenting that "the record of Congress is the best example of what women in leadership can get done." She did not think that differences in leadership styles were necessarily gendered, however. In her experience, corporate culture is a strong driver, and in her industry there are very few women. Women who are in leadership positions in her industry tend to display more stereotypic male characteristics. She totally gets it that some very competent women may be put off by a competitive, aggressive, loud, and outgoing style in some environments, but sees the differences mainly between quiet and profile-oriented styles and personalities who are attracted to her industry.

When asked about leadership aspirations, a surprising find of our survey was that women aged 21–30 were more positive, 2 to 1, about their future leadership opportunities than women in all other age groups. Those younger women were more apt to say they have a clear sense of the role to which they aspire, and that their desired position is a "visible position of leadership." Sean O'Keefe thought this was common today among young women in the aerospace industry, largely due to a decade-long "conscious industry-wide reversal" that occurred when organization leaders realized how thick the glass ceiling was for women and how few of them were pursuing engineering and technical-related opportunities. Susan Schwab agreed and disagreed with this sentiment, saying that while product development is fairly supportive of women, engineering is a tough sector for women, largely due to corporate culture, the need to relocate, and the low percentage of women in the field. She reported that she has been concerned by what she perceives as a deficit of women aspiring to visible positions of leadership in that field.

Tied in with this, another surprising find is that close to two-thirds of our respondents indicated that they had turned down leadership positions, but the reasons why they had done so were unrelated to whether the women reported being parents. Instead, women discussed their choices in terms of fit of opportunities with their values, style, and goals. Not all leadership positons are created equal and our respondents displayed a sophisticated ability to analyze whether a position was authentically right for them by assessing a wide range of variables.

Our retired HR executive for a federal agency challenged our finding of lack of fit with values. "Few are comfortable with all priorities of an organization" she said.

> ... [What] this seems to say to me is that there's an inability to compromise. Maybe not in terms of values, but in terms of priorities of the day. That can be a very fine line for women in leadership roles who may disagree with a direction that's being taken. But once the decision is made, they need to take the organization and lead it in the most appropriate path consistent with that direction. Certainly, from my point of view, one of my emphases was "no I can't agree with every priority at any given time, but there are ways of leading the organization so that you are consistent with priorities but also consistent with your underlying values that keep the organization on as steady a path as possible."

Both Sean O'Keefe and Susan Schwab expressed the opinion that many babyboomer women were cautious about, or even turned down, leadership positions because they did not want to be seen as the 'token'. "I had to convince them," O'Keefe said, that "they were going to have the standing necessary in order to credibly lead and be viewed by their peers as being selected because of their expertise or talent ... No one wants to have to demonstrate every day that they are worthy of a job." Susan Schwab phrased it a different way. She talked about "the rule of three." "Once there are more than two women in the room, it is a transformative experience" she said, and so easier for women to lead.

Her Stories

Chapter Five presented stories from, and discussion among, women who have all led in place in a variety of work settings—public, private, and non-profit—most paid, some volunteer. What surprised us the most was the consensus that women are already leaning in, but not necessarily in designated positions. Rather, they are leading in place, and are often not recognized for doing so.

Discussion concerning whether leadership is a position or a behavior in Chapter Five ended with the consensus that it is both. One certainly can and should lead in place, our interviewees concluded. Our retired federal HR executive told us that to some extent—possibly more with the baby boom generation than those coming along behind, "in terms of leading in place, certainly in certain stages of their careers, I do think a lot of women try to do that." She has seen many women opt to "exert influence from a lower-level position than they might otherwise be qualified to fill."

Early on in her career, she made such choices, opting for deputy-oriented positions, exerting influence through her secondary role. This was partially attributable to the culture of the organization in which she was working, and serving as secretariat for a prominent, powerful group was a critical opportunity. She saw her role as feeding information to make sure the policy-maker actually received the necessary input to execute his role. "I do believe that a lot of women from the baby boom generation spend a lot of time thinking about how to influence rather than lead," she said. Some of it has to do with large-scale responsibilities at home. "I did not want to take on leadership responsibilities that would have required putting more time in at work than I wanted to put in" she told us.

In hindsight, there may not be such an absolute trade-off required, she said. "To some extent, it is something women tell themselves. They don't necessarily let themselves take on the level of responsibility required. I see less of this in more junior level people coming up through the ranks now." Instead, she sees young women who are interested in taking on leadership roles, and actively seeking out leadership roles. "It's not possible to generalize", she told us, "as not everyone chooses the same path, either sitting back or stepping forward." Individual choices are influenced by cultural, organizational, and professional messages.

Sean O'Keefe validated this in his review of our research, but added that he has seen both men and women lead in place. Leadership on teams is a prime example. "Inevitably it falls in the category of 'let's assign it to so-and-so because they always get it done right'." A default pattern occurs in which individuals are leading, but don't have a position. This is especially important in crisis situations, O'Keefe said, and this phenomenon shows no gender or ethnic bias.

The software entrepreneur who reviewed our research agreed with O'Keefe's sentiments, telling us:

> You've hit on something, but it's not gender-specific ... That's my take on it. I do believe that there are women who exert this within their team structure. But I also believe that there are men that do that too ... I work in high-tech. I find that as many men as women tend to lead in place ... I see more that there are certain men and women that don't like to deal with the conflict that can arise in making decisions and driving things ... And yes, it's true that we tend not to reward leading in place. What I found is that I've had to create special positions for people to lead in place. But this is true for men and women.

The HR executive from the global manufacturing corporation, however, said she saw women leading in place more than men: "Yes. It's so prevalent, the phenomenon of women leading in place." She told us that she sees it all the time. Her biggest challenges and efforts are aimed towards "recruiting women into [her male-dominated] industry, and retaining them." Preparing them for leadership roles is a whole other challenge. She told us:

> The most frustrating thing is that organizations do all this great work, but often have the prerequisite that in order to move up the chain you have to already be a manager or a leader. We have all these extremely talented women who are doing great things in the organization but they don't hold formal roles, so they don't have access and might not be considered for top spots.

Also, she told us there is insufficient thought and attention given to the prevalence of the male prototype leader. There is too much emphasis on traditional male characteristics, requiring everyone to "fit a model of traditional leadership. How do we create space for a different style of leadership? I think reliance on the traditional [male prototype] negatively impacts the selection process."

There is also the challenge of some women's confidence and sometimes insecurity, she said. Women are more inclined to ask: "Am I really capable of this?" Women want to be very confident and knowledgeable before they take a leadership position, many of those interviewed told us. Others told us that men apply if they are 60% qualified and women will sometimes apply if they are 100%, sometimes 110%, qualified. Those who raise their hand are typically male, even if they don't meet the qualifications, whereas a woman's tendency is to screen the qualifications and assess whether she has everything on paper, before she chooses to go for it.

Susan Schwab had a different opinion of this issue. While she did see women leading in place in the State Department, she did not see it very often in her work in trade policy. Trade policy and negotiation is a "very user-friendly field for women" Schwab said. In fact, it is dominated by women. Most trade agreements in recent history have been negotiated by women, she pointed out.

Clearly the phenomenon of women leading in place varies and is influenced by industry and organizational culture. It is also highly intertwined with one's individual characteristics and life circumstances, likely with variation also by generation. Returning to our earlier discussion of theory and the emergence of a modern paradigm, our research demonstrates that the phenomenon of women leading in place is best understood as a spectrum with both women's stories and practitioners' feedback pointing to the imperative influence of context on leadership. The upshot is that yes, there is a mix of positional and 'in place' leadership that moves organizations forward. Organizations benefit from both, and leading in place is not unique to women.

However, leading in place should be either an explicit choice, or a predominant organizational model (such as in holacracies). It should never be the default for women (or any demographic category) because skewed systems or practices preclude access to leadership positions. In order to ensure that they are getting and retaining the best from diverse talent pools, organizations have to check both the underlying prototypes *and* processes by which individuals access leadership positions. Otherwise, women get closed out of opportunities; there continue to be too many such stories.

For example, a highly ranked public affairs graduate school recently did an international search for a Dean—the top position in the school. In the end all who applied were rejected—including an internal female candidate with many years of successfully leading academic programs within the school. She was told by a member of the search committee that she was rejected because she talked too much about herself in her interview. Instead, the Provost, in consultation with the President, chose the straight, white, male chair of the search committee who had not even applied for the job. This was done without the approval of the rest of the search committee and without vetting the man with the faculty, a long-held tradition in academia. This is an apparent example of gender bias that was implicit rather than overt, largely due to the lack of transparency at the highest level of the university. It is not dissimilar from the story of Sabine that we shared in Chapter One. As the former senior talent management executive for a public-private corporation (now a consultant) told us, processes are all too frequently skewed in ways that confine women to leading in place instead of climbing the ladder to top leadership positions:

> Junior level positions in most organizations today are posted. That creates transparency of opportunity and in many cases a more level playing field for interested applicants. Requirements for a role are posted, you can apply for the role, and in many cases you get some kind of feedback after you apply on whether you're going to be interviewed. Or, after you're interviewed

sometimes there's feedback about why you didn't get it. But at the top, the really interesting roles tend to continue to be filled by a much more biased process, which is the person doing the hiring knows someone that they want to hire, who often looks and leads in the image of the hiring manager. So the process that works so well at lower levels is far less often used at the very levels where we're not making progress [in getting women into positions of leadership]. So the positions that women especially want more access to, to be aware of, to be considered for, to get feedback on when they are not selected, they never even hear about them until the announcement is made.

When the internal woman candidate who applied for the deanship followed up and asked someone familiar with the final deliberations why not her, she was told that the person chosen "impressed the right people." Our former senior talent management executive (now consultant) continued, commenting on a similar case:

> This is where it breaks down. When you're asked to explain to female candidates at highest rungs 'why not them' . . . They just skipped . . . [important] steps. This is where implicit bias comes in. You look around and you see someone [and you give them the opportunity/role]. This is how lack of diversity becomes replicated . . . Opacity or incompleteness of decision process is how women get overlooked. It definitely disadvantages women. I see it over and over. The person doing the hiring sees someone just like them, maybe with a career path like them and so it fits well enough and they just make a decision [to hire]. [There is] bias in the lack of transparency in [access to] the most coveted positions. They tend to be the senior ones . . . Women tend to be thought of for staff positions but not for business heads or always client-facing roles. Some of the most significant opportunities are withheld from women by lack of transparency. What women want is a chance to be considered and to have access to positions at the top, and to understand when not selected what they have to do to be more successful next time. I think of that as inclusion that leads to diversity. When they feel like their organization won't even allow them equal access to the opportunities, they will sometimes leave. They feel like the system doesn't allow them to even be considered for what they're qualified to do.

She echoed that sometimes an "impulse to protect" women is also a problem. "What would happen if you looked at your process?" she asked. So many organizations would have to say 'we do it with three guys in a room'. For me transparency is the biggest opportunity to drive inclusion and diversity. And it's not just about women . . . The lack of transparency keeps people in roles . . . and allows you to hide from . . . difficult conversations."

Leadership is developed through access to opportunities and through performance in a role.

To the extent that women—or any demographic—is kept from a mix of opportunities, they are being disadvantaged. Many organizations offer leadership programs for women, but they can't access them unless they already have a formal position. So, the very population that needs and is hungry for such opportunities may get shut out.

Organizational culture, informal rules and networks play a huge role in determining who gets into leadership positions. Making sure that women are not differentially disadvantaged is a real challenge. The HR executive for a global manufacturing corporation put it this way:

> I think of it as a perpetual cycle. If an organization's demographics are heavily male, it's hard to break the cycle . . . For example, what are the implications of either boys club or girls club cultures? I just think about how the drinking culture, or an after-work/after-hours culture affects who gets opportunities to lead. How do different family obligations and even just comfort level (being a sole gender representative) . . . impact your ability to get the best information through those informal channels where a lot of key information is transacted and decisions might even be made? This is so real and pervasive.

Organizational leaders need to critically examine whether their model of leadership assumes a male prototype, and consciously make room for other styles of leadership. This is critical at the point of selecting leaders and is complicated by a pipeline that may be artificially skewed. The male prototype, and similarity bias, can skew who has access to leadership opportunities because of relationships.

The Pros Offered Not Only Insight, but Also Advice

We asked our six executive reviewers for advice on women leading in place. The HR executive for a global manufacturing corporation talked about the importance of role models and relationships. It's important to ensure women have diverse role models.

> Care about sponsorship and mentorship. This is definitely a hot topic in my company, and there's definitely a skepticism about whether traditional mentorship programs are effective. But I do think that really, at most organizations, work gets done through relationships, and we know most leadership models emphasize relationships: a foundation of trust and credibility are essential. People with strong and broad cross-functional relationships in an organization can get exponentially more work done.

She also talked about the importance of data in order to really make a change.

> There's bias training, there's all these traditional things in our corporate world. But it's definitely data, data and metrics, that [promote] change. So we really need to make a business case for those leaders who believe strongly in a meritocracy. Approaching [effort to ensure diversity in the executive cadre] so it's not seen as a deviation from meritocracy, but seen more as conscious effort to better represent your market, better represent your customer base and have the best ideas. That it is more innovative. That's one of the biggest challenges we face. It's so subtle, and it's so sensitive. It's never about hiring a women or having a quota. It's about diversifying your channels, your pipeline, your network. It's getting leaders great data and case studies and messaging that they can relate to, to understand, to embrace it rather than resist.

Sean O'Keefe told us that professional development is important, so women can "understand beyond their function." Also important is offering a broad range of opportunities to women, because succession planning "is always going to be limited to those who have had a broader range of opportunities."

> The general tendency within organizations confronted with gender or other bias is that they then try to correct by emphasizing that 'we need to pick from an excluded category'. That's not the point. That serves to stigmatize the chosen candidate and diminishes the credibility of the individual. A stronger technique that worked very effectively in almost every selection process [I was involved in] was to require the search committee to always ensure a representative sample, a diversity within the field. Then choose individuals from that broad range. This allows everyone to start from an even playing field. Word floats quickly … 'we had a broad range in the selection pool'. We need to set individuals up for success. We need to ensure open, equal access to candidacy.

Our retired HR executive from the federal government said that we

> … don't do enough to select for individuals who will question the priorities of the day, or question authority when they need to do that. Nor do we select necessarily for leaders who are willing to have people under them who question their authority, call them on assumptions if they're incorrect. I would really like to see future organizations do more of that because that's how you actually prepare people for leadership—to give them the ability to think for themselves, to question directions with an eye to the future rather than an eye to the past.

As to increasing diversity in the executive cadre, she told us that "the answer may be a little different between public and private sectors. If you wish to have diversity in the leadership cadre, first of all you need to have diversity elsewhere in the organization." As to developing leaders, she advised that we:

> . . . have to give people the opportunity to do a variety of different things. Anyone who does exactly the same thing for 20 years or 30 years will get bored and stale. If you want to have leaders with imagination, they need to have a good grounding in the work of the organization from a variety of different perspectives. Some opportunities are made available, some are self-created. Anything that gets you out of your own organization, and limited concerns of that small organization, will develop you as a leader.

As to traditional male stereotypes of what makes a good leader, she advised:

> The stereotypes of the leader are just that: stereotypes. Part of good leadership is really understanding what the people around you do, and how you can support them in doing that. Truthfully, most of the really good ideas about where to go, and new directions, don't come out of a single mind. The stereotype of the leader who can have all the ideas, and do everything, and be all things to all people is very damaging. Without having more collaborative approaches, and working towards the kind of engagement of employees that the federal government has been talking about, I don't think any leader can be as effective as possible.

Our HR executive from the global manufacturing corporation realized early on that women need opportunities to lead, so she partnered with outside organizations that do programming to support women to create committees. Females in the industry then have leadership positions, and can take advantage of some of the development opportunities. This is important because the demographics in her particular organization are tough.

> [There are] no women on the senior management team. The numbers get better at mid-level. Yet there is really high credibility for women in individual contributor roles. This really resonates with my experience and observation. We have to get women into streams to move up in the organization.

The former senior talent management executive, turned consultant, agreed and added that organizations need to take a hard, critical, look at their hiring processes. "Transparency and careful structuring of such processes where there is an openness that will engender an alignment between needs and candidates—all the way up to the top jobs in the organization—can actually eliminate bias," she told us.

A more transparent posting of opportunities and requirements and then more development of the capacity to explain to unsuccessful candidates why they were not selected is very important. Many people in the private sector who do the hiring express fear that too many people might apply if processes are opened up, when in reality they often do not have the skills to tactfully have conversations with unsuccessful candidates. But these skills can be learned. In other cases, fear of lawsuits keeps those who hire from having transparent conversations. Transparency is one key to getting women into positions of leadership.

Balancing Work and Life Constitutes a Gender-Neutral Reality

Most of our commenters said that in order to ensure fair access to leadership positions for women, our society needs to do more to enable men to do more of the child-rearing and childcare so that there is an expectation that the full burden doesn't fall on women. Yet Susan Schwab worries about some of the flextime/telecommuting options saying that "It may just raise expectation that women will do more of [family care], and men will be showing up in the office." Often women who work from home work harder than if they went to an office. "They end up working as hard or harder, with less recognition, if you're doing it at home," she told us:

> There should be a facilitative role for telecommuting, but not making it so easy that women are doing that and men aren't. This will set back women. Women will not be motivated to or expected to move forward in terms of advancement because they will not have been in the office and the jobs that involve advancement will be in the office. Higher level leadership jobs cannot be run from a distance. Unless you have as many men doing the part-time, distance component jobs, it's going to end up coming back to bite women.

Our HR executive for a global manufacturing corporation disagreed, pointing to the cost of the lean-in attitude:

> The Zappos model is conceptually, in an ideal state, a great way to go, the idea of work being freelance and people tapping in where they have skills. This is almost a network of logistics Uber-style, where you have such a sophisticated system of efficiency where you can connect and tap and have people contributing in a much more fluid way.

While "you have to be present to be a part of the group, to hear things" she said,

> I don't agree [with Susan]. One of the things I find concerning is the sort of pendulum swing among ambitious women . . . Today I was just talking

with a woman who was really struggling to identify a mentor, a female mentor, who could show her work-life balance, because in all the organizations she works with, the women in leadership, her role models basically, they're saying you really have to stop talking about not spending enough time at home. You've got to focus on work, you've got to do this, do that.

This is the perceived cost of the lean-in attitude. She continued:

What I have been really inspired by is thinking about this: for women it's really about getting comfortable with *you*, and what the right balance for you is. So, I think it's scary if women don't have role models that say 'yes, work from home', or [any message that allows them to find and lead from *their* place of strength]. In my organization our top leaders work from home one day a week. That empowers me to make similar choices. I don't worry at all about missing out. If you work in a global company, it's more about off-hours. It's more about relationships and sponsorship. So what I see is that guys become friends, they go to the lake house outside of work. Those are the guys getting sponsored for things. It's quite different than introducing work-life balance. I think the direction is becoming so much more flexible across the board that I don't worry about [women taking advantage of locational flexibility.] 'Leaning in' is not the only way forward for women. It's interesting to me that highly successful women can't find a role model [that reflects that it is possible to] spend time with your 1-year-old and also care about work. There should be room for that, I think. The leaning-in mentality is not the only way. Women need to be true to themselves, be what they want, and not feel pressure [to be or do otherwise].

As we walked out the door together Susan Schwab offered one last piece of advice:

Rewards and incentives matter. Mid-level managers have to be asked "how many women, how many people of color did you consider in that search?" We need to get more in the pipeline. Longevity [within an organization] matters. In terms of taking formal leadership positions, women need to get the message "try it, you'll like it." If you haven't tried it, you have no idea you'll like it.

In her experience, "when senior men pay attention [to diversity] and object [to practices that constrain it], then it gets attention." Men on corporate boards have particular power to push for improvements in diversity in the executive cadre. "It's imperative that issues of diversity be addressed in business school", she said. "What are students learning about leadership, and metrics for diversity? They're used to being evaluated (e.g., 360s), but what do they learn about promoting diversity?"

Our software entrepreneur ended with this insight about men's discomfort with women leaders:

> In the workplace, men in leadership roles do see women that have potential. They are uncomfortable with it. If they're not forced to go and confront this discomfort and act to get past it, they just shuffle those people off to the side. Those women end up—if you're type A, you're type A—exerting themselves to lead in place. If you're a leader, you're compelled to lead. In large companies I think it's easier for executives to not look past their discomfort, emotional discomfort, and act on putting the right people in the right place.

This is often how and why we see women leading in place instead of from senior positions.

What are the Implications for Research and Practice?

Based on our survey results and insights gleaned from interviews—along with our combined 60 years in the workforce, both leading in place and in formal positions of leadership—we offer suggestions to help improve knowledge and understanding of the phenomenon of leading in place.

Continue building robust findings on the effects of biases and prototypes in talent management practices (e.g., selection, development, promotion). It is hard to overstate this need, already well-recognized by researchers and practitioners alike. Practices need to reflect how leadership actually plays out outside hierarchical position structures, and to integrate women's perception of leadership, as well as mitigating impacts of unconscious biases (including of women themselves).

Organizations of the 21st century share little in the way of context and environment with those of the 20th century. Fascination with 'generalizability' needs to be more assiduously, thoughtfully challenged (not abrogated) in order to serve organizations in practice. Specifying boundaries of inquiry can actually increase the utility of findings. For example, tools appropriate to private sector organizations that operate in dynamic environments and maintain minutely detailed results metrics should be transferred to public sector organizations with great caution. Relative boundaries and cautions should be spelled out. Similarly, it's not necessarily a problem if research subjects' leadership prototypes are unknown; but that they are unknown and could significantly influence findings needs to be laid out. A path of intriguing and challenging interdisciplinary work lies in front of researchers and practitioners alike. (See Box 8.1 for illustration of possible questions likely to build knowledge and serve practice.)

While it post-dates our research, the late-2017 rash of revelations around (and firings of) high-profile apparent serial sexual harassers highlights two realities to which researchers and executives responsible for talent management need to attend. First, unfolding social transformation has significant implications (as we

BOX 8.1 ADVANCING PRACTICE AND KNOWLEDGE

Acknowledging the gender-neutral phenomenon of leading in place raises a wealth of questions. Straightforward practice questions arise for organizations such as how to assess operative leader prototypes, how to recognize and develop those who lead in place, what are the implications for power dynamics if organizations acknowledge those who lead in place? Much of what is already known about assessing systems and individuals can be applied to answer such challenges.

Research questions are extensive. For example, do deep-level individual differences drive preferences for leading in place or is it a strategic response to contextual and environmental factors? In particular, do differences exist in cognitive proclivities such as analogical and abductive reasoning? Do gender differences in perceptions of power and harassment artificially constrain opportunities available to women? What are the respective developmental needs for those who lead in place as opposed to those who only have interest in trajectories aimed at formal positions? Do organizations benefit differentially from the behaviors of these cohorts? How can the value-add of each cohort be measured? What are the implications for the full range of talent management practices—and how should implementation differ between public and private sectors? Tackling these questions is necessarily an interdisciplinary endeavor.

contended in opening this book) for views and expectations of leadership. Second, power dynamics as they actually play out in organizations cannot be ignored in either practice (selection and assessment of individuals) or research.

Measure thoughtfully. Counting who holds top spots is too little too late. Monitoring should cover who gets in the door and who doesn't; distribution of gateway opportunities for all contributors performing at an acceptable level; distribution of sponsor attention. Assessing how systems in use have performed is a good starting point; are competency models creating a robust, diverse pipeline or are they replicating biased prototypes (from the past)? In this age of data analytics, this is ever easier. There are models out there of companies that are using people data to constantly improve.

Mitigate predictable consequences. For example, mentoring programs should incorporate hands-on guided development opportunities to build leader self-efficacy of mentees. They should also guide mentors and mentees alike in examining and stretching habits of thought (not just to be aware of specific biases). Designing mentoring, and leadership programs more generally, to promote cognitive complexity and perspective-taking skills will position individuals not only to ensure that similarity bias is not restricting access to opportunities and skewing pipelines, but also to be more able and willing to engage in difficult conversations that promote shared sense-making for inclusive, effective organizations.

Equally important is changing performance management practices and systems to promote, recognize, and reward those who lead in place. This may be the area of greatest potential pay-off for organizations and individuals alike. There is plenty of room for enhancing organizational effectiveness by the widespread use of what we have learned in the selection, development, and recognition of engaged emergent leaders of both genders. It is, equally, at this moment the most ill-defined and messy of the paths forward.

Collaborate to collect and analyze data to build robust theory. Particularly with unfolding shifts in both social expectations and models of employment, pushing the boundaries of theory along two fronts may best serve the world of practitioners. Methodical examination of prototypes across units of analysis, their implications, and possible mitigation strategies comprises one of these fronts. The other is expanding work in contextual theories. This is a gender-neutral need: it is about the 21st century reality of dynamic, adaptive, and inclusive organizations.

EPILOGUE

Letter to Our (and Others') Daughters

This research benefitted from the generosity of literally hundreds of women. In addition, we each had years of personal experience watching leadership unfold— or remain absent—in all spheres of experience over the course of our lives. One of us (Rosemary) first worked as an attorney and a high-level administrator in the public sector, went back to school to earn a Ph.D., took an academic job out of graduate school, and pursued a straight track to a very successful academic career, having a daughter along the way. The other (Rita) opted for the world of practice after earning her Ph.D., spending 15 years at a multilateral international development organization, having two sons and a daughter along the way . . . but then stepped sideways and made a career change largely for family reasons. This led to years of practice in the leadership development field, first as a coach and independent consultant and then as a practitioner within organizations In the course of writing this book, we maintained our 'day jobs', endured the death of parents, moves and renovations, and became empty nesters. "Life has interfered with my life," became our mantra.

We each had views about women and leadership, about what needed to be different for our daughters and their rising generation. We each have seen capable powerful women thrive and take positions, or step away from positions, whether in the workplace or the volunteer sphere. We've also seen similar women overlooked and devalued by individuals and organizations. For years we'd been hearing and having conversations with friends and colleagues about the challenges of women and leadership. The publication of Anne Marie Slaughter's *Atlantic* article (2012) the same year our daughters graduated from high school— quickly followed by Sheryl Sandberg's *Lean in* (2013)—motivated us to move from observing and sharing anecdotes to influencing others, hoping that our efforts may empower them.

What Is Leadership?

Rosemary: In co-authoring this book, the following stood out to me as personally compelling and meaningful. First, leadership is a status quo changing behavior that can occur with or without a formal position of leadership. At the same time, a formal position of leadership can yield power and resources that make it easier to change the status quo. Second, to obtain leadership success we need both good process and good results. In the end, results matter, and in today's world most workers expect and even demand a process that allows them the opportunity to weigh in on the direction and the means of getting there. Third, values matter in leadership. As one of the women we interviewed commented, whether they know it or not, leaders set the tone and culture for an organization. Everything counts. Every step you take, every comment you make as a leader—formal or informal—will be observed and absorbed by your organization. The women we interviewed described accepting and rejecting leadership positions based on their own personal values and the values espoused by the organization. It is important to lead with values.

Rita: My view, based on decades observing leaders of both genders in organizations as well as watching women give their time and talents to support children and communities to thrive, often while caring for elderly or dying parents, was confirmed by what we heard from hundreds of women in the course of this research. Leadership is largely about behaviors one exhibits, the degree of open-mindedness and perspective-taking one is willing to strive for, and how one chooses to interact with others in solving problems and accomplishing goals. These have to arise from a place of integrity or things inevitably go off the rails either for the individual or for those around them. Leaders who always strike me as most effective and satisfied—whether leading from position or leading in place, paid or unpaid—are very clear about why what they're doing is worth effort.

I fully agree with Rosemary that healthy alignment with personal values is part of the equation. But always be sensitive to the reality that the range of choices available to individuals can vary. Some may face external demands that constrain their employment/activity choices: Do what you can to support them to thrive. Ralph Waldo Emerson's sentiment "Do not go where the path may lead. Go instead where there is no path and leave a trail" may be supremely bad advice for backwoods hiking, but it is wise and empowering advice for a life of leading.

What Choices and Trade-Offs Do Women Make in Order to Lead?

Rosemary: Life is about choices and trade-offs, no matter what you do or where you go. Time was the trade-off mentioned most often by the women we interviewed in deciding whether to take a formal position of leadership: time for other pursuits, time for family, time for avocations. I was struck by the fact that most of the women we interviewed who are my age felt a trade-off between family and taking formal positions of leadership when they had children at home. I have to admit that one reason I became a college professor is that after having experienced work as an attorney for four years, I was turned off by the lack of time for family, friends, and pursuits outside the organization. I wanted a more flexible lifestyle. Ironically, I have found that I work just as many hours (if not more) as a professor, but at different times of the day. It was not unusual for me to write a book chapter or grade papers at midnight after my family was asleep, for example.

This perceived trade-off was articulated less often in the responses of the under-30 women we interviewed. It will be interesting to see if your generation can create organizations that are more people and family friendly. Bottom line: You will be making choices and trade-offs your entire life, inside the world of work and outside. Choose wisely and choose the path that is right for you, based on your values.

Rita: I do not know a woman who invested in higher education, and subsequently had children, that does not at some point feel some ambivalence about their choices. It's simply part of the equation. There is a certain amount of privilege in being able to trade-off distribution of time and effort: if it's a power you have, use it. You can adjust your choices along the way, adapting them to your priorities, individual circumstances, and commitments to others. There isn't just one way to navigate life and career.

If you do face opportunities to take on a visible leadership role, don't fall into the trap of equating more responsibility with more hours and effort. Taking on higher positions requires individuals to learn new behaviors and adopt new perspectives. The challenge is seeing the bigger picture and keeping others moving with you towards the horizon—not doing it all. Be thoughtful, do not hesitate to make choices that work for you and remain ever aware you're living a life not a career.

What about Leadership and Power?

Rosemary: Power is not a four-letter word. Power is necessary to get things done and there are many sources of power. Formal positions of leadership may give you power, for example in the form of resources and people, as well as legitimacy and access, to accomplish desired goals. And at the same time there are sources of power available whether you have a formal leadership position or not: The power of a good idea, the power of creativity, the power of persuasion, the power of collaborative problem-solving, the power of having multiple options, and the power of having the energy and drive to never give up. Don't shy away from power and don't underestimate your power. You are powerful.

Rita: As Rosemary eloquently writes, power comes from many sources. Do not shirk from positional power, but recognize and own the personal power that comes from creativity and modeling constructive behaviors with others. Position matters more in some contexts than others, but it alone is never enough. Watch those who purport to lead you in any sphere of life, and remain vigilant of how they deploy that power. Learn from those who do it in ways you respect; shy from those who use it for corrupt or self-aggrandizing purposes. Position and power do not leadership constitute. The founding fathers provided a brilliant framework for democracy; protect it even if those in positions do not.

Do Others Need to Recognize Your Leadership to Validate it?

Rosemary: Others do not need to recognize your leadership to validate it. Leadership is leadership. But at some point in time leading without validation may become self-defeating. As our airline pilot who voluntarily revised the pilots' handbook but received no recognition for it indicated, after a while the lack of validation can make you never want to lead in place again. One point of this book is that we as a society need to validate and reward those who lead in place, as well as those who lead well in formal positions of leadership. Those we interviewed indicated that men tend to be socialized to self-promote more so than women. Strut your stuff. Don't be shy about professionally pointing out your awesomeness to the right people.

Rita: Self-promotion appears to be becoming more of a gender-neutral phenomenon in the US, but it is culturally bound and there will always be those who are not comfortable with it. If you lead in place and it's not recognized you've got three choices: 1) stay, grow, and stretch to use new behaviors that gain recognition; 2) stay and contribute to changing the environment; or 3) move on. If you can't remain positive and motivated to pursue the first or second option, you're in the wrong organization. It is not the job of others to make you feel good. Position yourself to thrive—keep working towards that even when the going is not smooth. One of our respondents said it better than I ever could: "1) Motivation is an internal drive, do not seek it externally; 2) Make mistakes, but always learn from them; 3) Be open to critique—you don't always see your weak spots."

What about Biases?

Rosemary: Biases abound in every culture. The bias of the enduring 'great man theory of leadership' has been offered to explain why some women voted for Donald Trump. As a brand of 'successful businessman' he represented what some women want their husbands and sons to achieve . . . so strongly that they were able to overlook his mocking of the disabled, his demeaning comments about women, and his company's refusal to rent apartments to people of color. Laura Morgan Roberts and Robin Ely explain this in a *Harvard Business Review* article published just ten days after the 2016 election:

> The second largest contingent of women supporting Trump was white women with college degrees. Forty-five percent of them voted for him.

While some were likely attracted to Trump's fiscally conservative policies, research suggests an even more pervasive gender dynamic at play. Women and men have been socialized by family members, educators, and the media to associate leadership with a particular version of masculinity, an image Trump exemplified in his persona as the supremely successful businessman. He reinforced the masculine, leader-as-savior image with repeated claims that he alone could make America great again. Those drawn to this view, by extension, place a higher level of scrutiny on those who do not fit their image of success. Thus, Secretary Clinton's handling of her emails was considered far more egregious than anything Trump had done, an assessment fueled by his systematic dismantling of Clinton in virtually every stump speech.

Many women (and men) who supported Trump bought into the false dichotomy that a woman leader can be either competent or likeable, but not both. What came into question was Clinton's character—so much so that her competence became a moot point. In contrast, while almost 25 percent of Trump supporters said he was not qualified, they voted for him anyway.

(Roberts & Ely, 2016)

It was easy for me to condemn the biases of those who still believe in 'the great man theory of leadership', but hard to confront my own biases. When I worked on the NASA Return-to-Flight Task Group created after the Columbia space shuttle disaster, for example, I befriended a woman astronaut with three children who had traveled to the international space station many times. In a conversation with her, I made a remark that she interpreted as being disparaging of stay-at-home mothers. "Don't be critical of stay-at-home moms," she said to me.

Because of stay-at-home moms I can travel to the space station. They carpool my children when I'm gone. They take my kids to soccer practice when I'm in training. They volunteer in the classroom when I'm in space. I could not do what I am doing without stay-at-home mothers.

She was right, of course. We all have biases. We need to acknowledge them, learn from them, be aware of them, and hopefully grow beyond them.

Rita: Gender is not the issue. Rigidities and unexamined limitations in flexibility of thinking and perspective-taking are the issue. I have worked with fabulous leaders and managers, male and female. I have worked with men who felt free to systematically freeze women out of opportunities and say things like "women just need to smile" or worse. What they meant is "I feel better if women behave to make me comfortable, conform to my expectations . . . completely independent of the contribution they're making." I have worked with women who seemed to suffer from 'queen-bee syndrome', going out of their way to belittle and cut off other women. Regardless of gender, the behavior revealed significant limitations, and a lack of self-reflection and self-management that foisted costs on others. Ultimately, failure to get everyone past such behaviors costs organizations: They skew their own pools of available talent as women who expect more professional behavior move on.

I find leaders not intimidated by having themselves challenged on any level, like the software entrepreneur interviewed at the end of this book, to be the best and most interesting. He could have grown into a male who expected women to make him comfortable; instead he faced his own discomfort and grew beyond it. Those who will take perspective on themselves, how they're thinking about an issue, a challenge, an individual, and on their own behavior, are the ones who attract good people. 'In-clubs' and closed networks of any gender operating in contexts and environments that do not expect individuals to reflect on their own thinking and perspectives are the problem. Interestingly, I view Hillary Clinton's defeat as an illustration of being captive to 'in-group' bias. While a highly qualified consummate machine player, Hillary appears to have surrounded herself with so many like-minded individuals, freezing out others, that in the end she and her team were tone-deaf to the fact that the machine was out of tune. They had every opportunity to hear it: Bernie was quite literally shouting. Always check your own biases and work against the blinding effects for yourself and those around you.

In the course of this research, I was particularly struck by the insight that we really do get to make sense of our own experience, even in the face of bias. I walk away truly impressed with the grace with which some of our respondents faced biases but refused to be defined by them. These women shared stories of professional setbacks and how they had navigated those. To me, the reported experiences clearly included racial bias (whether conscious or unconscious), which caused me to feel anger and indignity at a lack of fairness. My impulse was to urge these women to take action, to demand different treatment. But I realized this was not the sense they chose to make (at least not in speaking with me). They chose instead to go forward and make constructive professional moves, refusing to be defined or derailed by others' biases. It was a powerful illustration for me that I both always need to check the biases I bring to a situation, but also monitor that I do not box myself in by the way I respond to others' biases. The extent to which we challenge and stretch our habits of thinking influences our interactions and experience. Yes, it takes effort, but it's worth it. Good leaders model this for others.

What Else Have We Learned about Leadership?

Rosemary: In my 30 years in the workforce as an attorney, public manager, consultant, and as a professor, I have led in place and through formal positions of authority. I have learned that above all else you must know yourself and your values, and lead in a way that is authentic. You have to be comfortable in your own skin.

Rita: If you care about an endeavor, stick with it. This project was interrupted at times by professional and family obligations Rosemary and I each had. It was intellectually messy and simply time-consuming. There were several points at which we asked ourselves the question "should we give up?" For me, the answer was always "no" because of the gift so many women had given us by sharing their time and stories. I felt honor-bound to respect that gift by seeing this through to completion.

Rosemary and Rita: As many of our interviewees told us, it's really about getting comfortable with *you*, and identifying what constitutes a good fit and the right balance for you. If you want to reach for a position of leadership, go for it. We need more women in leadership positions. Make sure you are either in a system that creates transparent access throughout the pipeline, or you are willing to meet the prevailing norms of the informal system. Position and power are related, but influence is also power. Leadership is more than a position—it arises from behavior. If you are fulfilled by leading in place, then lead in place.

We were each fortunate enough to work with Elinor Ostrom early in our careers, before she was a Nobel Laureate. We each benefitted from watching her pursue her work despite the fact that early on she was, at best, ignored by 'mainstream' thinking. If you find yourself at a time in your life where it is most appropriate to follow, remember her sage advice: "There is a time to lead, and a time to follow." As your life ebbs and flows, you will find yourself choosing many different ways to contribute to your organization, your family, and society as a whole. In the end, the test is whether you can look yourself in the mirror and know that you have pursued the right path for yourself, made the difference you want to make by how you show up in the world and how you interact with those around you. To thine own self be true.

Reference

Roberts, L. M. & Ely, R. (2016, November 17). What's behind the unexpected Trump support from women. *Harvard Business School*. Retrieved from http://hbswk.hbs.edu/item/where-did-all-those-women-voters-go. Last accessed: January 9, 2018.

APPENDIX: THREE WORDS OF WISDOM

The question "What three words of wisdom would you give a young woman starting out on her leadership journey?" opened our survey. There was some unevenness, but the answers comprise a rich panoply of women's perspectives on how to develop and thrive as a leader. Distinct themes come through: learn from others as you develop your leadership style; master confidence, make choices to which you can and do commit; respect others, develop robust communication skills (including listening) and build relations; keep your eye on the big picture and the horizon, don't get stalled by details or setbacks, maintain integrity and perspective; learn and grow from others and from failure, develop resilience; and make sure that you expend your effort in a way that works for your life, not others' expectations. In addition, there are several tactical insights provided. Taken together, the advice extends beyond, but to some degree echoes behaviors of leading in place highlighted in Chapter Five.

Women were so generous and thoughtful in their responses, we wanted to ensure they saw the light of day. If you are starting your leadership journey, or supporting others doing so, here are three words of wisdom, from hundreds of women, verbatim.

- Lead by example. Practice the Golden Rule. No one is perfect. When you make a mistake, own it, learn from it, apologize if necessary, and move on.
- You can be strong and assertive without being 'mean'. This can be difficult for women, especially those early in their career. Confidence in conviction goes a long way when leading individuals.
- Her journey is her own, only take others' experiences not advice. A mentor is one of the best investments and it should equal disciplined bouncing

ideas/strategy time. Sponge all the info you can but keep learning to trust in our own gut instinct.

- Honesty, fairness and equality, respectful of diversity.
- Follow your passion. Politics and relationship-building are just as important, if not more than, technical expertise at the leadership level.
- Who to rely upon, When to lean in, How to take criticism in good stride.
- Gather information wherever you can (even boring meetings can prove useful later). Don't compromise your standards . . . ever. But be willing to compromise/ seek consensus.
- Keep breathing, keep moving forward, remind yourself of your goal every day (and/or revise it, if needed).
- Don't be afraid to fail, ask questions, even the ones you think are stupid, fake it till you make it.
- Know your core values and do not compromise them. Develop relationships. Thinking deeply is often more important than speaking quickly.
- Find a mentor. Honesty and ethics matter. When faced with questionable ideas or suggestions, do the right thing. Don't know the right thing? Go ask your mentor. Have a clear vision of where you want to go professionally.
- Tell the truth and your stories will never change. Stand your ground and support your choices. Treat everyone as you want to be treated.
- Watch the leaders around you. Watch each level of management and leadership to get a sense of the organizational style and culture. Begin to understand what you are comfortable with and what you are not and why. Communicate with others and learn from them. Become the person that others talk to and trust. Give the organization a break; try to understand what the organization does, why they do it, how you can contribute to its success.
- Be an active listener.
- 1) Learn to compromise without becoming compromised. 2) Learning is an ongoing process and can come from unlikely sources. Be open to new people and ideas. 3) Give yourself and others a break. Mistakes are to be learned from, not dwelled upon.
- 1) Always be open to feedback, both positive and negative. 2) Don't hold back. 3) Be communicative and responsive; ask questions and answer questions.
- Ask questions. Offer assistance. Work for the greater good.
- 1) If not you, then whom? 2) Don't think of relationships or opportunities as zero sum. Think first about growing the pie. 3) Don't be afraid to ask for help. You aren't weak if you ask your mentors for advice or are honest with your uncertainties and fears—rather the opposite.
- Be empathetic, but don't lose sight of the bigger picture. Think before acting or opening your mouth. Take an extra moment to decide the best way to communicate or do something before starting. Maintain perspective—there's a lot to juggle between working towards goals, leading a team, and everything

else that comes with professional leadership. Reserve time for yourself outside of that context and allow yourself to step away from time to time.

- 1) Motivation is an internal drive, do not seek it externally. 2) Make mistakes, but always learn from them. 3) Be open to critique—you don't always see your weak spots.
- Always listen to people that have been in your shoes already. Be willing to take compliments along with criticism. Put others before yourself, and in the long run, it will pay off.
- Leading from behind is honorable, hard work, and is a great place to observe what it takes to lead from the front. Ground yourself in something more significant than yourself and your own aspirations. Leadership can come from anywhere in an organization—the top, the middle, or from the bottom.
- Be bold; Be assertive; Take initiative.
- Become engaged and invested in your community whether it is workplace, community, or family. Just because you are 'leading' does not mean you are always right, always know what is best, or are better than others. To lead is to inspire.
- Your personal life is not separate from your work life. Everything you do is part of who you are, segmenting yourself into separate pots will most likely leave you feeling unfilled and disjointed. Embrace who you are and let that fill every part of who you are and what you do. When you are at work, school, home, tending children, reading, exercising, or down time, all are fulfilling your role as a leader.
- Don't be dragged down by the cynics sitting on the sidelines. Pick your battles. Take the time to relish even the small victories.
- 1) Self-knowledge, i.e. have a road-map for 'walking around' inside yourself, otherwise, your personal 'stuff' will get in the way of your capacity to lead others. 2) Effective decision-making is based on viewing the world through four lenses i.e., Political, Human Resources, Symbolic and Structural. [see Bolman and Deal's 'Re-framing Organizations; Artistry and Choice in Leadership.']
- 1) Do not strive to 'have it all', just the things that you want. 2) Determine your own standards for success. 3) Do not let anyone impose glass ceilings or walls.
- Clarify your strengths and passions, and be able to articulate those clearly. Outline a 3–5 year plan (know before you start a new job how long you plan to stay and what you plan to get out of it). Surround yourself with similarly goal-oriented peers that can help spur you on when work becomes difficult.
- Be confident, be positive, put forth your best always.
- Don't give up your beliefs to go along with the majority if you disagree. Balance your time at work and play. Learn from your mistakes—don't beat yourself up about them.

- 1) Make yourself available to people and be open to their ideas and concerns. If someone feels they have been heard, they will be more likely to support what it is you are trying to do. You may also learn something! 2) Make time for yourself. Charging yourself will allow you to deal with the issues of others. If you are on the brink of collapse, you won't have anything to give in the support of others. 3) Know the network you are working in. You don't have to have all the answers, but you do need to know where to go to learn the answers and be willing to search them out.

- Fake it till you make it. But seriously, be confident and have faith in yourself and your good sense. Be open to all opinions but understand how to manage that and assert the final decision.

- Believe in yourself and your vision. Seek out and learn from your elders/ people whose work you admire. Learn how to delegate.

- Don't worry, act.

- Hang in there—often your greatest success comes on the back of your biggest failures, and usually when you feel on the brink of defeat, you are closer to success than you realize. Be unreasonable—feedback and constructive criticism is welcome, but feel ok with being unreasonable and dismissing naysayers. If you are trying to change something, a lot of people will think you're crazy and unreasonable. Embrace this, you might be crazy to think you can change something, but since only the crazy are willing, you are closer than others. Make your own choices and own your mistakes. Go with your instinct rather than external 'should' pressures. If you make a mistake, own it and use it to get better. You can fail without being a failure.

- Don't be afraid to speak your mind.

- Never dictate your days based off a man. Do as much as you can when you can. Breaks are essential. Turn your stress eating into stress-releasing exercise.

- 1) "The mind will not be cultivated at the expense of the heart" 2) "Consider that you might be wrong" 3) Mistakes that she's made along the way—not so that the younger woman/mentee doesn't make the same ones, and not even so the younger woman can see 'value' in the mistakes; but mostly so the younger woman sees the leader as human, and can aspire to a similar position despite minor embarrassments, mistakes, disappointments that might otherwise get her down and hold her back along the way.

- Don't plan too far ahead. Take advantage of opportunities. Don't sell yourself short.

- It is difficult to strike a balance between the traditional male-female leadership expectations.

- 1) How to assert oneself in the workplace as a female and address being labeled as a bitch. 2) What is the biggest challenge of being a female leader? 3) What are the most necessary/crucial soft skills that a female leader should develop?

- 1) Be confident in who you are before allowing others to define you for themselves. 2) To not be afraid of conflict or the need to address a problem; speak out. 3) Not everyone will like you or agree with you; it does not mean you are not a good leader.
- 1) Be aware of your weaknesses but don't let them discourage you. 2) Fake it until you make it! 3) You CAN do it.
- Stay focused, work hard, have a sense of humor.
- While many women today would like to believe the push for equal access and rights is behind us, we still have a lot to fight for. Opportunities are available to women, but they still must work twice as hard as men to prove themselves and make the most of those opportunities.
- Prove your worth, then don't accept less. Be a confident leader that others will wish to follow. Demand the level of respect that you offer to others.
- Believe in your worth. Do not preface every statement with an apology. Listen more than you speak.
- It is a man's world, sexism is everywhere, go around the bastards.
- Always dress more professional than you think is required for the occasion. Assistants are the key to success. Be nice to all of them. Yours will make or break you and being nice to other people can get you a lot of help. Building relationships is a very important part of being a leader.
- 1) Try not to sweat the small stuff. 2) Understand that not everything is in your control. 3) Always push yourself to be better.
- Don't be too quick to judge others' motives. Listening to others' ideas and considering them will pay off in the long run. You don't always need to 'prove yourself' by being better than others, it is often better to coordinate something with others included than to do something by yourself.
- Be true to yourself. Hold strong to your values. Don't pay too close attention to what others say about you.
- It's good to be friendly in the workplace but do not allow those friendships to impede your professional progress. Have a clear goal and work towards it, even diagonally, until you are satisfied or you choose another goal. As you rise through the ranks, be careful who you surround yourself with. They will reflect on you. It's important to remember that being a woman in a male-dominated field is tough, but those that do well in those fields stand out as proof that it can be done. You'll have to work harder than friends in other fields, but if it's what you want it's worth the hard work.
- Never stop following your dreams/goals. You will face obstacles and you will learn and grow from them. You are a great person and a natural born leader so go, do and excel.
- 1) Never give up! 2) Don't let the discussion of family planning rule your life. 3) Work hard, but do not overwork yourself or else you'll burn out.
- Know yourself, know your strengths, and don't be afraid to share them or be proud of yourself. Be sure you know how to take care of yourself and who

you can lean on for support. Make a place for yourself at the table (make sure your voice is heard). Don't be afraid to advocate for what you deserve. Ask questions. Seek advice from mentors/advisors. Don't sell yourself short.

- Listen to others, but make up your own mind. Do what makes you happy, even if it is a less prestigious job. You can be a leader amongst your friends, family, work, anywhere.
- Don't be afraid to chase your dreams. Don't let others tell you that you can't do something. If you want it badly enough, you can find a way to get there. Don't be afraid of taking a different route. Sometimes your original plan is good, but the right way to do something is better or unexpected.
- Set your sights on the next promotion. Plan your goals. Don't compromise integrity for success.
- Be humble and willing to listen. Be confident in your abilities but always open to new ideas. Be able to see people's talents and delegate. You can't do everything on your own.
- Stay focused on your goal. Always keep learning. Be humble.
- Don't let your fears hold you back—decide what you want to do, work out what you need to do to get there and do it. Create a support network of positive, encouraging role models. Be very clear about what you want to achieve and why it matters to you.
- Speak up. Have confidence.
- Be yourself. Never let work be the only thing in your life. Set audacious goals.
- Continue learning, don't be afraid to try to learn from others.
- Follow your gut. Never settle. Do what makes you happiest.
- Be patient. Ask for feedback. Do NOT give up.
- Listen carefully to what you hear. Always remember there is more than one point of view. If you want to influence outcomes, listen to what is important to others and at the least understand the impact your decisions will have on others.
- Be yourself. Expect to be overwhelmed. You're not alone.
- Be patient and give yourself time and space to grow. Focus on the strengths you have and try not to compare yourself to others. Be humble enough to have people around you who have different strengths and let them shine.
- Don't be afraid to give things a go, and apply for jobs you're interested in even if you don't think you have enough experience. Go on training and seek advice but don't feel you have to change your personality to be successful— you can find ways to be successful and still be yourself. Seek advice from every leader you respect, be they male or female, old or young, and whether they have a similar leadership style/personality type to you, or a different one.
- Focus on building relationships/your network. Grow by challenging yourself, stepping out of your comfort zone. Don't let mistakes knock your confidence, learn from them.

- Surround yourself with good people; Take care of your personal life first; and Get a good mentor.
- Do what you need to do to sleep at night. Know that you can be overruled by those higher up the ladder. Listen.
- 1) Be so good they can't ignore you. 2) Develop a good support system (find a mentor and be a mentor) 3) Be proud to be a woman, do not try to be more 'man-like'. We bring a specialization to the table that is lacking sometimes, so own it and be proud.
- Always ask for what you want. You meet people at least twice in life along your career path so treat everybody well. Take risks.
- Watch, listen, and observe those around you in leadership positions.
- Build bank accounts, listen with intention, create open dialogue.
- Advocate for yourself. Don't be afraid to speak up, even if you may ruffle feathers. Always treat people with respect and always do your best.
- Be persistent. Be flexible. Lean In.
- Don't be afraid to take risks. Say "yes" when opportunities come your way. Don't second guess your skill set—you're more capable than you think.
- Confidence comes in its own time and its own way. There's no rushing it, until one day you realize you have it. Then use it to do not only what you are good at, but to bring the good work out of the people around you as well. Forgive yourself. You will make mistakes. It's OK. Repeat constantly in your mind. You will never, EVER, be able to have everyone like you or your decisions. Accept it. You'll be looked at as cocky by some, as a b%*%# by others, and other women (unfortunately) will be your worst critics. But if you know in your gut that you made the right decision for the right reason for that very moment in time, let other people's opinions of you go. You've got more important things to concentrate on.
- 1) The path may not always be straightforward, sometimes you take a left or right turn and use those opportunities to get back to forward momentum. 2) Get Better, Not Bitter. 3) Don't be afraid of change; it is what shapes you.
- You may be presented with many leadership 'opportunities' and you should weigh these carefully . . . not all opportunities are beneficial for your short-term and long-term goals. In fact, taking on too many opportunities, or the wrong kind of opportunities, can sometimes be more harmful than helpful. Don't be afraid to be yourself. Think about who you want to be in the future and plan a path to get there. That journey starts with understanding who you are today and what you need to do to reach your potential. Take care of yourself first; no one else can do that for you. You will be your best self, and able to do the most good, when you prioritize self-care.
- Learn from every experience. Never think you cannot learn something from someone else. Be willing to go above and beyond without being asked.

- Understand the challenging balance for women in the workplace—read *Hardball for Women*. Recognize and avoid dangerous people—read *The People of the Lie*. Learn to 'manage from below'.
- Hear others' feedback, but don't let it deter you from doing what you know is right. It's okay to admit you've made a mistake and try something else. Find others who have nothing to gain by your success or failure who can provide you with feedback and who will bolster your confidence when you need it.
- Take chances and sometimes go beyond your comfort zone—you may be surprised what you learn about yourself. Constantly re-evaluate your goals, as you progress in your career, what matters to you may change. 'Having it all' isn't possible so don't beat yourself up when you have to make compromises in order to maintain your sanity.
- Listen to wisdom of others, but don't be afraid to go after what you want.
- Find out what motivates people.
- Have confidence. Take the bad with the good. Stay informed.
- 1) Be positive and helpful by anticipating needs. 2) Seek promotion—don't wait to be asked to lead—but don't dictate. 3) Challenge yourself because that is how you grow your skills.
- 1) Observe, listen, act. 2) Do not be reactionary. Get all facts first. 3) Trust your instinct.
- Be true to yourself. Do what you believe is right always. Use your platform to change the world!
- Get involved in something you believe in. Ask for help along the way. Don't be afraid to get out of your comfort zone.
- 1) You always have the right to change your mind. 2) Leadership is an act of service that calls on you to continually ask your ego to step aside and to be your authentic self. 3) Leadership is only seen in conversation so work on your conversation skills.
- 1) Be confident in self-talk, attitude, words, and actions. 2) Be gender-blind—recognize that both men and women can be intuitive and both men and women can be assertive. 3) Seek out examples of the kind of leader you want to be and get to know them (either in person or through information-gathering).
- Find a mentor (formally or informally) who is able to support your career goals.
- 1) Do your research/analysis etc., but also listen to your instincts—they are usually trying to tell you something for a reason. 2) You will need to work through some periods where things aren't clear (that's how the world often is) but always try to be as clear as you can about the problem you are trying to solve. 3) Hone your communication skills—be good at listening/thinking about who you are communicating with, their context/drivers as well as crafting what you want to say.

- Co-create your own job—work with your employer to make your career what you want from it. Have clearly defined roles—don't be too nice to everyone, because they will come to you for absolutely everything, when you need to focus on the important. Rather, direct people to those best placed to help them. Work on the hardest things first—just as an athlete trains their weaknesses so as to improve the fastest, you need to get better at things that are difficult. Includes working with ambiguity; trying to influence people who won't budge; making decisions about the future with limited foresight available . . . or it could be stuff like time management, or relationship skills.

- You don't have to know everything, you just need to know where to go to find the answer. Acknowledge when you don't know something, you are after all human and not a machine. Learn to not take things personally—this comes with experience. Always treat people with dignity and respect. You never know when you might need someone's help.

- Be deliberate about moving, and get varied experience (move quicker than you think). Position yourself for people to sponsor you. Make and take opportunities.

- Always be humble and grateful for what people contribute and achieve. Share your vision often. Make it fun.

- Your success comes through making it easy for others to succeed. Think about every interaction with others an opportunity to influence: what do you want the person to think, feel and/or do. Ask questions and keep asking (especially 'why')—don't hold back because you are concerned that people will think it's a dumb question.

- Focus on your people. Provide the environment for them to thrive professionally. Stars are made, not born, you do have to put the hard yards in.

- Voice your position. Negotiate. Volunteer to lead and not just assist.

- You are better than you think you are. Make sure you can live with the choices you make. Be confident about the fact that things will change.

- Find leaders that you admire and learn from them; learn from your mistakes (everybody makes them); and don't be afraid to make a decision—inaction can be worse than getting it wrong.

- Find work you love. Pursue it with passion and commitment. View your employment history as a process of building up a toolbox of skills and capabilities that you can take with you from role to role. This will help you be nimble in our modern economy and in our ever-changing workforces.

- Network with other leaders, try and choose a limited amount of things to do exceptionally well, never try and be one of the boys.

- Trust your gut/intuition. Get to know yourself very well (and don't measure yourself by others). Work out what you love doing.

- The most important decision you make is who is to be your life partner. They effectively operate like leverage. They can support/help/guide you in your journey or they can undermine/distract you. You may well have to make a trade-off in your personal life. You rarely see very senior women with children and still in their first marriage. It can work if your husband is prepared to carry more of the family load—see first point; choose wisely. As you move up the hierarchy, you will do less of the doing and often the doing is much more fun. Don't be blinded to climbing the ladder for the sake of climbing. Always check you are enjoying what you are doing.

- Believe that you can change and grow; your major limits are the ones you set yourself. "It's not this battle, it's the war"—prioritise long-term outcomes/ relationships over short-term but transient 'wins'. Listen to others—you don't know it all, everyone has insights.
- Make connections with people. Get back to people on things quickly. Think big.
- Be yourself, even if you feel pressure to conform to others' expectations. It will be harder for you than for a man. Set your own goals and priorities.
- Watch, listen and learn first (before seeking to give advice). Do not assume that the new cannot learn from the old (whether the new is new people or new ideas). Make sure you know what you value and that you hold true to your values.
- Speak up—don't hint at things and hope someone will get it—but be pleasant not demanding. They might say no and you need to be okay with that. Thank people as often as you can— gratitude is in short supply and you will be remembered for it. You are not entitled to anything so don't be insulted by other people's attitudes or assignments—just do a great job with a good attitude no matter what the work is. If you don't like it, you learned that you need to make a change but it's not someone else's fault.
- Always look to preserve the dignity of others, seek guidance from varied sources, don't be afraid to lead with authority.
- Help one another to bring out the best in each other, healthy competition, not spiteful competition.
- Have courage and be willing to try things and do things at which you might fail—it's the best way to stretch yourself and grow. Happiness comes from doing what you love—your work should, at some level, be sustaining to you and give you some sense of fulfillment. Think hard about how you want to balance work with family, especially if you plan to or already have children. Achieving this balance is the toughest juggling act a woman often does throughout her career and it does help to think about how you'll do this and how you can best achieve it.
- Develop relationships with and seek input from subordinates, peers and seniors. Keep your word and don't give it lightly (maintain and guard your integrity and reputation for honesty). Smile!
- Work hard and be nice . . . these two qualities will get you far in your leadership journey.

- 1) Don't be afraid to lead as a woman. 2) Watch, listen, and learn from women and men you admire. 3) Don't be afraid of failure: Failure isn't Fatal—it's a weeding-out process.
- You are NOT always right. Listen to others, be kind.
- Surround yourself with people who know more than you do. Define the needs of your target group. Don't ever stop growing or taking chances.
- Listen to feedback and be flexible. Know your internal and external audiences and what motivates them. With every situation, look back and ask yourself what worked and what could be done better next time.
- Fairness, concern during decision-making, public values, building expertise.
- Focus on honing your soft skills as you will use them in almost everything that you do. Listen twice as much as you talk. Communication at all levels is key to success.
- Listen more than you talk. When you do talk, be impeccable with your words. Share with everyone the mission and how it will be achieved.
- The effect of gender. Diversity. Best work habits.
- Lots of things will go wrong, don't let it shake you.
- Be yourself. Trust that you know the answers. Keep moving forward, even if it's small steps.
- Listen before you act. There are always two sides to every story. Be honest.
- Understand your context; leadership is about understanding the setting and being strategic with your actions in that setting. But also know yourself. Invest in becoming conscious of what you are good at, and what you are called to do. The best leadership emerges when you are clear about your skills, your heart, and the problem the Universe is asking you to stop out on and be of service. Trust the inner compass and have regular practices—journaling, exercise, art, being with friends—that ground you in wise action.
- 1) Above all, learn self-love, self-acceptance and self-confidence. 2) Find what you love and learn to do it well. 3) Study human behavior enough to learn to manage your mental state and deal with challenging people and circumstances.
- Listen and communicate well. Know and be who you are unapologetically. Be excellent at what you do.
- Don't take things personally. Be yourself, you don't have to act or be like the men in your profession in order to achieve what you want. Continually educate yourself—never stop learning.
- Seek folks with talents different from your own, facilitate collaborations, be prepared to provide the tools your team needs—even before they know they need new tools.
- Don't get caught up in the power issues. Treat everyone on the team as if you're all in it together. Men can still be sexist jerks. Call them on it.
- Seek out challenges—if you don't, no one will have confidence in your leadership potential. Speak honestly. Consider the motivations of others carefully to move them to your side.

- 1) While I want you to focus on this job, please remember that you're pursuing a career, not a job. 2) While you are pursuing a career, please remember you are making a life. 3) There's no such thing as work-life balance. There's only work-life 'fit', and the weight and intensity of each may shift and change over the years.
- Always own your mistakes, don't belabor them, learn from them and move on. It's hard to earn trust and respect but easy to lose it—keep true to your word and don't lie. Don't get caught up in negativity, gossip or other non-productive activities—you can bond with others in the workplace without being part of these conversations. Be polite, set a good example.
- Don't be afraid to ask for what you want. Do your homework (don't go into a meeting unprepared). Listen and learn from others.
- Express confidence in what you know. Listen to others. Be flexible.
- Development of leadership is a process—have patience, take time to ask questions and learn—demonstrate your skills by working hard.
- Listen, reflect, and instill values.
- Stay focused on what matters; keep a sense of humor; don't let the perfect be the enemy of the good.
- Know yourself first. Understand your strengths and weaknesses (as a communicator, as a team member, as a supervisor and your natural inclinations (habits, tendencies, ways of perceiving, stereotypes of others). Treat every experience as an opportunity to learn and give yourself time to reflect on what worked and what didn't work as well as you would have liked. Keep a diary/log/journal of the lessons and strategies. Don't be afraid to make decisions or mistakes. But do pause for a moment before making a decision and ask yourself if you will comfortable explaining your rationale and defending that decision to your family, friends, colleagues, or the media.
- 1) Stand tall (don't couch your ideas or your accomplishments). 2) Listen and get input, but don't heehaw about making a decision. 3) Develop your own style, but aware of political, symbolic, human, and structural elements in leadership.
- Don't try to be something you're not (i.e., one of the guys). Always keep learning. Do the right thing.
- Build competence . . . learn, ask questions, listen. Don't be afraid to speak up and contribute/display confidence. Build relationships, network, seek out mentors.
- Develop self-confidence, align career goals with your interests and strengths, seek out 'stretch' assignments/projects to challenge yourself.
- Be honest with yourself, treat people with respect, work hard, play, ask questions. Don't be afraid to be wrong, don't be afraid to be right, speak up. If someone has a job you want, don't be afraid to talk to them about it, you can do anything you want to work at.
- Be true to yourself, learn at least one lesson from people you cross path with in your journey and treat everyone with respect.

- Believe in yourself! Do it with Passion. Have a positive attitude.
- Listen to everyone and all levels of staff. Be patient and wait before making decisions. Gather all information and review details. Don't try too hard. It will come to you. Gain as much knowledge as you can from your surrounding colleagues and staff.
- Be bold and take the opportunities on offer. Trust those who think you can do it, even if you've never tried it before. Try stuff outside your comfort zone at the beginning but still be excellent in something.
- Stay focused and work hard. Be honest. Listen and learn from others, ask questions, get involved.
- Keep an open mind, both at work (people, solutions) and career. With each job you take, more doors will be open and paths you may not have considered. Network and maintain relationships. To the extent you can, make your relationships two-way or 'value-added'. For example, I let clients/acquaintances know about articles of interest they may not have seen.
- Be confident. Be assertive (not abrasive). Look for opportunities to learn and grow.
- Don't try to control your future; be flexible as opportunities arise. Learn when—and how—to say 'no' effectively. Not everyone is going to like you, so get over it.
- Be sure to take care of yourself, else you cannot care for others; seek out advice of those you admire; know your values and stick to them.
- Aim high. Collect supporters. Learn from failure.
- Believe in your own talents. Don't expect others to tell you it's ok to lead—you have to just do it. Speak up at meetings.
- Believe in yourself. Respect others and value difference. Be willing to be visible even if it's hard.
- Leaders don't do the work—their job is to enable/facilitate/help others (their staff) to do the work, i.e., leader as servant model. Leaders help others build their skills to become the best they can be, and by providing support to staff to help them get ahead builds trust between manager and staff that is returned by greater effort and commitment to the team/organization. Leadership is a long apprenticeship, and you should look to learn from all your experiences, with failure providing the best lessons and reflections.
- In your personal life, try to surround yourself with friends and partners who are willing to be there as a sounding board during difficult leadership moments and who are secure about their own identities and who do not interpret your sounding-off as an indictment of them. You need them as emotional infrastructure (and hopefully you can be the same for them), not as emotional roadblocks. Lean in. Assume you are an equal partner in conversations that involve the management of collaborative projects. If you suspect that you aren't an equal partner, however, then find a private moment after the fact to inquire as to what your role really is and to explain your impressions

of possible marginalization/misunderstanding. If you don't know where you stand with your peers or 'superiors', then it is very difficult to be consistent and to offer transparency to those for whom you have leadership responsibilities. Push back against attempts within professional relationships to 'maternalize' you. Simply because you are a woman, you should not have to be—by default—a shadow advisor, the collector of waifs and strays that the boys have rejected (there are sometimes very good reasons why someone has been dropped by an adviser), or a mental health counselor. If you want to be those things, fine—but learn to recognize when you are being cast into those roles, and push back if you don't feel comfortable about it, especially on being a mental health counselor. But know the names/places to refer people when they are in crisis and remain understanding.

- Be honest, accept defeat, celebrate success, and always carry on. Empower others to be more than they thought they could be.
- 1) There's no such thing as 'working smarter, not harder'. There is no substitute for extremely hard work and if you're not prepared for that, don't aspire to senior leadership positions. 2) Never lose sight of the ideals you held at the start of your career. If you've lost a sense of why you're doing this, step aside for a while and recharge your moral batteries. 3) Don't hop onto every bandwagon going around in your organization and/or sector (you can easily fall off a bandwagon). Stay iconoclastic and skeptical in your approach.
- Back yourself. Think of the women who forged the path before you and work to create pathways for the women who will come after you. Balls are an advantage but not a necessity.
- There is always a 'them and us', no matter how inspirational a leader you are, because you have to make the hard calls. Never mistake popularity for leadership. Lead by example.
- Get a mentor, be a mentor, trust but watch your back.
- Keep your sense of humor at all times. Be courageous, follow your heart and take creative risks. Be authentic, people respond strongly to, and follow, authentic leaders.
- Get into leadership for the right reasons, be yourself—don't try to be like men.
- 1) Find people that have more experience than you, seek their counsel, and take their advice. All too often young people try to figure it out themselves or recreate the wheel when they can get fantastic coaching from mentors who have been there before. 2) Always, always do the right thing. 3) Never hire someone or work for someone without breaking bread together first. You learn so much about someone through the conversation that happens over lunch or dinner, it will help you make a good decision about the work relationship. AND ... CAN I ADD A FOURTH? 4) Stay out of the weeds. Do not let others drag you into their drama, poor decisions, or bad work habits.

- Ability to instill confidence. Able to lead by example. Empowerment.
- Be approachable. Be decisive. It's okay to be thoughtful.
- Find a mentor or colleague you connect with and maintain that relationship over the course of your career; network, network, network! Join professional organizations, meet peers and seek advice as you are learning your way through your chosen profession; always dress professionally when it matters most, be on time, meet all deadlines!
- Listen to others, keep an open mind. Actions speak louder than words.
- Know your core values and do not compromise them. Develop relationships. Thinking deeply is often more important than speaking quickly.
- Be yourself. Don't be afraid of challenges. Let negativity from others roll off your back but don't be afraid of criticism (particularly constructive criticism).
- 1) Get a mentor. 2) Honesty and ethics matter. Don't know what to do when faced with questionable behavior or ideas? Go ask your mentor. 3) Have a vision of your leadership. Don't know where you want to be when you grow up? Maybe that mentor can provide some insight.
- Be true to yourself. Don't let others dissuade you of your dreams/goals. Have fun with your choices.
- Believe in yourself, even when others have doubts. Don't do things half-way—that's not what God wants. Never lose sight of your vision. You may have to change how you get there, but don't lose sight of where you are going OR why.
- I think young women must understand that they are known by their reputation—so the quality of their work, their ability to work with others, and their willingness to work for the betterment of the organization not just themselves is very important. It is very important to be positive in their approach to problems and they must be respectful of others in all situations. It is important to do the best job they can in every job, not just those they think will make them successful—this goes back to the reputation issue.
- Have a mentor you trust to help with the inevitable problems that will arise on your journey, continue to learn to make time for yourself.
- 1) Out-work everybody. 2) When you make a mistake, admit it, and make it right. 3) Play fair, always do the right thing.
- It's a man's world: Go around them.
- Seek out a sponsor and mentor, speak up about the good work you are doing; DON'T wait to be noticed for doing good work. Find leadership roles as soon as possible, whether in your organization or not—community groups, religious or professional organizations—get leadership experience.
- 1) Be prepared for anything, be flexible. 2) Join various professional organizations that will help you stay current in your field. 3) Find and reach out to other women leaders and network with them.
- Don't back down from your beliefs/ideas, let your voice be heard, don't let anyone tell you that you can't succeed.

- Know yourself and your vision and be able to share that vision with others. Treat everyone with respect and fairness and show others that they are valued. Communicate and build trust.
- 1) Use your mind and heart, not your ego. 2) Know your people and care. Intention always surfaces attitude. 3) Practice balance.
- Demonstrate competence. Be assertive and speak up. Cultivate relationships with peers and superiors.
- No one is expected to have all of the answers. Listen to the people you work with. We are always stronger merging many minds and many ideas. You won't always be right. Don't be afraid to admit a mistake. Your team will respect a leader with the maturity to admit making the wrong decision much more than a leader who argues and justifies validity of a poor decision. Display empathy and understanding for your team. Everyone has strengths and weaknesses. Everyone has crisis at some time in their lives. We need to embrace our differences and appreciate where people are in their lives and how that impacts their work performance.
- Always do your best work. Don't get caught up in negative talk/gossip. Take every opportunity.
- Be open. Be flexible. Look for possibilities.
- "Be kind because everyone you meet is fighting a harder battle" (Aesop). Don't ever be too busy to give a kind word or extend a helping hand. Always set aside time for yourself—sacred space— that is written in stone and non-negotiable. This is time for you to stop, catch your breath, and get your bearings; because the work will always be there waiting for you, and setting aside a small part of your day for you will keep you centered and make you more focused and productive. Don't ever sacrifice your family nor your health to succeed.
- 1) Persevere! It's a journey, not a sprint. 2) Surround yourself with great teammates—immense joy comes from achieving together. 3) Maintain work/life balance—rest and relationships are key!
- Integrity, flexibility as to goals and how to obtain them, and keep learning.
- 1) Be yourself. 2) Believe in yourself. 3) Do what you think is good.
- Be generous to subordinates. Promoting their best qualities supports the team mission.
- 1) Focus on your primary goal/job. 2) Know the strengths/weaknesses of others and use accordingly. 3) You cannot do your job alone, learn to work with others.
- Set goals. Be bold. Don't sweat the small stuff.
- Listen, but do not be shy about expressing your opinions/advice when you know your advice will advance the success of the effort. Show up for anything that you feel you can make a contribution to the successful accomplishment of, speak truth to power.
- Be willing to take risks, learn how to be strategic with your own career, you may not be able to do it all.

- Learn and understand what the support staff does and how to do it yourself. Learn good body language—show you are attentive, listening, paying attention. Prepare—if giving a talk, prepare your talking points, use relevant examples, and DON'T tell jokes aimed at only one part of your audience.
- Watch and learn from other leaders. Work hard. Listen to advice and concerns of others.
- Be persistent. Be willing to learn, change and adapt. Don't be afraid to ask questions, seek help, develop a variety of professional/career advancement relationships.
- Think outside the box for creative solutions to problems. Put together a network of people to bounce ideas off of one another. You are part of a team. You are not alone. Seek guidance and advice from others that have gone before you.
- Set boundaries. Develop a thick skin. Choose priorities strategically.
- Speak up. Don't take conflicts personally. Treat everyone with respect.
- Network, get to know people in your field and other fields. Learn as much as you can about everything. Don't sell yourself short, have confidence in your abilities.
- Have a plan but stay flexible. No matter where you are on your career path, you are a role model. To be a teacher you must continue to be a student.
- Build relationships across lines of difference (with 'the other'). Give back to others/mentor others. Trust your gut.
- Don't be intimidated by those in authority. Try to find the underlying problem, not what people say the problem is. It takes time and effort.
- 1) Admit you're wrong when you are. 2) Listen. 3) Keep good records.
- Establish and protect your reputation for good work. Hone your social skills—they'll take you farther than any other skill. Be kind.
- Work your butt off. Try to anticipate what is needed. Be flexible.
- Work hard, dream big, believe in yourself.
- Be aware of (office) politics but never discuss it. Develop your own relationships with co-workers and clients. Present ideas and solutions in writing—even if after-the-fact.
- 1) Have the courage to THINK critically. 2) Have the COURAGE and the wisdom to know when/how to be present and speak into situations, especially challenging ones. 3) Have compassion for yourself, in addition to the compassion you have for others.
- Be comfortable in your skin, realize everyone feels inadequate sometimes—we just cover it up in different ways. Be curious.
- Believe in yourself. Others believe in you, otherwise you would not have been given this post. So make the most of it. Don't be afraid to ask questions and opinions from subordinates and superiors. This is NOT a sign of weakness but a sign of a well-balanced person wanting to ensure they have sufficient data before coming to their conclusion. Give informal feedback regularly to your subordinates—do not wait until a formal meeting.

- Stay true to yourself, aggressively seek opportunity, build for the long haul.
- 1) Be a good listener; experts are available, but you have to make decisions. 2) Include people in the planning phase; people are likely to follow you if they feel part of the plan. 3) Make decisions that affect short-term and also help your long-term goals; some organizational changes such as software tools take time and are painful but, in the long run, pay off.
- Have confidence in yourself, be a good listener, be willing to acknowledge a mistake.
- 1) Be reliable and take ownership; recommend solutions and don't kick problems to supervisors or others. 2) Be collaborative and pleasant; share knowledge and ideas rather than be competitive. 3) Take responsibility for your own learning and seek out what you need rather than wait for training or knowledge to be 'given to you'.
- Learn to become aware of each individual person's gifts. Keep the group's goals and values as a priority in your interactions. Have patience when leading a group, ask questions leading to collaboration, consensus.
- Don't give up! Do what you love (have a passion for). Build a support group, and mentor each other.
- Seek a good mentor willing to be available and offer solid critique. Conduct 'information interviews' with persons in leadership positions in the organizations/ business you aspire. Keep updating your career goals with specific education, skills and abilities that will start the growth you need.
- To persist in the face of success and failure. To dream and aspire. To work hard, especially when others are not.
- Know your stuff. Consult your elders/former mentors, often and as needed. Try to be inclusive of all team members and further team work as much as possible.
- Learn from your mistakes, watch successful leaders and try to see what makes them that way, don't overthink decisions.
- Be true to yourself and stand firm in the face of criticism. Know you have inner power and use it, aka self-esteem. Build the self-esteem of others and reap the rewards.
- Show that you are an exceptionally hard worker by your actions, not by saying how hard you work. Treat subordinates as well as you do your supervisors. Compromise when needed, but avoid compromising your principles.
- 1) Be honest. 2) Know your stuff. 3) Don't take things personally (know how to go to the balcony and not be reactive).
- Listen. Communicate. Lead.
- Hold tight to your own integrity—believe in yourself. Keep moving forward even if the path looks a little uncertain. Don't give up your dreams.
- Learn all that you can about the subject matter, listen to other opinions and ideas, and don't be too sensitive to criticism.
- Be present to people and events; while recognizing the problem make every

effort to be part of the solution; do not underestimate yourself, get the help that you need (professionally and personally); take time out, read.

- Attentiveness to the needs of others.
- That women can do anything that humans can do if they set their minds to it. Do not let others define what you can do. You stand on the shoulders of others who came before you and you can be the stepping stone for women who come after you. Be faithful to yourself. There will always be others who tell you what you should do, what you can't do, what your life should be— listen, accept what advice fits into your life plan and then do what you want. You want to go through your life so that, at the end, you have no regrets for what you didn't do.
- Look for and strengthen your passion(s). Learn to say 'no' when it is not possible to do well what you are being asked. Be certain to let others know your strengths and weaknesses so they can match you with their needs accordingly.
- "I can only live one life"—engage people in issues that will affect them, don't decide for them. Seek out those with a different perspective from yours and learn what truth they bring. Don't be afraid of chaos; it's where new life grows.
- Listen closely to your co-workers; surround yourself with wise colleagues; treat everyone you meet with dignity and respect.
- To succeed, you must step up and lead. Force yourself to overcome bashfulness. Think of how your words/actions affect others.
- Always be gracious and thoughtful to those you are leading. Acknowledge mistakes and rectify them quickly. Listen to others from whom you can learn good ideas.
- Connect with and show caring for people (including the 'least ones'). Listen to, as well as give direction to, those one is leading. Be open to and responsive to feedback.
- Women are not supported in the same way men are—so just get used to that. Women's perspective is valuable and undeniable. Women will lead the world to sanity.
- Be organized. Always deal with people fairly. Look for the positive in any situation.
- Stand with, learn to focus, be yourself.
- Arm yourself with a good education, be open to other people's opinions, learn to be strong, yet kind.
- Try out different roles and approaches to see which is most comfortable for you. Find someone to share experiences. Don't assume that others (particularly men) are as secure as they may seem.
- 1) Don't lose sight of your goals. 2) Be open. 3) Never give up.
- Listen. Have confidence. Take risks.

INDEX

emotional intelligence (EI) 15–19, 118,
128–129, 137
emotions *see* affect
empathy 16, 94, 106, 118, 120, 128, 137,
162, 176
employment 11, 35, 58, 60, 97, 110, 112,
113, 117, 122, 123, 126, 153, 155, 169;
changes in landscape 26–28; of survey
respondents 93
empowerment 21, 55, 71–72, 84, 87, 108,
116, 117, 150, 154, 155, 174, 175
engagement 3, 18, 20, 26, 28, 30, 52, 66,
97; disengagement 98, 101, 115–116,
121, 148; 'grass roots' 66–67
ethnic minorities 45–46, 81, 92–93, 121,
126, 137
expectations 10, 26, 31, 34, 35, 44, 47, 51,
59, 70, 96, 105, 116, 120, 121, 153, 158;
of customers/stakeholders 35;
employment relations 27–28; factors
influencing 15–17, 144–146; of male/
female leaders 108, 116, 152; of
leadership 94; of survey 94; of
achievement 114; three words of
wisdom 161, 164, 170

failure xi, 3, 4, 7, 23, 159; of leadership
10–11, 18, 36, 84, 98, 117; productive
18; three words of wisdom 161, 164,
168, 171, 173, 178
'faking it' 42, 162, 164, 165
family 16, 55, 57, 68, 84, 137, 146, 149,
158, 160; balance and 80, 112, 117, 119,
119–121; choices and trade-offs 27, 77,
85, 112, 122–123, 124, 154–156; of
survey respondents 93, 94, 96, 97; three
words of wisdom 163, 165, 166, 170,
172, 176; *see also* eldercare
federal sector 18, 39, 69, 93, 101, 137–138,
139, 141, 142, 147, 148
feedback 27, 36, 47, 75, 96, 101, 102, 103,
128–129, 130, 132, 135, 144–145; three
words of wisdom 162, 164, 166, 168,
171, 177, 179
fit 3, 4, 8, 17, 18, 32, 34, 43, 59, 75, 104,
107, 116, 119, 123, 131, 132, 139, 143,
145, 158, 160, 172, 179; refusing roles
and 124, 125, 141; transition and
10–11
Fletcher, J. K. 107, 111
flexible work 27, 35, 41, 58, 149–150
followers 3, 12, 13, 14, 15, 16, 20, 21, 23,
61, 78, 87, 136

Forgas, J. P. 16
Forsyth, D. R. 31

gender x, 30, 31, 34, 36, 55, 106, 107, 114,
116, 118, 126, 130, 140, 142, 146, 153,
155, 158, 159, 168, 171; and bias 121,
122, 124, 138, 142, 144, 147;
counterproductive messages 104–105,
138; differential evaluations 32, 110;
experience of leadership roles 45–46,
58–61, 113; gender-neutral x, 4, 6, 52,
114, 119, 135, 149, 152, 153, 157;
interaction styles 103–105; of leaders
worked for 97, 96–97, 98, 99; leadership
styles and 101–102, 102–103, 107,
108–109, 110, 138–139, 140; people
management and 51; recognition of
leading in place 52, 99–100;
transformation of roles 35; uneven
distribution of opportunities 35–36
generational differences 26, 27, 66, 75–76,
116, 123, 142; aspirations 114, 140–141;
culture and 119; effectiveness of leaders
97–98; experience of stereotyping
105–107, 106, 138; gender-based
leadership styles 107; perceptions of
leadership 94, 95; recognition of leading
in place 99, 144; satisfaction 95–96; in
the workplace 66–67
Gilligan, C. 55
goals 19–22, 35, 55, 58, 59, 65, 78, 87, 88–89,
91, 95, 112, 116, 124, 141, 155, 156; three
words of wisdom 162, 165, 166, 167, 168,
170, 172, 175, 176, 178, 179
Goleman, D. 16
Google 33–34
'great man/woman' perspectives 110;
leadership styles 109, 157–158; moving
beyond 18, 57; *see also* prototypes
'groupthink' 35

Hackman, J. R. 19
Hansen, M. T. 6
health 17, 18, 26, 135, 155; individual 15,
33, 55, 56, 119–120; three words of
wisdom 170, 174, 176; community/
organizational 8, 52
Heiney, M. M. 31
heuristics *see* prototypes
Hewett, S. A. 59
Hill, L. 52
Hogue, M. 57
Hoyt, C. L. 18, 32

recognition as benefit of leadership 116,
117; of leading in place 36, 78–81, 85,
98–101, 137–138; reward and 82, 150;
of subordinates 109; validation and 157
relationships building 20–21, 43–44, 46,
83; leadership development 128, 130;
managing problems 70–72, 73–74, 84;
with seniors 120–121; success and
87–88, 89–90
research overview 1–38; summary 11–12;
biases and 7, 30, 32–33; business/
management approach 17; case study
approach 17–18; discussion of findings
136–137; field study, 14; generalizability
29, 151; implications of study for 126,
151–153, 152; influence on practice
28–34; methods 14; psychological
approach 13–17; recurring themes
19–22; reliability of findings 31;
replicability of studies 28–29; varied
findings 18–19; see also confidence
respect 20, 42, 46, 76, 82, 87–88, 98, 157;
three words of wisdom 161, 162,
165, 166, 167, 169, 172, 173, 175, 176,
177, 179
revolutions in concept of leadership xi, 4,
6, 34–36, 61
reward xi, xii, 5, 7, 36, 52, 60, 78, 79, 80,
81, 82, 107, 116, 135, 143, 150, 157, 178;
see also recognition
Roberts, L. M. 157–158
role models 166, 177; importance of 146,
149–150; leadership development 129;
parents as 40–41, 43, 45; success and
86–87
Rosie the Riveter 56

Sandberg, Sheryl 5, 6, 18, 61, 76, 154, 160
satisfaction 15, 28, 92, 95–96, 111, 113, 116
Schwab, Susan 135, 138, 140–142,
143–144, 149–150
scientific revolutions 34–36
selection xi, 6, 7, 8, 17, 18, 28, 30–31, 32,
33, 53, 57, 58, 59, 97, 131, 138, 143,
144–145, 146, 147, 151, 152, 153
self-awareness 15–16, 19–20, 23, 32, 102,
109, 128, 137
self-doubt 108
self-efficacy 14, 15, 23, 55, 88, 94, 114, 137
self-esteem 129, 178; see also confidence
self-management 15, 128, 159
self-management structures 21
self-promotion 120, 130, 157

self-reflection 41, 129, 130, 159
sense-making 17, 19, 20, 21–22, 23, 35, 52,
54–57, 55, 83, 153
sexual harassment 151–152
Shipman, C. 23, 119
similarity bias 138, 146, 153
Simon, S. 18
simulations 131–132
skills, communication 17, 43, 44, 55, 67,
69, 70, 77, 83, 94–95, 103, 109, 110,
115, 120, 125, 137, 149, 161, 162, 164,
168, 171, 176; constructive xi, 126;
decision-making 17, 20, 31, 33, 36,
39–40, 68, 104, 110, 117, 122, 163, 164,
167, 169, 171, 172, 174, 175, 176, 178;
emotional intelligence 15–16, 17, 18,
19, 87, 106, 118, 128, 137; leadership
(generic) 40, 43, 45, 68–69, 74,
115–116, 173; management/technical
42, 79, 87, 149, 167, 168, 178;
perspective-taking 6, 19–20, 51, 152,
155, 158; relationship 79, 120, 131–132,
169, 177; see also leader characteristics
Slaughter, Anne Marie 5–6, 61, 154, 160
Smith, Vernon L. 54
social media 23, 115–116
speaking up 77; discouraged 103, 104–105,
118; encouraged 103; making changes
and 68, 69–70, 82–83, 84
spheres of leadership 7, 11, 12, 16, 20, 22, 29
sports 12, 39, 40, 45, 73, 82
Stacey, R. D. 51
Staines, G. 111
status quo, challenging 67, 83, 87, 155
stepping back 16, 33
stereotypes xi, 32, 33, 55, 57, 85, 101–110,
116, 120, 121–122, 123, 139–140, 148,
172; see also biases; prototypes
stories xi, xii, xiii, 8, 9, 23, 34, 39, 51, 61,
63, 67–74, 83, 91, 92, 93, 98, 99, 102,
110, 115, 116, 118, 119, 120, 121, 123,
124, 126, 142, 144, 159, 160, 162;
importance of 54–57; women and
leadership 53–54, 57–58
student studies 14
success 6, 10, 22, 29, 30, 40, 43, 46, 47, 60,
70, 71, 76, 79, 82, 102, 106, 107, 115, 124,
131, 136, 138, 145, 147, 150, 154, 155,
157, 158, 162, 163, 164, 165, 166, 168,
169, 171, 174, 175, 176, 178; experiences
as leader 113, 114, 116–122; perspectives
on 86–90; without being CEO 76
Sullivan, Teresa 10–11